MASKED SCHIZOPHRENIA

Margaret O. Strahl, M.D., is Associate Clinical Professor of Psychiatry at New York Medical College. She had two years psychiatric residency at New York State Psychiatric Institute. She received her analytic training at the Psychoanalytic Clinic for Training & Research of Columbia University, adopting the biological theory of adaptation conceptualized by the clinic's director, Sandor Rado, M.D. Dr. Strahl then joined Dr. Paul H. Hoch's research team, and compiled the clinical material on a 5-20 year follow-up study of treated patients, which led to the publication of *The Course and Outcome of Pseudoneurotic Schizophrenia*. Since Dr. Hoch's death, Dr. Strahl has co-edited (with Nolan D. C. Lewis, M.D.) two volumes: *The Complete Psychiatrist—The Achievements of Paul H. Hoch, M.D.*, and *Differential Diagnosis in Clinical Psychiatry—The Lectures of Paul H. Hoch, M.D.*

MASKED SCHIZOPHRENIA
Diagnosis and a Unified Method of Treatment

Margaret Olds Strahl, M.D.

SPRINGER PUBLISHING COMPANY
New York

To

George Daniel Olds, Jr.,
in appreciation of his
contagious intellectual
enthusiasm.

Intellectual curiosity is a delicate plant—
to be cultivated early, not crushed.
—*Albert Einstein*

Springer Publishing Company, Inc.
200 Park Avenue South
New York, New York 10003

80 81 82 83 84 / 10 9 8 7 6 5 4 3 2 1

Library of Congress Cataloging in Publication Data

Strahl, Margaret O
  Masked schizophrenia, diagnosis and a unified
method of treatment.

  Bibliography: p.
  Includes index.
  1. Pseudoneurotic schizophrenia. I. Title.
[DNLM: 1. Schizophrenia, Latent—Diagnosis.
2. Schizophrenia, Latent—Therapy. WM203 S896m]
RC514.S823   616.89'82   80-10338
ISBN 0-8261-2820-3
ISBN 0-8261-2821-1 pbk.

Printed in the United States of America

Contents

v

vi   Contents

Introduction

This book evolved from a lecture series titled "Therapeutic Approach to Pseudoneurotic Schizophrenia," presented to physicians in the Psychiatric Residency Training Program of New York Medical College. The lecture series described in detail a unified method for treatment of the pseudoneurotic as well as the many other forms of schizophrenia that manifest nonpsychotic symptoms but do not show gross psychotic symptomatology. I adopted the term "masked" forms of schizophrenia because the nonpsychotic symptoms in these syndromes so dominate the clinical picture that the underlying symptoms of schizophrenia are often obscured from plain view.

Under the heading of masked schizophrenia are included a great many patients placed in the long-time controversial diagnostic category of "borderline"—the symptomatology initially being considered to lie on the border between the neuroses and schizophrenia. The term "borderline" currently refers to a disorder that is assumed unlikely to develop into schizophrenia (American Psychiatric Association, in press). "Schizotypal" currently refers to a disorder that is more likely to develop into schizophrenia due to a greater genetic propensity, as shown by familial incidence of schizophrenia (Kety et al., 1968). However, any probable relationship between these prevalent disorders is unclear insofar as their clinical criteria overlap.

In this writing, special emphasis is given to what can loosely be termed borderline syndromes that manifest a predominance of neurotic symptoms—the pseudoneurotic form of schizophrenia (Hoch & Polatin, 1949). Pseudoneurotic schizophrenia is extremely prevalent and frequently is encountered in clinical practice. Furthermore, due to the predominance of neurotic features, this form of schizophrenia is all too often diagnostically confused with the neuroses—which require a radically different treatment method.

I had two main reasons for writing this book. First of all, there is a pressing need to dispel existing confusion as to the nature of the dynamic mechanisms that give rise to the various clinical pictures we are dealing with when treating the so-called borderline patients who are actually schizophrenic. As I shall demonstrate, in these patients the nonpsychotic symptoms develop as defenses against the pan-anxiety generated by the schizophrenic dynamic processes. Secondly, there is an expressed need for a workable unified treatment method: one that is applicable for dealing with dynamic mechanisms of the basic schizophrenic symptomatology underlying the masking façade of neurotic or other nonpsychotic symptoms. Many experts in clinical psychiatry and psychoanalysis have contributed theoretical and empirical schemes for a therapeutic approach in dealing with one or more specific symptoms occurring in so-called borderline syndromes. However, an explicit unified method applicable for dealing with all the underlying schizophrenic symptoms and their interactions is needed. Therefore, I present a single treatment method based on a single theoretical frame of reference.

The unified method I have formulated is structured on the late Paul H. Hoch's concepts of the dynamic mechanisms of schizophrenia, which he postulated in accordance with his etiological concepts of the disorder (Hoch, 1957). It is in tune with Kurt Goldstein's holistic, biological study of the individual because, as was later pointed out by Hoch, these masked forms of schizophrenia manifest the typical schizophrenic thinking and disturbance of Gestalt described by Goldstein in 1939. In some patients this organic disturbance is obvious; in others, careful scrutiny is required to disclose its presence. Ongoing neurochemical, neuroanatomical, and neurophysiological research affords increasingly supportive evidence that Goldstein's organismic psychology and Hoch's subsequent theory of the dynamic mechanisms operating in schizophrenia are essentially valid.

My lectures proved of practical value to psychiatrists in training; in book form I hope they will be welcome to general psychiatrists and psychoanalysts, who find themselves increasingly confronted with the problem of treating schizotypal and so-called borderline or pseudoneurotic and other masked schizophrenic patients—a great many of whom respond minimally, or even unfavorably, to the established supportive and psychoanalytically oriented methods applicable for treating the neuroses. This book will also serve as a practical guide for therapy supervision of clinical psychologists and psychiatric social workers, and as a source of clinical insight for registered nurses holding a master's degree in psychiatric nursing.

I am greatly indebted to the late Paul Hoch for his inspiring teaching in years past and for affording me the opportunity to collaborate with him in research on pseudoneurotic schizophrenia (Hoch, Cattell, Strahl, & Pennes, 1962). I am also indebted to Dr. Nolan D. C. Lewis who, during the years following his retirement as Director of the New York State Psychiatric Institute, has been a steadfast friend and has encouraged me in this and other works.

Secretarial friends, Sally Morrow, Louise Mussolini, and Carol Jeffcoat have been indispensible in their expertise and willingness to type the drafts and finalized manuscript.

The psychiatric residents who have attended the lectures on treatment of pseudoneurotic schizophrenia deserve repeated thanks for their questions, comments, and criticisms over the years—all of which served as valuable stimuli to further my learning. I am also grateful to my patients, many of whom inadvertently taught me how to treat them and inadvertently rewarded my efforts by successfully realizing their potentials and becoming able to live adaptively without the pleasure-eroding tyranny of pan-anxiety.

Part 1

RATIONALE FOR THE TREATMENT METHOD

CHAPTER 1

Origins and Symptomatology of Schizophrenia and Development of Masked Forms

A very large number of psychiatric patients come to our clinical attention who appear to be suffering from a neurosis or a depressive disorder, or who present a picture of sociopathic personality or some other non-psychotic psychiatric disorder. Many of these patients are actually suffering from schizophrenia. They do not manifest hallucinations, they do not manifest delusions, but they are schizophrenic nonetheless.

This large group includes patients placed in the controversial diagnostic category of "borderline," a term initially referring to patients in whom the symptomatology was considered to lie on the border between the neuroses and schizophrenia. Other terms employed to designate this group include "ambulatory schizophrenia" (Zilboorg, 1941), "as-if" (Deutsch, 1942), "pseudoneurotic schizophrenia" (Hoch & Polatin, 1949), "borderline states" (Knight, 1953), "borderline personality" (Kernberg, 1967), and "borderline patient" (Perry & Klerman, 1978). There is no assurance that these terms refer to separate clinical entities. In fact, very probably the various investigators each have described the same disorder but, due to its complex and varying symptom manifestations, have simply given it different designations and selected different diagnostic criteria.

I eschew the currently accepted term "borderline" because it suggests that the patients so designated belong in neither the diagnostic category of the neuroses nor that of schizophrenia, yet it gives us no clear-cut direction for emancipating them from a diagnostic state of limbo. By analogy, one might have to assume there is such a thing as borderline pregnancy, or borderline syphilis, for instance. In any case, a patient's condition either belongs in one diagnostic framework or some other, but it is not on a "borderline" regardless of how incipient or subtle the signs and symptoms of the clinical entity appear. In actual fact, the clinical picture of many medical disorders is often masked by a facade of symptoms characteristic of some other type of disorder: an enlarged uterus of pregnancy with placenta praevia can simulate endometrial tumor; anxiety dreams occurring with brain tumor can simulate neurosis, and so forth.

Based on an assumption that the majority of patients placed in the category of "borderline" are actually suffering from an underlying schizophrenia, I have chosen as a more fitting descriptive term for this large group the "masked forms" of schizophrenia. This term indicates that the schizophrenic symptomatology is more or less concealed by symptoms characteristic of some other disorders—such as neuroses, depressive states, sociopathic personality, or other nonpsychotic entities. Basic signs and symptoms of schizophrenia are present in these individuals but are masked by an overlay of nonpsychotic symptoms. Furthermore, the basic schizophrenic symptomatology is indeed active; the schizophrenia is not "latent" (Bleuler, 1930, p. 239) any more than a snake in the grass is latent; it is there to be perceived if one knows what to look for. In many psychiatric circles the basic schizophrenic symptomatology is disqualified as having no particular diagnostic significance, partly because of the vast disagreement among clinicians and investigators as to what they should include. But the fact remains the symptoms exist, and turning our backs on them will not make them go away.

In masked schizophrenia, it is often a temptation to make a diagnosis of psychoneurosis, for instance, on the basis of one or two predominant neurotic symptoms, or on the basis of obvious early environmental factors that influenced the development of these symptoms. This is an easy way to overlook the presence of the underlying schizophrenic process. This mistake is often made even by experienced therapists—few of whom relish accepting the label of schizophrenia for their patients because of an unsure footing as to a treatment method. Thus, many a pseudoneurotic schizophrenic patient is misdiagnosed as suffering from a form of neurosis and treated accordingly, employing the Libido hypothesis or whatever other psychodynamic hypothesis the therapist considers applicable. However, when this is done the patient may gain insight but very often loses ground. As we shall later discuss, psychoanalytically oriented treatment aimed to resolve the neurotic symptoms can rob the schizophrenic patient of his compensatory mechanisms of defense against the underlying pan-anxiety; the patient can thereby decompensate into a state of massive psychotic confusion and develop psychotic compensatory symptoms such as hallucinations and delusions.

When we discuss the dynamic mechanisms of schizophrenia, it will become apparent that they differ very markedly from the mechanisms responsible for the formation of symptoms that develop in the neuroses; that neurotic symptoms in schizophrenia and in neurosis develop along entirely different dynamic courses. (Incidentally, there can be no such thing as a purely "functional" mental or physical disorder, insofar as every dynamic functioning process—even in the neuroses—requires morphological substrata.) The important thing to realize is that treatment methods must always be formulated according to the dynamic mechanisms appropriate to the diagnostic framework of the disorder treated.

You will find that the diagnosis of schizophrenia is not based on any single symptom (with the exception of the conceptual thinking disorder peculiar to schizophrenia, which can be minimal and not readily discerned). And the diagnosis is not based on any single laboratory finding to date. Unfortunately we do not have such a thing as a litmus test for diagnosing schizophrenia. Actually, in schizophrenia the diagnosis relies on a constellation and configuration of symptoms. The basic symptoms of schizophrenia—which indeed are present in all forms, including masked forms—afford some clue to the motivating factors (not to be confused with the etiological factors) from which they evolve. In turn, the motivating factors afford clues to some of the dynamic mechanisms from which the schizophrenic symptoms are derived.

BIOLOGICAL ORIGINS OF SCHIZOPHRENIA

As has been mentioned, the dynamic mechanisms characteristic of a psychiatric disorder will determine the treatment procedure of that disorder. Thus, in selecting the appropriate procedural method for treating schizophrenia, whether masked or another form, one must be familiar with the dynamic mechanisms involved in the schizophrenic disorder per se. And when we discuss these "schizodynamic" mechanisms it will become apparent that the same dynamic processes exist in the pseudoneurotic or other masked forms as exist, for instance, in the overtly psychotic forms: schizophrenia is schizophrenia, despite any overlying masking symptoms. However, in order to have formulated the dynamics, one must have arrived at a definition of the schizophrenic disorder.

Schizophrenia is a complex disorder that readily assumes such a large number of clinical pictures that it is difficult to arrive at a nicely concise definition. Bleuler (1930/1950) referred to the disorder as "the group of schizophrenias"; they have to be classified phenomenologically due to the fact that we do not as yet know the etiological factors involved.

Schizophrenia is defined as basically an organic disorder of chemical intermediary metabolism involving the brain: The diencephalon and mesencephalon are involved, and also the reticular system which, in turn, influences the cortex. Probably the normal relationship between the subcortex and the cortex is disrupted by a deficiency of integrative capacity. This special form of integrative impairment is inherent in all forms of schizophrenia and manifests itself in many ways: Stimuli from the external and internal environment are most likely screened differently than they are in normal individuals and cannot be fused in an integrative and organizational manner. Consequently, a disruption of homeostatic mechanisms in response to stimuli occurs on all levels of the nervous system—thought, affect, sensorimotor, and vegetative. The most outstanding feature in schizophrenic individuals is the dysregulation in any ability to fuse in a homeostatic fashion that which is going on in the external environment and that which is going on within themselves, as other individuals are able to do (Hoch, 1961).

It is interesting that the proportion of involvement in different areas of the brain seemingly varies quite considerably among schizophrenic individuals. If it is assumed that the integrative impairment varies in degree and configuration among schizophrenics, it follows that the manifestations of homeostatic dysregulation vary accordingly. For instance, the thinking disorder may be prominent in one schizophrenic, while in another the thinking disorder will be minimal but the individual may suffer marked emotional dysregulation in response to stress-provoking stimuli, and so forth. And in each case, this may bear some influence on the type of compensatory defense symptoms the schizophrenic individual will construct—whether psychotic or nonpsychotic. It could be postulated that this sheds partial light on the fact that the symptomatology in schizophrenia takes so many forms.

The concept of an inherent defect existing in schizophrenia is generally accepted. Many investigators have proposed the theory that a recessive factor is primarily involved, and others suggest that a dominant gene is involved, with or without a recessive contributing genetic influence. Still others have proposed that there is a separate gene responsible for each subtype of schizophrenia (Buss & Buss, 1969). Observations and opinions to date have not discredited nor displaced the theory based on the first great study on genetic factors in schizophrenia, which was done by Franz J. Kallmann (1946).

Kallmann accumulated evidence from studies on twins. In monozygotic twins he found that in 86% both twins manifested schizophrenia when one did. In fraternal twins only 7% of both showed schizophrenia

when one did. Kallmann maintained that the main gene in schizophrenia is autosomal, specific, single, and recessive (Kallmann, 1946).
He believed that the schizophrenic personality has this gene, but that it
is only expressed fully in interaction with some secondary genes that deal
with "constitutional resistance." In other words, some people inherit
genetic factors giving them physiological resistance—mesenchymal
defenses—which begins to explain why it is that many schizoid individuals do not develop schizophrenia while others do, and why it is that
some schizophrenics are able to develop nonpsychotic defenses while
others are not (Kallmann & Barrera, 1942). More research is needed to
fully answer the question of why different individuals develop different
forms of schizophrenia.

OVERTLY PSYCHOTIC AND MASKED
FORMS OF SCHIZOPHRENIA

For treatment purposes, the group of schizophrenias can be divided into
two main clinical categories: (1) the overtly psychotic forms, and
(2) the masked forms of the psychosis. Occasionally one encounters
patients who will vacillate from one category to the other in their clinical course. First I will briefly describe the overtly psychotic forms; then
I will define the masked forms and describe in some detail the development of their symptomatology.

The overtly psychotic forms of schizophrenia are characterized by
signs of massive personality disorganization, with symptoms of confusion and all-pervasive anxiety, usually psychotic compensatory symptoms of defense form, such as hallucinations and delusions. In other
words, the predominant symptomatology consists of the "hard"
symptoms of schizophrenia, which include Schneider's (1959) criteria
for the presence of schizophrenia. These patients are unable to make
appreciable reality contact with the therapist and require a preliminary
course of drug therapy before they are able to become engaged in psychotherapy. In fact, only when these patients have responded to major
tranquilizers to the extent that gross psychotic symptoms no longer
dominate the clinical picture can they become amenable to psychotherapeutic influence—providing, of course, that predisposing and precipitating stress factors are also removed from the patients' lives.

It should be mentioned here that the marked reduction in the number of classical forms of the schizophrenic psychosis observed in recent
years is partially related to the preventive efficacy of available neuroleptic drugs. Many of these patients who would otherwise "break" with
reality are seemingly enabled to cope on a more integrative level, and

even to construct nonpsychotic defenses, by means of drug support, despite their marked inherent integrative deficit.

The masked forms of the schizophrenic psychosis are characterized by the presence of nonpsychotic symptomatology—neurotic, depressive, sociopathic, and so forth—which dominates the symptom picture. In some cases the nonpsychotic symptom picture shifts from one form to another during the course of the disorder. The "hard" symptoms manifested in the overt schizophrenic psychosis are not present, although occasionally, when under extreme stress, a patient may experience a brief micropsychotic episode, following which non-psychotic symptoms will again prevail. Most patients, however, will maintain symptom pictures resembling those that occur in one or another nonpsychotic disorder. Nevertheless, an underlying constellation of basic symptoms of schizophrenia are always present, the content and process of which have all been comprehensively studied and documented (Hoch & Cattell, 1959). We might refer to these as the "soft" signs and symptoms of schizophrenia. They are quite easily detected in some patients; in others they are very subtle and require experience to recognize.

In masked schizophrenia the nonpsychotic symptomatology is actually only a thin façade overlying the basic symptoms of schizophrenia. It serves as a mechanism of defense against the disintegrating forces of pan-anxiety. Those schizophrenic individuals who are able to construct one or more nonpsychotic defense symptoms seemingly possess more integrative potential than do overtly psychotic schizophrenics. In other words, they are somehow able to compensate for (counterbalance, deflect, offset) the defects inherent in the schizophrenic psychosis by means of channeling much of the anxiety into specific nonpsychotic symptoms, which become a masking façade superimposed on the basic schizophrenic symptomatology. These individuals are the subject of our thesis, because a large number of them respond to our unified method of treatment approach. They have not severed contact with reality; they are able to make contact and form a working relationship to the therapist and engage in the therapeutic process.

DEVELOPMENT OF SCHIZOPHRENIC SYMPTOMATOLOGY

Now let us examine the development of the so-called "soft" signs and symptoms. First, we shall describe the schizoid personality organization, which always exists to a greater or lesser extent in all individuals who inherit a propensity for the development of schizophrenia. Secondly, we shall describe the early stages of schizophrenia, during which period the basic symptoms give rise to mounting all-pervasive anxiety. Thirdly, we shall discuss the nonpsychotic mechanisms of defense against pan-anxiety that evolve in the masked forms of schizophrenia—with emphasis on the pseudoneurotic form.

In order to recognize the developing signs and symptoms of schizophrenia, thorough exploration of the patient's background is essential. The importance of taking a careful history cannot be overemphasized. One must explore the heredito-constitutional factors, taking into consideration the patient's physical diathesis (which, incidentally, gives clues to an individual's physiological compensatory resistance factors for a number of disorders) and also one must pay attention to the family history. One must explore the early environmental stress factors—life stresses stemming from the external environment, and stresses stemming from the internal environment, such as endocrine or other somatic disorders. In taking a history we study the evolution of the patient's symptoms, namely, the type of onset and course of various symptoms in relationship to any predisposing and precipitating factors. While doing all this, we are very likely to note that the schizophrenic patient's symptoms developed in the framework of a peculiar personality organization termed schizoid. The schizoid personality organization is usually found to have been evident in early childhood, but very often schizoid features first become markedly apparent during the stress period of adolescence.

Schizoid Personality Organization

There is a typical configuration of traits characteristic of the schizoid personality. The individual is often colicky when a baby; often he is described as "unbelievably good," passive and compliant. He is shy as child; withdrawn, shut in, he prefers to play by himself, finds it difficult to relate to others, and has one or no close friends. It is as though he is "allergic" to people, or "phobic" for people. The child tends to be fearful in general; he avoids social turmoil; he avoids meeting strangers. He dislikes any changes in his environment. He may not be accident prone, but he is certainly anxiety prone.

Marked mood fluctuations are typical of the schizoid personality. Mood fluctuation is rarely mentioned in texts; its presence indicates an aura of apprehensiveness in which anxiety is often precipitated by small and seemingly irrelevant events. Sensitivity is very marked: the child tends to take everything personally, as though directed toward him; he is easily hurt and tearful.

Energy output can be variable: some are hyperactive, reminding

one of the so-called minimal brain dysfunction or the thalamic syndrome. Some persons, on the other hand, are abulic—seemingly "born
tired." Many of them lack enthusiasm except perhaps for matters not
involving other people, such as music, science, or the arts. Many are
unable to sustain active interests for any protracted period of time in
their lives.

A great many schizoid individuals begin to develop phobic reactions
very early in childhood. For instance, if the one-year-old child falls
while learning to walk, he may not attempt it again for 3 to 6 months.
When school-aged, he will avoid contact sports and any semblances of
violence. The schizoid child also tends to be phobic regarding his body;
he tends to exaggerate his aches and pains and is often hypochondriacal.

Vegetative homeostasis is often poor—when very young, these
people frequently suffer with gastrointestinal disorders, vasomotor
lability, and tend to have severe reactions to bacterial and virus infections. Homeostatic dysregulation seemingly points to some enzymatic
disturbance which, of course, is probably basic to schizophrenia.
Throughout childhood the schizoid personality may suffer more than
an average share of nightmares, sleepwalking, or insomnia with brooding and fear of death—all indicative of a great smoldering anxiety. In
adolescence, there often develops a tendency for sleep inversion, and
occasionally the individual's circadian rhythm may gradually become
so reversed that he feels the urge to sleep during the day and at night is
wide awake and relatively free from anxiety. Here again, the schizoid
personality tends to shy away from the stress of interpersonal relationships.

In taking histories, you will find that these features recur with a
monotony which leads us to connect it with some future development
of schizophrenia in *some* of these people—but not in all. No one can
predict who will and who will not develop schizophrenia. Moreover, if
schizophrenia does emerge, no one can have predicted what form it
would take. Nevertheless, we do know that schizophrenia develops in
the schizoid personality only. Naturally, the majority of people have a
few of the early characteristics described in the schizoid personality.
They are not diagnostic in themselves, although they are indicative of
an individual's proneness to anxiety reactions. If, however, an individual develops a mental disorder *and* if careful history-taking discloses
the pre-existing schizoid pattern, it is a fair hint as to the nature of the
disorder. The schizoid personality is basic to the individual; it is not
secondary to environmental stimuli. However, its presence is an indication that there is a genetically determined propensity for the individual to react in a disintegrative and dysregulative way to internal
and external environmental stimuli.

Clinically, all schizophrenic individuals show more of these basic schizoid symptoms, at least in a diluted way, than do persons who do not develop schizophrenia. Here again, no single schizoid symptom is, in itself, pathognomonic for incipient schizophrenia.

The schizoid personality organization points toward schizophrenia; it is not schizophrenia per se. However, it gives us a clue in making a diagnosis, for instance, between neurosis and pseudoneurotic schizophrenia, and it indicates that we should search for additional evidence of schizophrenia—specifically, the symptoms of early schizophrenia— the actual schizophrenic process.

Early Schizophrenia

Early schizophrenia is not just the schizoid personality; it is not the masked form of schizophrenia, nor is it the overt psychotic form. The term early schizophrenia applies to schizophrenia in its early stages of development—comparable in medicine to early syphilis, early tuberculosis, early hypertension, or the stage of appendicitis before it is perforated (Strahl & Lewis, p. 724, 1972). Early schizophrenia implies, one might say, that the disorder is at a stage before it is "perforated" into a definite form—either that of an overt psychosis on the one hand, or a masked form on the other hand. In other words, it is the stage of schizophrenia before symptoms have become "crystallized." This crystallization into a form of schizophrenia can develop very gradually or it can occur very quickly.

Early schizophrenia develops in an existing schizoid personality framework only. Symptoms can emerge in all areas and on all levels of functioning. They commonly begin to appear at an early age, especially during adolescence, and the illness is quite often ushered in by symptoms of depression. When this occurs it is well-differentiated from the manic-depressive psychosis by the fact that the latter rarely develops in persons under the age of 30. As early schizophrenia progresses the emerging symptoms are, of course, aggravated by life stresses.

To give you a rough outline of the symptom constellation existing in early schizophrenia, I shall briefly define a few important symptom configurations. Their treatment shall be discussed fully in Part 2.

A *self-esteem problem* becomes apparent in the early stages of schizophrenia and is always present in all forms of the disorder. Strong feelings of inferiority are deep-rooted in these individuals and become conditioned early in life due to a continual inability to function adequately in many areas. They are confused regarding a sense of self, or "ego"; they are confused about their bodily integrity and function, and confused about themselves in relation to their social environment. Reality is confused with unreality, which adversely influences major areas of functioning and compounds their profound sense of failure.

Intellectual impairments are always present. Objective signs and subjective symptoms of this vary in degree and pattern in different patients. Objectively, one can observe that these patients cannot perform consistently and realistically to the full potential of their intelligence. Subjectively, patients can be painfully aware of difficulty in concentrating, of confused thinking, and some complain of feeling "doped" or "dazed" from some vaguely defined "outside force" which they do not even try to explain. (By the way, in treating such patients, question their sensations, not their thoughts; then you are able to interpret to them what is going on inside them and they will have greater confidence in your understanding. For instance, you can explain, "You *feel* you lack control of your thoughts, and in your anxiety tend to assume you are being controlled".) These patients also readily feel detached, and, unlike the neurotic, react to experiences of depersonalization with marked anxiety. Of course, the conceptual thinking disorder, which we shall later describe at length when discussing treatment, is unique to schizophrenia. In some patients it is quite obvious, and in others so minimal that it is difficult to discern until the patient is well into treatment.

Emotional dysregulation is a common manifestation of early schizophrenia, although, here too, it varies in extent in different individuals. True anhedonia does not develop in early schizophrenia; in fact, it is one of the late signs and indicates deterioration is in progress. In early schizophrenia the patients are highly emotional. They often have great difficulty in expressing their feelings, due to blocking caused by a tremendous undercurrent of anxiety. Some patients, however, will display intense emotions that are inappropriate in quantity and quality, with marked and unpredictable ambivalent swings. Their ability to make emotional contact with other people is usually impaired due to intense anxiety, confusion, and feelings of isolation. Nevertheless, these schizophrenic patients do have an inherent capacity for experiencing affectionate bonds and pleasure in many things, but it is usually dampened by anxiety.

Chaotic concepts of sexuality make their appearances in early schizophrenia when patients relate their sexual attitudes, fantasies, and behavior. Due to confusion concerning the anatomy and functions of the body and its parts, concepts of that which is sexual and nonsexual, male and female, normal and pathological are often quite contaminated in these patients. And sexuality is always fraught with anxiety: on the one hand, they view sex as "evil" and imbue it with destructive aggression, and on the other hand they seek sex as desirable. Although some patients lead a relatively normal sex life, a great many resort to sexual perversions in desperate attempts to override anxiety and attain some amount of pleasure.

The anxiety structure in schizophrenia is not mentioned in many texts, yet it is the most disabling symptom the patients experience. In early schizophrenia anxiety is diffuse and all-pervasive, rising and falling like ocean groundswells, but always present. These people are fearful despite the fact that many of them are able to present a picture of outward calm and poise. It is a pan-anxiety: it permeates every area of thinking, feeling, and performing—especially in the tasks of relating to people—and cripples their capacity for pleasure and adequacy of functioning in major life areas.

Ambivalence goes hand in glove with the massive anxiety and plays an active role in all the symptoms of early schizophrenia mentioned. Later on, when we discuss treatment of the masked forms, we will find that actually half of the therapeutic process focuses on influencing ambivalence conflicts. On the intellectual level, schizophrenic patients are ambivalent: they swing to contradictory extremes, and they tend to be indecisive in everything—with an inability to distinguish the important from the unimportant. They are continually weighing pros and cons in attempting to cope with environmental stimuli, which compounds the existing anxiety, and a vicious circle thus develops because the anxiety in turn feeds the ambivalence. On the emotional level, schizophrenic patients are also ambivalent: they want and don't want, love and hate, fear and desire, all at the same time. The emotional dyscontrol is characterized by polar swings. Naturally, along with intellectual and emotional ambivalence there is ambivalence in behavior. In their anxiety they tend to construe the world of interrelationships as a kill-or-be-killed proposition. These are the people who are described as reacting too much, too soon or too little, too late. They swing to extremes with the all-or-none policy so typical of schizophrenia.

In summarizing the symptomatology in early schizophrenia, we can state that schizophrenia is a disorder affecting the whole personality; that afflicted individuals have an autistic-dereistic way of life with pan-anxiety and massive ambivalence in the foreground—and that this is much more extensive than is ever observed in neurotic patients.

Now, with the understanding of the development of schizophrenia in general, we shall go into considerable detail describing the development of the masked forms in particular.

Symptomatology Development of the
Masked Forms of Schizophrenia

At some point during the early stages of schizophrenia, a large number of individuals are somehow able to "crystallize" much of the vague and diffuse anxiety into tangible and nonpsychotic symptoms with which they are better able to cope. During the early stage of the disorder they become afraid of everything in general and unable to cope in any area in particular. Then, perhaps quite quickly and in response to some stressful life situation, certain definitive neurotic or other nonpsychotic symptoms emerge and are superimposed on the existing schizophrenic symptomatology. These nonpsychotic symptoms actually predominate the clinical picture and thereby serve as a mask which covers over the underlying schizophrenic symptomatology.

When these superimposed symptoms develop, they seemingly serve as posts onto which the schizophrenic patient is able to hitch his anxiety. In other words, pan-anxiety becomes largely channeled into one or two specific areas, rather than flooding all areas in the patient's life; it is directed onto certain concrete and tangible symptoms upon which the patient can focus his anxious attention and cope with it, to some extent. Without such nonpsychotic compensatory symptoms, an otherwise intolerable pan-anxiety is likely to cause the patient to "break" with reality—to decompensate into an overtly psychotic state.

The various forms of masked schizophrenia are properly labeled according to the predominant symptomatology manifested. If the predominant symptoms are neurotic, the disorder belongs in the category of pseudoneurotic schizophrenia; if a sociopathic picture predominates, the disorder is termed pseudosociopathic schizophrenia. These two forms are extremely prevalent in our culture today. There are a number of other masked forms of schizophrenia, however, including those manifesting predominantly depressive, phobic, somatoform, vegetative, or psychosexual symptoms.

Patients who suffer the masked form of schizophrenia do not manifest frank, overt psychotic symptoms, but they are psychotic nonetheless, insofar as they are relatively incapacitated in most of the main areas of functioning—social, sexual, intellectual, or occupational. Despite their nonpsychotic defenses, their lives are considerably disrupted due to the inherent disorganization of the personality. In other words, the "soft" signs and symptoms of schizophrenia continue to exert a disruptive force as an undercurrent, although masked by nonpsychotic symptoms. However, the fact that these individuals are able to construct nonpsychotic defenses indicates that their integrative capacity is comparatively stronger than that of persons suffering the overtly psychotic forms of schizophrenia and that they are therefore less readily devastated by anxiety-provoking stress.

In masked schizophrenia, the nonpsychotic symptoms render the patient only relatively free from pan-anxiety—and I say only relatively because the "crystallized" symptoms such as a phobia, an obsessive-compulsive symptom, or a hysterical one fails to fully absorb all the free-floating anxiety as it often does in the neuroses. Thus, despite any display he may make of outward calm, it is correct to assume that the schizophrenic individual continues to suffer anxiety in daily life.

It must be kept in mind that all schizophrenic individuals have a low tolerance for tension and frustration, and it does not require much environmental stress to foment a great deal of anxiety. In the masked forms, when stress factors in life grow so great that they outweigh the schizophrenic individual's powers of resistance, the nonpsychotic defenses may fail. On the rare occasions when this occurs, the individual may experience fleeting micropsychotic episodes, or even decompensate with a more protracted period of acute psychosis. However, the fact that these individuals had formerly been able to construct nonpsychotic defense symptomatology is a good prognostic sign to indicate that they will probably rebound from the psychotic state—especially when provocative stress factors are removed and when expedient therapy is afforded the patient.

Particularly in the case of the pseudoneurotic form of schizophrenia, it is not rare that one observes symptom shifts occurring in the course of the patient's illness. Sometimes, for instance, the neurotic symptom will shift from predominantly hysterical features to obsessive-compulsive ones, or even shift to sociopathic or phobic manifestations. In fact, in some patients a group of nonpsychotic symptoms can occur simultaneously, or in sequence. These phenomena can confuse the diagnostic issue and confound the treatment program for therapists who are not fully aware of the underlying schizophrenia in the patient.

Here, a useful diagnostic point must be mentioned. In the neuroses, one does not observe marked shifts in the character of the predominant symptoms—for example, from hysterical to obsessive-compulsive. Should such a drastic shift in the symptom picture occur, it is a clue to the existence of an underlying schizophrenia. In the neurotic patient, a consistent symptom pattern develops that is quite stable because it evolved along an established psychodynamic structure based on early environmental determinants. However, the neurotic symptoms that develop in the pseudoneurotic schizophrenic patient evolve along a far different dynamic structure from that of the neuroses, as we shall discuss.

Another important point must be mentioned. Depression is a symptom everybody experiences at some time or other, regardless of its diagnostic setting. And depression is a very common symptom in schizophrenia. When it recurs in schizophrenia, patients are all too often placed in the diagnostic category of manic-depressive psychosis. Therefore, because treatment method should be dependent on the diagnostic disorder to be treated, it is important to search for, and rule out wherever possible, any existing underlying signs and symptoms of schizophrenia before proceeding to establish a treatment regime.

It is interesting to note that in the neuroses and in the masked forms of schizophrenia, the type of symptoms individuals develop tend to be influenced not only by their somatotypy and genetic predisposition, but also to some extent by environmental and cultural determinants. For instance, the Scandinavian cultural groups seemingly are prone to the development of depressive symptomatology (Hendin, 1965). The peoples of Latin cultural background tend toward hysterical personality organization and high emotional expressivity. Furthermore, whether in the framework of a neurosis or pseudoneurotic schizophrenia, it appears to me that persons in every culture tend to develop symptoms "in style" with the times as well as the mores. Over the decades there has occurred a general shift in psychiatric symptomatology. For example, during the first quarter of the 20th century, hysterical dissociation and conversion symptoms were in vogue in the Western world. During the middle of the century, psychosomatic symptoms became very popular (as perhaps Freud's findings on hysteria and the unconscious were put in perspective). Throughout the Western world in the past two decades, we find an increasing number of people manifesting sociopathic acting-out symptoms, particularly those of crime and drug abuse. And we also find that depressive clinical pictures increasingly demand our professional attention.

Regardless of the prevalence of certain symptom pictures in any given period of time, our attention must focus on the patients who complain of depressive, neurotic, sociopathic and other nonpsychotic symptoms who are actually schizophrenic. On the psychiatric ward one will encounter many schizophrenic patients who are temporarily decompensated or who have compensated psychotically with hallucinations and delusions, and in these patients the diagnosis is obvious. However, also on the ward and very commonly in the outpatient clinic one will encounter many schizophrenic patients who have functioned and continue to function fairly well, with nonpsychotic compensatory symptomatology that deceptively masks the schizophrenic disorder.

The pseudoneurotic form of schizophrenia is especially important insofar as the diagnosis is very often mistakenly assumed to be that of a psychoneurosis. It cannot be overemphasized that when treatment of these patients is psychodynamically oriented to focus attack on the neurotic symptoms, the patient's neurotic defenses become undermined and he is likely to decompensate into a full-fledged psychosis. A medical analogy is useful here: a mole on a patient's face may clinically resemble a simple freckle, but before you excise it you would make certain of your diagnosis and rule out melanoma—because you would not risk decompensating your patient.

It goes without saying that in psychiatry, as in any other branch of medicine, careful diagnosis is of utmost importance because selection of treatment method is reliant upon it. Moreover, one should never attempt to arrive at a diagnosis on the basis of any assumed dynamic formulations. In fact it is quite the reverse: There is a specific dynamic structure in each diagnostic category—even though the clinical symptomatology can appear similar to that occurring in a number of different disorders. Thus, the method for treating the masked forms of schizophrenia is determined by the dynamic structure of the schizophrenic disorder—regardless of any neurotic or other masking façade. The dynamic mechanisms in schizophrenia are unique for that disorder and differ vastly from those postulated in the neuroses. Therefore, the method for treating schizophrenia is basically different.

CHAPTER 2

Dynamic Mechanisms of the Schizophrenic Integrative Impairment

Schizophrenia is a disintegrative disorder and its symptoms are protean, sometimes mimicking the neuroses and other nonpsychotic psychiatric disorders. Therefore, diagnosing the masked forms is often a difficult procedure. However, it is of utmost important to recognize the presence of schizophrenia because the diagnosis pinpoints the dynamic pattern of the disorder, and treatment method is reliant on the dynamic mechanisms—irrespective of any neurotic or other nonpsychotic symptomatology present. These dynamic mechanisms are unique to schizophrenia and differ vastly from those postulated for the neuroses. The method for treating each of these disorders is basically different.

My viewpoint here differs from that of those treating the so-called borderline disorders who base their diagnosis on psychodynamic theories, such as the theory of object relations (Mahler, 1968; Masterson, 1976). This theory postulates that the borderline individual's ego development was arrested or fixated at a growth state of separation-individuation, and assumes that the failure of normal integration of intrapsychic structures is largely on a psychodynamic basis. The theory is undoubtedly applicable and yields good results in treating "borderline" patients who are not basically schizophrenic. But, among those "borderline" patients who belong in the category of masked schizophrenia, my contention is that the integrative deficit is based on inherent constitutional factors, not psychodynamic ones; that infantile conflicts of environmental origin may only serve to precipitate or exaggerate its manifestations, not to cause them. Therefore, the psychodynamic theory is not applicable for formulating a method of approach in treating masked schizophrenia.

In the neuroses, the symptomatology is largely determined by environmental dynamic influences, particularly during the individual's formative years. This is not to deny that other factors, such as constitutional makeup, play some role as well. For instance, it can no longer be assumed that environmental factors fully account for the development of hysterical as opposed to obsessive-compulsive symptoms in a neurotic individual. To put it more simply, environmental influences alone cannot explain why it is that one child reacts to something threatening by running in fear, yet another child in a similar situation responds with fighting rage. Moreover, a considerable bombardment of stress is required for the development of full-fledged neurotic symptomatology in an inherently well-integrated individual. The schizophrenic, on the other hand, suffers an inherent defect in the ability to cope adequately with various environmental stimuli from the very beginning, and for this type of individual slight problems often loom as enormous stresses.

Schizophrenia is much more clearly an organic disorder. Inherent organic predispositional factors are the main determinants for symptom development. Environmental influences are not determinants; they serve merely as stress factors that may aggravate the schizophrenic process and precipitate the symptom picture. Schizophrenia is not "caused by" environmental stress, but can be precipitated by it. Similarly, physical stress can precipitate a heart attack in a person, but the "cause" is usually that the heart has been weakened by some disorder. Otherwise an enormous number of active people would be dropping like flies all around us.

RECOGNIZING THE DYNAMIC STRUCTURE

Patients who present very similar symptom pictures can actually be suffering from different disorders, each of which has its own dynamic structure. A hypothetical example can illustrate this. Patients A, B, and C are all individuals in their thirties who suffer obsessive-compulsive symptomatology and seek treatment due to recent onset of depression. Their histories disclose that each had experienced considerable parental demands, prohibitions, punishment, and emotional rejection during early childhood. The cultural backgrounds and socioeconomic situations were quite similar for each, and all were afforded similar educational and social opportunities. Further observations, however, point to how the diagnosis and dynamic structure differs in each case.

Patient A developed obsessive-compulsive symptomatology gradually during childhood, and the symptom contents did not shift. The onset of depression occurred clearly in direct relationship to losing his job. Based on this and further evidence, patient A's diagnosis is psychoneurosis, obsessive-compulsive type, with reactive depression. The psychodynamic mechanisms can be outlined as follows: in early childhood, Mr. A reacted with rage against oppressive parental authority, but a growing guilty fear of their retaliation caused such mounting anxiety that he defensively repressed feelings of rage and its connected ideation. The impulse remained, however, and under continuing environmental stress, his frustration and tension mounted. In order to protect himself from an emergence of the repressed ideation and rage connected with the impulse, his "ego" constructed obsessive-compulsive mechanisms of defense, which he carried throughout childhood and into adulthood. Then, the recent job failure struck a chord in the unconscious: the childhood rage with its guilty fear of further "punishment" was mobilized in the unconscious, and an attempt to make restitution by expiation to an unnamed authority led Mr. A to turn his rage inward against himself, part of which became manifested by feelings of depression. Appropriate treatment should aim at the target of the depression and obsessive-compulsive symptomatology, and guide the patient to trace the neurotic dynamic mechanisms back to their origins in early childhood.

Patient B resembled patient A in that his obsessive-compulsive symptoms developed gradually along a similar dynamic pattern traceable to early childhood parental pressures. However, patient B's obsessive-compulsive symptoms were mild and overshadowed by the depression. The history disclosed that patient B had suffered two previous episodes of depression within recent years. The family history disclosed evidence of manic-depressive psychosis in the collateral line, and one parent suffered regular periods of depression during middle-age. Mr. B's current depression, similar to the two preceding episodes, developed gradually over a period of weeks, and as depression mounted he found himself unable to maintain his compulsively high level of work performance. The diagnosis of unipolar manic-depressive psychosis was correctly made. Although the dynamic mechanisms for the obsessive-compulsive symptomatology were similar to those for patient A, these mechanisms failed to explain the cause of depression in Mr. B, and no precipitating factors could be perceived. Actually, the depression was the cause, rather than the result, of B's work inadequacy and perhaps imminent job loss. Psychotherapy aimed to relieve him of his obsessive-compulsive symptoms would be appropriate, and lithium carbonate could be used to control his affective disorder.

Patient C differed from A and B uniquely: History disclosed that the obsessive-compulsive symptoms did not appear until adulthood, although throughout childhood he was anxious, phobic, shy, and veered away from social contacts. As an adult, patient C suffered pan-anxiety, and in recent years began to practice rather bizarre obsessive-compulsive ritualistic behavior, especially in the area of sexuality. He related poorly to his peers and changed jobs several times due to conflicts with authority. The onset of depression was very sudden, and patient C was unable to relate it to specific stress factors. The diagnosis is schizophrenia, pseudoneurotic form, complicated by depression. In dynamic terms, depression developed secondarily to a chronic all-pervasive anxiety—an anxiety too strong to be adequately "absorbed" by obsessive-compulsive neurotic symptoms of defense. Treatment must first aim at the target of the pan-anxiety underlying the neurotic defense symptoms.

These briefly outlined case examples serve to illustrate that in each mental disorder the treatment approach is determined on the basis of the diagnosis, *not* the predominant symptom picture. It bears repeating that *the treatment approach for each disorder is reliant on its diagnosis, because the dynamic mechanisms which gave rise to the symptomatology are specific for each diagnostic entity*. In the case of schizophrenia, the dynamic mechanisms are specific for schizophrenia in general, regardless of the form it takes—and regardless of the presence of nonpsychotic symptoms.

THE DYNAMIC MECHANISMS OF SCHIZOPHRENIA

It must be kept in mind that the dynamic mechanisms in schizophrenia originate from an organic disturbance that dysregulates brain functioning (see Figure 2-1). Schizophrenic individuals undoubtedly suffer from neurochemical alterations that influence the intermediary breakdown of certain brain enzymes—resulting in metabolic disturbances of function in varying areas of the central nervous system and in varying amounts in each individual. Many hypotheses are under investigation concerning, among other phenomena, the malfunctioning of the neostriatal thalamic system, reticular pathways, and so forth (Flekkoy, 1975).

Probably consequential to the unknown enzymal defect, the brain is unable to screen afferent stimuli appropriately: there occurs a faulty screening of stimuli that stem from within the organism as well as from the external environment (Strahl & Lewis, 1972, p. 724). The screening

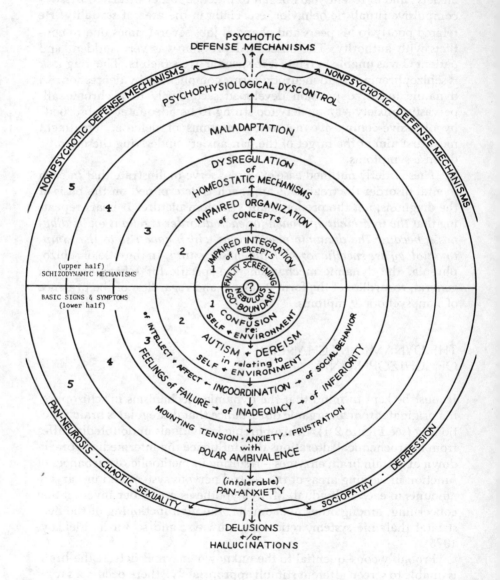

Figure 2-1. SCHIZODYNAMIC MECHANISMS: BASIC SIGNS AND SYMPTOMS.

disorder implies that the brain is unable to appropriately reject stimuli quantitatively. In analogy, it is as though the "holes" in the "sieve" of the afferent system are too large, allowing excess stimuli to pass through. In other words, in schizophrenia there is inadequate protection from a sensory overload. Excessive stimuli reach the level of perception, which leads to impairment in the schizophrenic's ability to select or to sort out appropriate stimuli.

Due to faulty screening, faulty integration of percepts occurs on the psychophysiological level. Naturally, the schizophrenic individual is thereby unable to fuse these internal and external stimuli appropriately in an integrated and organized way, qualitatively and quantitatively. This is the basis for the perceptual disorder in schizophrenia. Faulty integration is the problem of relevancy of percepts: irrelevant stimuli are fused with the relevant in the formation of percepts. Percepts that belong together are rejected and percepts that do not belong together are picked up.

The integrative impairment leads to a deficiency in organization of percepts, quantitatively and qualitatively. They are not set in appropriate order, and therefore are conceptualized in a faulty manner. Here one can glimpse the roots of the schizophrenic individual's confusion with regard to the self, somatically and functionally, and the interaction of the self with the external environment. A symptom peculiar to schizophrenia then emerges: the conceptual thinking disorder. Distortions of concepts accumulate and this, in turn, leads to faulty Gestalt formation. Gestalt capacity is impaired with regard to spatial relationships and body image, recognition of background versus foreground, and concepts of relevance and irrelevance. This shows up in sorting tests. Among other things, the disturbed Gestalt could well indicate that the integrational and organizational disturbances are connected to disturbance of synchrony in the interaction between the right and left cortical hemispheres in schizophrenia.

At the same time, the organizational deficiency leads to the most important dynamic problem: dysregulation of homeostatic mechanisms. This can be physiologically manifested on any and all levels of the nervous system in schizophrenia. On the psychophysiological level there is an inability to respond to percepts and concepts in a regulative way. The schizophrenic will overreact or underreact to stimuli, and with inappropriate timing. Qualitatively, the individual will aim attention in the wrong direction at the wrong time. On the affect level, intellectual and emotional incoordination—which Stransky (1929) referred to as "intrapsychic ataxia"—is manifested with both quantitative and qualitative inappropriateness. This problem is the source of the schizophrenic contact impairment, which Hoch termed "extra-psychic ataxia" (Strahl & Lewis, 1972). The schizophrenic individual is unable to relate to other people in an appropriate and consistent manner.

On the vegetative level, many schizophrenic individuals manifest considerable disturbance of metabolic functioning and endocrine regulation of one type or another. Dysregulation of energy output is often conspicuous, with tendencies for either abulia or hyperactivity. Many individuals experience misinterpretations or exaggerations of certain somatic sensations and an inappropriate disregard for others. On a motor level, many schizophrenics are slow in developing gross coordination and often maintain a deficit in this function.

Homeostatic dysregulation is most responsible for the development of all subsequent symptomatology in schizophrenia, and in treatment a great deal of attention is focused on the many aspects of this phenomenon. The symptoms that stemmed from the deeper dynamic mechanisms described have already fomented pan-anxiety. It can be understood, here, that the existing pan-anxiety further aggravates the homeostatic dysregulation and gives rise to massive ambivalence reactions. In other words, the highly anxious schizophrenic individual suffers intrapsychic incoordination with an inability to respond adaptively to stimuli on all levels, and this leads to "extrapsychic ataxia" (Strahl & Lewis, 1972), characterized by massive ambivalence reactions occurring on all levels of functioning. Polar swings occur in response to even slight stimuli, and, paradoxically, the schizophrenic often fails to react at all to gross stimuli, which is a part of the "ataxia."

As we shall later observe, a great part of therapy involves influencing and modifying these ambivalent patterns. Furthermore, therapy must deal with the ataxia as it is manifested by a form of splitting characterized by a lack of coordination between thought content and affect, as well as between thought content and behavior. For example, a schizophrenic patient will tell you she grieves over the death of her father, but she has the idea that the manner in which he died was ridiculous and she could not control her laughter when given the news. Incidentally, this differs from the usual display of inappropriate grimacing often observed in schizophrenia, in which the patient's seeming smile does not connote pleasure or amusement when relating a negatively charged emotional matter.

Bleuler's term, the "autistic-dereistic way of life" (Bleuler, 1950), refers to the primitive and unrealistic thinking and affect manifested in schizophrenia, all of which are explicable in reference to the dynamic mechanisms described. The peculiar thinking disorder is the only single symptom that is pathognomonic for schizophrenia. Emotional dysregulation interacts with the thinking disorder, and in conjunction with these phenomena there are behavioral reactions that are quantitatively and qualitatively inappropriate and maladaptive to the patient's situation.

THE SCHIZOPHRENIC PROCESS
IN LIVING PERSPECTIVE

If *you* were afflicted with schizophrenia, how would you feel about yourself, and how would you feel in relationship with your social environment? Assuming yourself a victim of the schizodynamic processes described, time after time you would observe that other people reacted as though they perceived that "something is wrong" with you; that you are "mixed up." You, too, would sense that "something is missing" in your mind but would be unable to define it. Because you are extremely sensitive to people's reactions, as well as to a vague feeling that you are different from others, your confidence and self-esteem would be continually undermined in your attempts to relate to others. You would feel unsure of yourself, terribly inferior, and confused about whom you are and what the world is all about.

First of all, your thinking disorder gets you into trouble. (If you understood its nature, which you don't, you would be able to correct it.) Your views on reality issues differ from those of other people and you find it difficult to make yourself understood. You often feel confused in trying to determine the priorities of issues before you while attempting to solve your daily problems.

Emotionally, you find yourself uncontrollably underreacting, then overreacting, and seemingly having the wrong feelings at the wrong time; people look askance and reject you; time and time again, you feel unacceptable and hurt. In your behavior, you make mistakes and in attempting to correct them you are sometimes too fearful to act; you become very passive in your anxiety and then, as tension mounts, you become aggressive, which lands you in further difficulties.

Self-doubts and confusion in everything you do has compounded your anxiety. You feel that you are a misfit. Social experience has taught you to anticipate hurts, rejections, and failures—so much so that you feel that any small achievements are not to be trusted. And, any "real" successes in life seem distant, vague, and unreal—success is only to be realized in frustratingly ephemeral daydreams of love, power, and glory. You have learned to be suspicious of people, interpreting their ordinary behavior as having negative implications in reference to yourself.

Small daily situations loom large; they all are problematic, confusing, preoccupying, and of great negative import. There is little room for pleasure in your life. You are on guard, always self-consciously on guard. With all this, you withdraw from social contact and then feel painfully isolated. Later on, as tension and frustration mount to an intolerable pitch, you crave stimulation and try to "break through"; once again you try to contact people—only to expose yourself to hurt and rejection, again to be reminded of your hopeless inferiority.

Anxiety permeates every area of your life, and self-doubts cause you to swing from one extreme of thought, feeling, and action to another. This compounds your coping difficulties—a vicious cycle heightens the anxiety, and further feeds into your feelings of confusion about yourself and the environment. The point comes when you whisper the awful idea to yourself, "I am cracking; I fear I shall go crazy!" Words of self-condemnation seem detached from yourself—almost as though not a part of you. In efforts to understand these things, you have fleeting ideas that perhaps your room is wired by people hostile to you.

Then something happens: You contract a bad cold and get the idea you may have cancer of the lungs because you smoke and you had learned that a cousin recently died of cancer. In a way, you feel somewhat relieved: at last you understand the reason for your anxiety. So, you begin a health regime: no smoking; no food additives, and you watch your diet and sleep habits very, very rigorously. You find you work slightly better on the job now because by taking health precautions you are less anxious and can think more clearly. It feels good to have *some* reason for *some* confidence, and you find you are less anxious socially. Although your friends do not agree with your health ideas, at least you are able to converse about them with conviction. When you feel tense and withdraw to your apartment, you read up on health matters. They interest you, and help you gain a feeling of self-mastery. Nevertheless, anxiety about your health forces you to constrict your daily life with increasing precautionary rituals. Finally you seek medical help, and go from one doctor to another attempting to find one who can diagnose your physical problem. Then a routine examination by a very prominent doctor includes a psychological interview, which discloses that your tension and anxiety are the cause of your physical problems. It feels so good to talk with a doctor who understands your feelings! At last you are going to be helped!

SCHIZODYNAMIC MECHANISMS AS
THE BASIS FOR TREATMENT METHOD

The psychiatrist investigating a patient similar to the hypothetical "you" described above will probably recognize the signs and symptoms of schizophrenia underlying the phobic and obsessive-compulsive symptomatology. Viewing this from the psychiatrist's position, what treatment method is appropriate for this patient? In other words, how does he treat the patient with pseudoneurotic schizophrenia or any masked form of schizophrenia?

First of all, the psychotherapist gathers sufficient data to make the correct diagnosis. Then, in this case, attention is focused on the dynamic mechanisms of schizophrenia, and the particular ways in which these mechanisms influence the patient's functioning in each life area. The patient's integrative capacity is appraised to determine the areas of integrative strength and the areas of relative integrative weakness.

By recognizing the patient's patterns of faulty integration, the therapist understands the patient's anxiety structure. The greatest amount of anxiety evolved out of the greatest area of faulty integration. In response to excessive stress, the patient suffering the masked forms of schizophrenia is then able to utilize one or more areas of relative integrative strength to compensate for, to offset, an intolerable pan-anxiety.

For instance, the hypothetical patient under review manifests massive emotional dysregulation but has significantly better integration on the intellectual level. He is able to construct obsessive-compulsive symptomatology. Now, at last, he can channel some of the diffused anxiety into concrete symptoms with which he gains a sense of mastery and, in fact, a tenuous sense of superiority. Thus, neurotic symptoms superimposed on the underlying schizophrenic symptomatology serve to defend the patient against the decompensating forces of pan-anxiety.

In conclusion, the dynamic explanations for the development of neurotic symptoms in a neurosis are not valid for explaining the development of neurotic symptoms that occur in pseudoneurotic schizophrenia. In treating schizophrenia, attempts to trace any neurotic symptoms along the lines of the psychodynamic mechanisms of a neurosis would not lead to the origin of the neurotic symptoms. Despite the fact that neurotic symptoms occurring in schizophrenia resemble those that develop in neuroses, they develop on a vastly different dynamic structure in each disorder.

A unified method for treating patients suffering with pseudoneurotic or other masked forms of schizophrenia must rely on the utilization of the schizodynamic mechanisms (schematized in Figure 2-1) that we have described. The evolution of all schizophrenic symptomatology, as well as the superimposed symptoms manifested in the masked forms of schizophrenia, can be traced back to their derivations in this theoretical model. The basis from which the nonpsychotic symptoms are derived can be understood when one recognizes that these symptoms serve as compensatory mechanisms of defense against overwhelming anxiety; that they protect the patient from decompensating into a frankly overt psychotic state. This explains, first of all, why it is of utmost importance for the therapist to avoid tampering with the nonpsychotic defense symptoms—no matter how temptingly they appear to be structured on neurotic dynamic mechanisms—but rather to aim at the underlying anxiety from which they emerged. Secondly, the schizodynamic mechanisms that gave rise to the pan-anxiety should then be dealt with actively in the psychotherapeutic process. Know the diagnosis and dynamic structure of the patient's disorder!

CHAPTER 3

Prognostic Factors and Treatment Goals

Prognosis relies on the diagnosis of a disorder and the nature of its dynamic mechanisms. The dynamic mechanisms of schizophrenia that we have discussed, and that were schematized in Figure 2-1, serve as the guideline for determining prognosis and for establishing goals when treating all schizophrenic patients, including those suffering from masked forms of schizophrenia. Prognosis and treatment goals are unique to quite an extent for each schizophrenic patient; both these matters are influenced by the patient's anxiety structure and the underlying symptoms of dysregulation patterned by the integrative impairment.

Sometimes it requires a considerable number of fact-finding interviews with a schizophrenic patient before the diagnosis can be established and prognosis determined. Prognosis must be considered fairly early in treatment, however, because the patient, as well as the patient's family, will surely ask, "What is wrong, Doc?"; "Will I get well?"; "Will I have another relapse?"; "For how long must I be in therapy?"; "What kind of treatment will I have?"; "How much will it cost?", and so forth. Generally speaking, you can rest assured that when the prognosis can be determined, it can serve as a fair indicator of the degree to which your patient will respond to therapy.

It is important to realize that no one is without bias in making diagnosis; bias always intrudes when prognosticating for our patients. Bias is due to many factors. First of all, the therapist's personality makeup is an important factor. If the therapist making the diagnosis is relatively stable, relatively normal, and anxiety-free, he is very likely to make a diagnosis on his patients that is slanted in a very optimistic way—especially if he is young, vigorous, dedicated, and hopeful. His prognostication is going to be optimistic, and usually there is nothing terribly wrong with this because of course the suggestive power of the therapist can have a constructive influence on a patient's attitude in therapy. However, any type of bias can lead to diagnostic error and treatment difficulties.

On the other hand, if the therapist's personality makeup is anxiety-laden, or depressive, or if he is schizoid, or if there is a schizophrenic member in his family, his attitude in making a diagnosis is unwittingly going to be influenced accordingly. He may overlook certain symptoms in his patients. He may be afraid to make a diagnosis of schizophrenia, in which case his prognostications would be inappropriate to the patient's schizophrenic disorder.

There is also the factor of the therapist's background training. If his background is in neurology, he is going to look for neurological disorders, which is fine, and diagnose the patient accordingly. If his background is internal medicine, that will carry influence. And, I do not hesitate to add, if a psychiatrist's background is confined to psychoanalysis, he may want to have his patient climb up and down the psychosexual ladder, and in fact will tend to diagnose his patients as psychoneurotic whenever possible (this can be quite unwittingly done) and prognosticate with the dynamics of neurosis in mind.

There is also the factor of fads, especially cultural and pharmaceutical fads. It is my biased opinion, for instance, that in some psychiatric circles at the present time it is the fad to see people as manic-depressive psychotic or as neurotic, and investigators tend to practice gymnastics with phenomenology in order to avoid the diagnosis of schizophrenia. There are pharmaceutical fads. For instance, since the advent of lithium treatment a tremendous number of patients have been diagnosed as having manic-depressive psychosis who would heretofore have been put in the category of schizophrenia or involutional depression, or psychoneurosis with depression, and so forth. Prognosis has a lot to do with the diagnostic category, so following fads is not good.

In our human fallibility, we can turn prejudice to advantage if we accept the following diagnostic credo: Assume the "neurotic" patient is schizophrenic, or otherwise suffering an organic disorder, until all the diagnostic evidence is at hand. In this way you will not make a detrimental error in your therapeutic approach and you will not make a major prognostic error.

PROGNOSTIC CRITERIA

To prognosticate, one must arrive at the diagnosis and determine the dynamics of the disorder as it applies to the particular patient. This requires investigating: The patient's heredito-constitutional background, his genetic propensity plus compensatory resistance factors; the early environmental predisposing stress factors; the evolution of the patient's symptomatology; and the symptom picture.

Now, assuming the patient is schizophrenic—even though you cannot predict if, when, or in what way he may decompensate—by exploring heredito-constitutional and environmental life stress factors and the dynamic evolution of the symptom picture, you are able to prognosticate with reasonable accuracy the outcome of the patient's mental disorder, despite the fact that your present diagnosis may be only tentative.

At this point I would like to cite an example by means of metaphor. Let us assume a patient begins to suffer certain schizophrenic symptoms. Let us picture the situation in terms of a diagram of a beaker. In that beaker are different levels of single factors, all of which add up until the beaker overflows—comparable to the patient's spilling over with symptoms of schizophrenia. The sequence of this development is as follows: At the bottom of the beaker are the hereditary factors, and in some patients they are a large component; in others the titer is very low. Poured on top of that are the formative years' stress factors, which of course influence a person's psychological predilection to symptom formation. Finally, there is added a precipitating factor consisting of exposure to sudden stress. If this factor is great, the fullness of the beaker becomes such that it spills over in terms of symptom manifestations.

With regard to schizophrenia, a number of different factors must be operating in the individual before there occurs an "overflow" in terms of clinical symptoms. The number and type of factors underlying the clinical symptomatology of the disorder give us clues to the prognosis. These factors are only generalizations. They cannot be assayed. A single factor is a single clue; it is not a sure determinant for prognosis, just as each symptom is a clue and it takes a constellation of symptoms to give you an indication of the diagnosis.

Heredito-Constitutional Factors

Heredito-constitutional factors consist of the numerous inherent mechanisms that determine an individual's resistance, as well as predisposition, to schizophrenia. A person must have inherited propensity
factors for schizophrenia in order to develop the disorder. The family
history of mental disorders, especially of schizophrenia, affords clues to
the possible amount of genetic propensity in your patient. By the way,
schizophrenia appears somewhere—in the immediate or collateral line
—in practically every family. The greater the family history of schizophrenia, the worse it omens for prognosis in your particular patient.

Then there are the factors of physiological compensatory mechanisms. The greater these are in a patient, the more it points toward
good prognosis. For example, there are what Kallmann referred to as
"mesenchymal resistance factors" (Kallman & Barrera, 1942): if the
patient's somatotype is mesomorphic with a good skeletomuscular
structural balance and a hypertrophic cardiovascular system development, somehow this indicates a strong structural and metabolic regulatory potential. These innate resistance factors are prognostic assets.

If the patient has a life history of good vegetative homeostasis, it is a
favorable prognostic sign. If he has not suffered obvious gastrointestinal
lack of homeostasis or cardiovascular lack of homeostasis, and if his
endocrine and hormonal balance is good and if his healing powers and
resistance to infections seem strong, the prognosis is likely to be better
than if the opposite were so.

Also, we have to consider the energy output, or "drive" potential,
in a person. The more assertive the individual and the more he achieves
in life, despite symptoms and despite the environmental influences, the
better the prognosis will tend to be. A person's potential for energy
output is to some extent inherent. Margaret Fries made an observation
that newborns differ in their response to the stimulus of a sudden loud
noise. Some babies automatically respond with an allover massive reflex
in response to the loud noise; at the other end of the scale, some babies
are passive and show no pronounced reaction. Follow-up on these
infants would probably show that later on in life the trends toward
assertiveness or passive dependency are directly proportionate to the
early trends. Also in terms of energy output, inherent as well as environmental determinants play a role in an individual's rage or fear reactions to threatening situations. Actually, environmental factors alone
far from explain why it is that from the very first time one child is confronted with danger he runs in fear and yet another child in the same
situation reacts with rage and fights. Whatever the basic personality

differences are between the two, those patients who have a history of positive energy output tend to have a better prognosis than those patients who have been passive-dependent. Similarly, patients who are "achievers" usually tend to respond better in therapy.

This brings us to the discussion of basic personality organization. On the psychophysiological level, this is an expression of the physiological compensatory makeup of the individual. The number and intensity of schizoid personality features present in early childhood is an important prognostic factor. The greater the extent of schizoid features manifested in early life, the worse the prognosis is likely to be for the schizophrenic patient, the indication being that the patient lacks adequate inherent resistance factors to schizophrenia. On the other hand, if a schizophrenic patient's basic personality makeup has relatively few, or mild schizoid traits, and especially if there is no schizophrenia discernible in his immediate family, he shows good resistance. Considerable life stress is required to push such a person over into developing any form of schizophrenia, and when that occurs he is likely to respond well in therapy.

Early Environmental Stress Factors

Early environmental predisposing factors, or life stresses, in the patient's external environment are of prognostic import. The so-called formative years of a child's development—the first 5 years of age—are critical times in that a milieu of chronic stress can seriously damage the person's ability to cope later in life. The first 2 years of life are particularly critical times. And I say that because by the approximate age of 2, the individual's brain development is such that he has formed an attitude about himself and the environment, an attitude that he is a "good" self, a strong self, or a weak self, a "bad self," and that the environment is gratifying or that the environment is dangerous. Now these attitudes are in large part instilled in the individual by the parental authority on whom, of course, the small child is completely dependent. If such early influences foment a stressful milieu and give the child a negative attitude about himself and the environment, naturally it interferes with emotional maturation and cripples the child's future abilities to cope in an adaptive way. His attitudes about himself and the world are also, of course, influenced by his inherent integrative capacity.

If any inherent faulty integration is present in the child, early environmental stresses will hit that hard—and schizoid symptoms will become conspicuous. Therefore, how the schizophrenic patient reacted to chronic stress situations and/or the occurrence of acute stressful events throughout childhood is important to note. Chronic stress can include parental rejection, excessive demands and punishment, or—what is even worse—an unstructured environment. Physical illnesses or handicaps during his maturing years are additional sources of stress. On top of that, if the child experienced acute mental or physical trauma, it is important to find out how he reacted to those events both in a quantitative and qualitative way. Were his responses withdrawing and phobic or did he tend to react with assertion and defiance? These data afford prognostic clues.

If life stress was so slight that the environment offered smooth sailing during childhood, considerable heredito-constitutional propensity must exist to push the person over into schizophrenic symptomatology. In such case, the patient's inherent deficits indicate that prognosis is unfavorable. On the other hand, if environmental stress was very marked and the going was rough during childhood, only a small amount of inherent propensity is required to provoke schizophrenic symptomatology. In such case, a good prognosis is directly proportionate to a patient's integrative strength. (Of course, in the absence of any inherent propensity for schizophrenia, a person who had a dreadful childhood is probably going to develop an emotional disorder, too, but it will not be schizophrenia.)

If the patient is schizophrenic and has coped with fair adaptation in a fairly homeostatic way despite life stresses, and if the patient made achievements in life despite his schizophrenia, you might say that the life stresses played some role in mobilizing the patient's innate compensatory strength—in other words, his innate resistance. He is not so likely to develop marked schizophrenic symptomatology and he may be able to develop a defensive façade such as neurotic symptoms.

This partly explains why the mid-European peasant, for instance, does not so readily manifest a schizophrenic disorder until middle age. In comparison, people reared in upper middle-class American society quite often develop their schizophrenic symptoms around the time of puberty: The Americans did not experience the daily doses of frustrations and deprivations that are common reality for people where life demands hard work and obviates the luxury of self-gratification.

Parallel to this, I am reminded that years ago little children used to dive off piers and swim in New York's East River. Today if a child were to do that he would probably be completely dissolved by the toxins in the water. Yet even 30 or 40 years ago the river contained considerable sewage and pollution, and perhaps those children who were weak succumbed to illness and we didn't see them swimming there any more. However, the stronger ones probably built up their resistances to all kinds of bacteria, viruses, and other toxins; daily doses of these things mobilized their potential for developing immunity.

Evolution of Symptomatology

The evolution of the symptom picture in the schizophrenic patient must be studied not only with regard to inherent and environmental predisposing factors, but also with regard to age and rate of onset and the nature of precipitating factors. They all afford prognostic signs. Age of onset is very important prognostically. The older the patient was before the onset of his schizophrenic symptoms, the better the prognosis. As we have mentioned, if the patient does not suffer symptoms until later life, it indicates a strong innate resistance enabling him to cope with a certain amount of stress for a long time. Conversely, if another patient experienced a similar amount of life stress and "breaks" at an early age—before or during puberty—it strongly indicates that he has relatively poor constitutional resistance, and prognosis is not so good.

Now what about prognostication in reference to the rate of onset? The more acute the onset of symptomatology—especially in the presence of clear-cut and strong precipitating factors—the better the prognosis. This is a general rule in medicine. Conversely, the more chronic and insidious the onset, the worse the prognosis, regardless of the factors of predisposing or precipitating influences.

Look for precipitating factors: They are very important! The greater the number or intensity of precipitating stress factors before the development of symptomatology, the better the prognosis. Precipitating factors can consist of physical or external environmental stress-provoking events, or perhaps largely of long-term accumulative minor stresses until a straw finally breaks the camel's back. But if clear-cut and heavy precipitating factors exist, the patient may be quite entitled to his symptomatology, in which case it is a good prognostic sign.

The clinical course along which the symptom picture evolved from its onset to the current state of illness varies qualitatively and quantitatively among schizophrenic patients. Symptoms in one patient may develop gradually and steadily, and in another patient remissions and exacerbations may occur. The latter symptom course is of considerable prognostic significance. For instance, there is the "three-day schizophrenia" syndrome, which usually has a sudden onset with massive symptomatology with decompensation. After a few days or a week the symptoms disappear as suddenly as they came, and seemingly there is complete remission. This indicates a good short-term prognosis. However, it tells you nothing about the patient's long-term prognosis. For one thing, future episodes cannot be predicted on the basis of a single event. Nevertheless, if a series of exacerbations occur, you are observing a trend sequence that forebodes an unfavorable long-term prognosis.

Incidentally, during the climacterium, the diminution of sex hormone production combined with environmental demands for role change can alter a schizophrenic patient's clinical course. For instance, a pseudoneurotic woman can react to these stresses in one of two ways: It can make or break her, so to speak. One patient may mellow and suffer much less pan-anxiety. Another patient may suffer an involutional depression or psychosis. The latter reaction can sometimes be predicted by the therapist on the basis of the patient's rigid personality organization and early attitudinal conditioning—usually obsessive-compulsive in character.

The greater the number and depth of regression symptoms occurring along the symptom course, the worse the prognosis. Note, here, that regression must not be confused with deterioration. The latter is a state of regression from which the patient cannot rebound. It does not occur in masked forms of schizophrenia. In simple regression the patient is reacting to stress and may behave on quite a childish level, but rebounds to a more mature level when the stress is removed or surmounted.

The Symptom Picture

Prognostic signs related to the constellation and configuration of symptoms in the course of the schizophrenic disorder are considerable. Several components in the symptom picture should be examined—the intellectual, affective, and behavioral components, and also their symptom mixtures.

First we shall appraise the intellectual component. In general, the greater the patient's intellectual integration, the better the prognosis and response to treatment. (There is one specific exception to this general rule: An acute schizophrenic confusion state bears resemblance to the delirium occurring in organic toxicity states, with clouding of consciousness. Such episodes usually clear up within a few days and the prognosis is good. However, the prognosis is good for that incident; the long-term prognosis depends upon whether or not the patient suffers exacerbations in the future.) It is very important to realize that the more often any type of intellectual disintegrative trends are manifested by the patient, the worse the prognosis. For instance, if the patient manifests massive thinking disorders, strong paranoid reactions, and obsessive-compulsive rigidity, the prognosis is not good. This patient may operate in a clear sensorium but he displays a certain lack of resiliency that indicates that he is not likely to budge in treatment. I must remind you that many obsessive-compulsive neurotic patients are so intellectually rigid and so lacking in emotional flexibility that, regardless of treatment efforts, the prognosis is not good. In fact, it can be worse than in the obsessive-compulsive pseudoneurotic schizophrenic patient—probably because the obsessive-compulsive symptoms in pseudoneurotic schizophrenic patients do not have deep dynamic "roots" and can be influenced in treatment. However, the pseudoneurotic patient whose obessive-compulsive symptoms serve as strong compensatory defenses can be far more difficult to treat than, for instance, the pseudoneurotic patient who relates in therapy with a strong affective component.

Now we shall consider the affective component. The greater the affective component of the symptomatology—love, hate, desire, resentment, or whatever—the better the prognosis. Perhaps such a patient is too flexible and sways to extremes with the slightest breeze, but the fact remains he has flexibility. The patient reacts; the patient responds to stimuli, including stimuli in treatment. Thus, the greater the show of emotional "incontinence" and emotional ambivalence and swinging back and forth of the compensated schizophrenic patient, the better the prognosis.

Note here that I have not mentioned anhedonia. Psychiatric literature usually claims that anhedonia is always part and parcel of schizophrenia. True anhedonia in schizophrenia indicates the presence of a deteriorative process. In compensated schizophrenic patients, there is no deterioration, but a blandness of emotional expression can occur; this is often mistaken for anhedonia. The patient can appear to be disinterested, bored, constricted in affect, and rather emotionally nonparticipating, but usually underlying this blandness the patient is a seething cauldron of feelings. When encountered in your social life, these individuals present a calm and controlled exterior, and you might remark to such an individual, "I certainly admire your calmness." And if the individual is a close acquaintance he might respond, "Oh, underneath all this I am very, very tense; I feel like a worm on hot coals, but somehow I cannot show it." Many such compensated schizophrenic individuals are able to maintain a calm façade even when under great emotional stress. However, if the patient's self-containment overlies strong chronic anxiety, which is on a more basic physiological level than actual affect, especially if the anxiety has no apparent basis in reality to explain it, the prognosis is not very favorable. Such chronic anxiety indicates that inadequate compensatory mechanisms are at the patient's disposal.

The behavioral component of the patient's symptom picture also contains prognostic signs. Generally speaking, the more aggressive an individual can become, or the more assertive he is in his general behavior, or the more acting-out symptomatology is present, the better the prognosis. Here again, the patient reacts; he has some strength and resiliency. Conversely, the more passive-dependency present, and the more the patient tends to cling, or withdraw and avoid any confrontations, the "weaker" the patient's ability to cope with stress and the worse the prognosis. In other words, you will not get so much motivational response from a patient who would prefer to sit in a corner and perhaps suck his thumb.

Interesting observations have been made concerning this acting-out behavior in patients. Years ago a colleague told me that when he was a prison psychiatrist, he observed that many of the prisoners who were acting out and disrupting the group were the ones given treatment, simply to make the managing of the prisoner group more expedient for the staff. And many of these patients responded surprisingly well to treatment. Then they found that when they placed the passive, compliant, well-behaving prisoners into treatment, there was not the same number of good results.

Now to mention the symptom mixtures. The greater the "purity" in terms of few and well-delineated symptoms, the better the prognosis. On the other hand, the broader the mixture of symptoms—the more areas involved (mainly, social, sexual, and occupational) and the more levels involved (mainly, thinking, emotional, behavioral, and vegetative) —the worse the prognosis. Obviously, patients with a broad mixture of symptoms are unable to develop serviceable compensatory defense mechanisms in sufficient areas on one or the other level. Quantitatively, therefore, the development of a broad constellation of symptoms, especially if they tend to shift in configuration, bodes for poor prognosis.

To reiterate: all that we have discussed are only general prognostic indicators. No one of these signs is a sufficient prognostic determinant alone. Furthermore, there are exceptions in the case of each. You must view them all together, in their constellation, as you view symptomatology in its constellation before you arrive at your diagnostic appraisal.

There is another important prognostic indicator: the patient's symptom picture as presented in the transference. Usually during the first interview, the manner in which the patient relates to you affectively becomes apparent. If he relates with display of affect—whether negative or positive affect—it is a good prognostic sign. On the other hand, the more detached, bland, or cold he appears in relating to you, the less favorable you can view the prognosis, generally speaking. Does he stir your empathy, your feelings of concern? Or, does he arouse your resentment because you feel unable to reach his emotions? And, of course, the more harmonious his emotional responses are in relationship to his thought content and behavior, the better you can view the prognosis. However, if there is a split between thought, feeling, and behavior—if the patient's display of affect is inappropriate to his ideation, while he behaves in yet a third way—you observe marked evidence of disintegration of the patient's total personality and the prognosis is not so favorable.

Prognosis also relies on the extent of the schizophrenic patient's integrative strengths and weaknesses as manifested in various life areas. These can be surmised by observing in which areas the individual is best able to function; in which he is least able to function; in which life areas he has suffered the greatest environmental stress; in which the least environmentally induced stress in the course of his life.

I would like to emphasize that it is important to rule out "untreatable" patients whenever possible. Not all schizophrenic patients who are compensated on a nonpsychotic level respond sufficiently to psychotherapy to warrant their going through with it. For instance, patients who accept their symptoms in an egosyntonic manner are usually not adequately motivated to work in therapy, but rather to try to manipulate the therapist to adjust their environment to suit them. This applies particularly to schizophrenic patients with sociopathic character and traits; they lack sufficient capacity for clinical insight and do not utilize interpretations constructively—unless the therapist is skilled in applying Aichhorn's (1935) technique, and even then prognosis is dubious.

Furthermore, in selecting patients one has to be very careful that one is not dealing with simple schizophrenia. Simple schizophrenics are usually difficult to diagnose and, when a façade of fleeting nonpsychotic symptoms appears, are readily confused with pseudoneurotic or depressive schizophrenic individuals. Seemingly, in simple schizophrenia the energy "batteries" are low; these individuals lack drive; they lack motivation; they lack depth of affect; and usually the symptoms are too vague to be dealt with. Treatment yields only tentative responses, if any, and long-term prognosis is very poor.

Should the prognosis appear obviously poor, you may decide the patient is not an appropriate candidate for psychotherapy in your office or the clinic, and you will have to decide upon referral to afford the patient an appropriate alternative form of therapy. However, should you determine that the patient has a fair or good prognosis and decide to treat him, then you establish treatment aims and goals in accordance with the patient's total personality configuration, with its assets and liabilities.

AIMS AND GOALS OF THERAPY

Aims and goals of therapy cannot be ascertained until one has arrived at the proper diagnosis and considered the prognostic criteria. Upon recognizing that you are dealing with a schizophrenic patient—of pseudoneurotic or any other form—you know that your patient suffers an inherent integrative impairment. You do not know the etiological basis for this impairment, so you cannot aim to remove it. But you do know the schizodynamic mechanisms derived from the integrative impairment, and therefore you know that you can to a greater or lesser extent influence some of its symptom manifestations. *Thus, the aim in therapy is to enable the patient to overcome some of the manifestations of the integrative impairment.* How is this to be accomplished?

It can be accomplished by applying the method for interpreting the various target symptoms that is consistent with the schizodynamic formulations we have discussed. Since the symptom manifestations occurring in all forms of schizophrenia are culminations of the schizodynamic process, a single unified method in accordance with these dynamic mechanisms is consistently applicable. Because these dynamic mechanisms differ vastly from the dynamic mechanisms of any other disorder, the method for psychotherapy of schizophrenia is basically unique.

In general, the procedure aimed to help the patient overcome manifestations of integrative impairment can be outlined as follows: Having appraised the patient's areas of integrative strength and weakness, you proceed to gradually teach the patient the nature of the dynamic mechanisms responsible for the symptoms that evolved from the inherent impairment—step by step, from superficial to deeper layers. You teach the patient to recognize his integrative strengths and to focus on developing and directing these strengths for improved adaptive performance in those areas. This serves to realistically enhance the patient's self-esteem and confidence.

Thus fortified with more ego strength, the patient is able to learn from you to recognize and understand his particular areas of integrative weakness. You then aim to teach the patient how to avoid involving himself in those areas of greatest conflict, wherever it is feasible. You further teach the patient, repeatedly and in many contexts, ways whereby he can utilize his existing inherent adaptive assets to somewhat compensate for his existing inherent adaptive deficits. Thereupon, the patient gains protection from much of the anxiety that had been fomented as a result of his inherent integrative impairment—and the patient is able to overcome some of its manifestations.

During this therapeutic procedure, you do not aim to diminish the patient's neurotic or other nonpsychotic compensatory defenses and, in fact, you may even condone the patient's fortifying these defenses, or constructing new defenses, when required for allaying anxiety during untoward stress situations. Once therapy begins to favorably influence the patient's compensatory adaptive behavior, you may want to re-estimate the prognosis and review the patient's symptom picture in order to establish treatment goals.

What should be the goals in treating the masked forms of schizophrenia? *The goals are to enable the patient to attain the level of adaptation appropriate to his particular integrative potentials.* Setting these goals will guide the therapist in determining when and how to eventually terminate formal therapy. Naturally, for as long as the etiological basis of schizophrenia remains unknown, the "core" of the disintegrative disorder cannot be eradicated. Therapists cannot expect schizophrenic patients to achieve "absolute" cure, regardless which form of schizophrenia they suffer. Yet, this need no longer discourage either the patients or their therapists. A large number of so-called borderline or masked schizophrenic patients are considerably benefited by the appropriate treatment method. Many become able to live relatively free from anxiety or other disruptive symptomatology. On the other hand, there are schizophrenic patients who are unable to benefit appreciably despite conscientious efforts of both the patients and their therapists. Nevertheless, therapists can anticipate that those patients who had been able to construct strong nonpsychotic compensatory defenses are usually markedly benefited by the treatment method outlined (which will be described in full later) and achieve what Hoch (Strahl & Lewis, 1972, p. 755) termed an "orthopedic" cure: They learn how to walk through life with merely a slight psychological "limp," or by using a modest psychological "cane."

In order to determine the appropriate goals, the therapist must know each patient's integrative assets and limitations as manifested by their symptoms of dysregulated functioning. The goals for the patient must not be set too high, nor set too low. If goals are set too high, the patient will feel unable to attain them and is likely to develop greater anxiety than that which was initially present. Feelings of disappointment in himself and the therapist can be very painful. The patient will become discouraged and depressed, because he feels that he has let the therapist down. Or, the patient may regress to a more childlike level of adaptation. Or, the patient may actually decompensate with symptoms of overt psychosis. Disaster can occur if the patient feels the therapist is pushing him, forcing him into some type of position wherein he is unable to cope.

On the other hand, if goals are set too low the patient will feel increasingly convinced of the inferiority that had plagued him extremely in the first place. He will become increasingly passive-dependent, feeling more and more helpless and more and more anxious. So, do not underplay the necessity of pushing the patient. The trick is to gauge how far to push each patient during the course of treatment, in what direction to push, and at what time to push in each life area. In other words, the aim of therapy is to reeducate, to recondition, the patient to reality in terms of his inner potentials to cope with environmental opportunities and limitations. And the goals of treatment are to enable the patient to cope adaptively to the extent of his particular inherent potentials. In this way, the patient will encounter minimal stress and experience minimal anxiety.

Of course, anxiety is a signal of distress that everybody experiences from time to time, and the patient must learn that fact, too. When the patient becomes able to function without excessive anxiety he, too, can learn to respond to the signal of anxiety by readjusting to the stimulus in an adaptive way. As the patient experiences less intensity of anxiety as a result of therapy, he becomes able to shed some of the compensatory neurotic or other nonpsychotic symptom defense patterns, which had originally developed as end-manifestations of the impaired integrative functioning. The appropriate goals reached will be those deemed suitable by the patient, not those foreseen as suitable in the mind of the therapist. Each patient is entitled to adapt in terms of pleasure and security according to his own particular style and value system.

Part 2

PRELIMINARY TREATMENT TECHNIQUES

CHAPTER 4

Initial Anxiety Reduction and Establishing the Therapeutic Relationship

A constructive working relationship between patient and therapist must be established before actual therapy can be conducted. However, treatment cannot even commence if the patient is unable to make sufficient contact with the therapist to form a transference relationship. In pseudoneurotic schizophrenia and other forms of masked schizophrenia, a patient is very often unable to make this contact, because of his intense anxiety: paradoxical as it may seem, the patient's anxiety must be reduced before therapy can begin the task of investigating the dynamic factors responsible for the anxiety.

Unless some measure is taken by the therapist to reduce the level of the schizophrenic patient's anxiety during the initial few interviews, the patient will soon begin to veer away from therapy. The anxiety will stir up ambivalent attitudes and feelings in the patient toward the therapist and toward treatment itself. After a few interviews, the therapist will find that the patient arrives late or skips appointments—offering weak excuses when questioned—and, in fact, within a few weeks' time the patient may cancel the idea of undergoing therapy altogether in final defense against exposure to further anxiety.

Before discussing methods for reducing anxiety, a few facts concerning anxiety patterns deserve review. First of all, a large number of attitudes, feelings, and behavioral patterned responses to the environment are conditioned in everybody over the years. In other words, everyone has developed assorted life habits. Similarly, psychiatric symptom patterns also become conditioned. And, especially in schizophrenia, a lifelong conditioned response to stress in the form of anxiety has in itself become a "habit."

Furthermore, the habit-response of anxiety has been aggravated over the years by "do-gooders" who have tried to influence the patient: they have tried to force the patient to give up his symptom defenses. For instance, a schizophrenic individual suffering from anxiety connected with social contacts may have developed a pattern of social withdrawal and constructed a compensatory defense consisting of composing music in solitary splendor, or delving into work as an expert CPA, or activating some other particular potential. Such maneuvers on the part of the patient thus serve to render him relatively free from anxiety, other than that which may occur in connection with career performance per se. But his family and friends want to change him; they want to make him happy. They continually "encourage" him: Over and over and over again they tell him, "Don't work so hard; take time off; take Jane to the movies; come to our party and relax," and so forth and so on. In resentment of him for his seeming rejection or independence, their efforts are augmented with intrusive and critical words of wisdom, such as, "You are selfish and rude to stay by yourself!" The unfortunate schizophrenic individual is thus made to feel increasingly resentful and guilty by a continual barrage of reminders that he is socially inadequate and inferior. Naturally, his anxiety connected with interpersonal relationships becomes more deeply grooved.

In the task of attempting to break any anxiety pattern, the therapist must recognize that many of the patient's symptoms are actually frozen reaction patterns. Conditioning has made them rigid. In the course of time, great intensity of anxiety can be aroused in the patient by even the slightest suggestion for change. Naturally, such a patient will fear that the therapist will also try to dictate changes. The anxiety thereby provoked interferes with the patient's ability to relate to the therapist. In this state the patient cannot possibly be motivated to explore the dynamic mechanisms underlying his anxiety, and therefore cannot gain insight into his symptom habits and learn ways of altering his life. So, the therapist very often must reduce some of the anxiety in order to reach the patient, to earn his trust, and to make it possible to establish a working relationship in therapy.

Of course, neurotic defenses in some compensated patients are rather effective and these patients seemingly do not suffer marked pan-anxiety. The therapist is able to relate to them in a short time, and they work well in treatment without medication or other anxiety palliative measures. But the large majority of compensated schizophrenic patients suffer a great deal of anxiety, even though they do not include anxiety among their complaints. To some extent, at least, they have had this anxiety all their lives and may not actually know what it feels like to be without anxiety—so they do not complain about it. However, when the therapist cuts some of their anxiety with medication, for example, the reactions are somewhat startling, as we shall discuss.

INITIAL ANXIETY REDUCTION

Two general approaches for initial anxiety reduction aim at some of the anxiety-provoking stress factors in the patient's life. The first approach aims to reduce stress stemming from the patient's internal environment; the second approach aims to reduce stress stemming from the patient's external environment, wherever feasible.

First of all, medication is usually indicated in order to reduce anxiety stemming from internal stress factors connected with the patient's integrative impairment. While considering which medication is appropriate for the patient, the therapist should make certain the patient has a complete physical examination; if any metabolic or other physical dyscrasia exists, the patient must receive appropriate medical or surgical treatment. Also, explore the patient's health habits—sleep patterns, diet, drug habits, and so forth. Patients often need some guidance in regulating these situations. At the same time, while considering how to diminish the intensity of the patient's anxiety, it is important to make very certain that whichever medication you deem appropriate is in no way contraindicated due to any existing medical conditions or to other medications the patient is currently receiving.

Keep in mind that medicating the patient to reduce anxiety is not treatment per se, any more than anesthesia is treatment for appendicitis. Nevertheless, medication can reduce the pain of anxiety to such an extent that perhaps for the first time in his life the patient becomes able to at least contemplate facing the possibility of changing certain patterns of thinking, feeling, or behavior. He will dare contemplate loosening his hold on rigid, conditioned anxiety responses. Thereupon, the physician can proceed with actual psychotherapy.

Before prescribing medication, you have to ask yourself certain questions. First, how do you approach the subject of medication (provided the patient has not already requested it)? Hear the patient out: see what symptoms are secondarily connected with the anxiety; for example, depression. Find out what tranquilizers the patient has taken in the past and is taking now, and how they affected him. If they have been beneficial, it might be foolish to prescribe a different formula. On the other hand, if the patient reacted to them adversely, naturally you do not want to put the patient through the regimen again and have him lose confidence in you. Explain the purpose of the medication you are about to prescribe: "This is to make you feel less tense and anxious." Then, tell him to take it regularly, as prescribed. Explain the type and duration of the common side-effects—but do not go to the extreme of giving your patient a long list of phenomena about which he might become hypochondriacal. Frame your explanation in a positive, matter-of-fact way, rather than conveying the idea that the medication may not work—the latter attitude will give cause for more anxiety and then you can be sure that the medication will not work. Maintain a positive attitude, assuming there is always some element of placebo factor involved. If the patient expresses a great deal of doubt, add, "Everyone is special and we shall find the medication suitable for you."

Second, what medication is the drug of choice for the particular patient who has come to you for therapy? This question is not easy to answer because many unsettled (and unsettling) factors are involved, including the patient's neurochemical requirements and the location of action in the central nervous system (CNS) of each drug and not omitting mention of the possibility of such harmful toxic effects as tardive dyskinesia and habituation (Levenson, 1980).

It has been my experience, especially in treating pseudoneurotic patients, that the use of minor tranquilizers will usually adequately reduce their pan-anxiety, and that some patients respond well with the addition of a tricyclic drug when secondary depression interferes with the patient's ability to make affective contact with the therapist. The benefits of medication outweigh the risks particularly if one follows the general rule that the patient receive the smallest dose required to alleviate anxiety and depression sufficiently to enable the patient to form a working relationship in the psychotherapeutic process. Dosages should be decreased or increased, respectively, when the patient responds favorably in treatment or when he suffers adverse vicissitudes during the therapeutic process. Naturally, the drug should be discontinued whenever harmful side-effects develop. If medication is still required, another drug should be prescribed and evaluated thoroughly in terms of its toxic potentials. (Although caution in prescribing drugs is necessary, I might add that caution is also very necessary in the application of psychotherapy; the wrong theoretical system applied in treating masked schizophrenic patients can also serve as a destructive force, as I have previously discussed.)

The third question you might ask youself is: What do you do if the patient refuses to take any medication? Never argue with the patient—ever! Ask the patient to explain the reasoning behind his refusal. Realize that many schizophrenics fear "outside control." Here you have to reassure the patient: "It will give you more control over yourself; by cutting your anxiety it will enable you to utilize your own strengths, which are now overridden by your anxiety."

Some patients have an hypochondriacal and in some cases realistic fear of possible chemical damage. Perhaps in their anxiety they equate medication to drugs such as LSD, "speed," "downers," or "pot," and these patients sometimes will not even indulge in an aspirin. So you could respond reassuringly, "Think of it as a tonic." Or, "Think of it as beneficial, similar to vitamins; it balances your metabolism; it moves you toward health." Which is to some extent true. You might want to ask the recalcitrant patient, "Do you drink coffee or tea?" And, if the patient replies "yes," you can answer, "The medication I am giving you is no more harmful than that as long as it enhances your functioning." You need not remind him that a cup of coffee or tea can contain 3¾ grains of a drug called caffeine.

Some patients express a great fear of drug dependency. Maybe your patient actually has been, or is presently, dependent on a drug. Provided your patient is not "hooked" on some drug, you can reassure him, "I won't let you become dependent on medication." And it is a good idea to add, "Actually, you are already anxiety-dependent, you know. Anxiety is like any other habit and your anxiety habit must be broken before you can really get well. Medication will help you overcome the anxiety dependency that so plagues you."

You might have to explain further: "Nature is on our side. By taking your medication regularly you will find that you cope better in daily life without undue anxiety. The time will then come when you realize there is no longer a need to continually react with anxiety. Gradually you will have established a new habit—an anxiety-free habit. When this time comes, you will want to decrease, and then discontinue, the medication, and will automatically continue to function on the anxiety-free level insofar as it is appropriate to do so."

Please note that schizophrenic individuals, in their ambivalence, very often do not take the medication as prescribed. For instance, after a few days of anxiety alleviation, especially should they feel drowsy with the medication, they will discontinue it. Then they will come back and report that they feel worse, without telling you that they did not take the medication. At another time they will go ahead and take three or more pills at once to "catch up"—and they will get all mixed up. Keep after them in this—every so often ask the patient, "Have you been taking your medication regularly?" It must be made clear to the patient that until his anxiety habit is broken, he should take the medication regularly, even on those days when he feels all right; that it is important to prevent the old anxiety habit from breaking through, especially because stress situations are bound to occur in daily life that could provoke it.

How should you react when all explanations fail and your patient refuses to take any medication? In such case the first thing to do is swing the patient's ambivalence—gingerly. (We shall discuss the ambivalence-swinging game at length later on.) If the patient flatly refuses medication, the first thing to do is to wait. In other words, when the patient backs up, you quickly back down, and quietly remark in a casual manner, "Okay, I won't prescribe it." Then, later, after you have made him aware how terribly his anxiety habit hurts and that he can be afforded relief, the patient may come forward. He often does. But he comes forward hesitatingly, usually. Then you come forward, hesitatingly, and at the same time you back down very subtly. For instance, if the patient indicates an interest in medication, you can suggest, "It might be a good idea," and in the same breath back down a little, "Maybe you would like to think about it." Play with the patient's ambivalence the way a fisherman plays with a baited hook. Dangle the bait: "A small amount of Valium® helps a lot of people—." Keep the bait not quite in reach: "—but not everybody." Entice with it: "You may want to give it a short try." Then if the patient is willing, make a time bargain with him. This indirectly, and in a small way, presents the ambivalent patient with the reality of a middle-of-the-road attitude in life. The time bargain could be done this way: "Take it regularly just for 3 or 4 days and then see how you feel." Should the patient comply, and if the medication influences his anxiety, his apprehension about taking it may cease, leaving him only with a complaint about drowsiness or some other mild side-effect. Reassure him then that within a week or two such effects will no longer be a problem to him.

Another question you might ask yourself is What do you do if the drug worsens the patient's anxiety? Keep in mind that the selection of a drug should be tailored to suit each patient. In some patients, Thorazine® produces tachycardia, hypotension, and results in panic. In some patients, Elavil® produces pathological sleeping or dizziness. In some patients, Librium® causes release of emotional restraints and the patient weeps or displays other signs of emotional incontinence. In other words, a drug that helps one patient may be "toxic" to another patient, although they manifest similar schizophrenic symptoms. If adverse reactions occur, immediately prescribe another drug derivative for the patient and explain to him what you are doing and why. Usually the patient will readily comply with your new prescription, although, here again, he will be cautious and is likely to take it sporadically, so follow through and make certain he takes it as prescribed. And, of course, be flexible about altering the timing or dosage to meet the patient's requirements. Do not "drug-hop." Strangely enough, if you do that, the patient will lose confidence in *you*, not in drugs. In fact, he may take the matter into his own hands, and borrow pills recommended by relatives or friends.

The next question: What do you do if the patient is relieved of anxiety with the medication, but presents *that* as a complaint? Why do some patients complain, "Doctor, the trouble is that these pills make me feel normal!"? At such a time, you look at the patient and you see he looks terribly anxious. First, ask the patient why feeling "normal" frightens him. He may state that it makes him feel detached. Or, he may tell you, "I feel all right but it's not the real me." In any case, a realistic interpretation is indicated: "Perhaps this is the first time you experienced freedom from anxiety, so it makes you feel that it is not really you. By being free from anxiety you are actually experiencing the 'real' you. This is what it will feel like when you become well." Here, you observe that a lot of patients feel anxious about no longer feeling anxious. Hypochondriacal fears that the drug has some powerful control over them are quite understandable, and reassuring interpretations are required.

In line with this, a patient often fears the normalization effects of medication because it makes him feel "off guard." In other words, anxiety has always served as an alert to danger; in that sense it arouses his defenses. The patient may explain, "Now that I don't feel so tense and anxious, I am afraid I will not be able to foresee situations that can get me into trouble." Then you can reassure the patient that he will automatically feel anxiety appropriate to situations that realistically require anxiety responses—just as other people do. The patient can respond to these interpretations, provided he has not been "drugged down" too much.

Another patient may tell you in a frightened way, "The medication helps. Good God, now I'm hooked!" Obviously, the patient now views the drug as very dangerous. In response to that, you might again point out, "Nature is on our side; when you are no longer anxiety-dependent you will discover you are not drug-dependent."

By the time the patient's internal stress has been decreased with medication, the therapist should consider ways and means to further reduce the patient's anxiety by influencing stress factors in the patient's external environment. When medication enables the patient to relate adequately in interviews, the therapist is able to take a careful history.

Ongoing external environmental stress factors should be clearly delineated. Only then is the therapist in a position to determine which situations in the patient's life can be influenced. Perhaps the family can be influenced to ease up on demands and pressures whereby they are unwittingly aggravating stress in the patient's daily life. Perhaps the patient can be influenced to avoid excessive demands in the social area, or to recognize existing opportunities for avoiding unnecessary pressure in the job area, and so forth. Observe, however, whether or not the patient is sado-masochistically "cruising" for some of these external stress factors. And go very gingerly at first.

ESTABLISHING A THERAPEUTIC RELATIONSHIP

Determining the Form of Psychotherapy

Having reduced the intensity of the patient's anxiety with medication and perhaps with some environmental manipulation, the therapist must then decide what form of psychotherapy is appropriate for the patient. Pseudoneurotic and similarly compensated schizophrenics vary in their basic personality configurations and symptom pictures, and a form of treatment for one might be somewhat inappropriate for another. The main treatment forms I am referring to are individual psychotherapy, group psychotherapy, family psychotherapy, and also psychotherapy with the adjunct of one or more organic agents (other than tranquilizers). These I shall touch upon briefly without going into any detail.

In my opinion, individual psychotherapy is definitely indicated as the main procedure for the large majority of patients suffering from masked forms of schizophrenia. The psychotherapy should aim at the target symptom—anxiety, but it should not tamper with any of the nonpsychotic symptoms of defense. It should be dynamically oriented and consist of reeducating these patients to basic realities—simple realities that schizophrenic individuals are unable to learn on their own, due to concept distortions that evolved from their basic integrative impairment. These patients usually suffer considerable contact impairment and have intolerable anxiety whenever attempting to cope in interpersonal relationships; they are thus likely to feel less threatened in a one-to-one relationship with the therapist. In such cases the therapist must first aim to lessen the patients' anxiety connected with the contact impairment by means of analytic interpretations and reeducation to the realities concerning social relations. When this source of anxiety is diminished, many such patients are able to benefit by moving into group therapy, where they can reality-test in a controlled setting.

There are many schizophrenic individuals, however, who suffer great anxiety connected with the threat of intimacy when engaged in a one-to-one treatment relationship. These patients will initially benefit when placed in group therapy for a period of time. The group setting appears less frightening to them, as they can "blend with the herd," and learn about themselves by hiding behind others who are actively relating in the group. This also enables many patients to gain insight into the important fact that they are not alone in suffering contact impairment; they are not alone in suffering pan-anxiety, and are not alone in suffering depression, phobias, compulsions, confusion, and innumerable other symptoms as well. Thus, group therapy can at least temporarily alleviate the inexorable feelings of isolation and loneliness that all schizophrenics experience.

Needless to say, the therapist must be skilled in monitoring group sessions. I have known pseudoneurotic patients to decompensate into a state of overt psychosis when exposed to what they interpret to be "verbal attacks" from seemingly aggressive members of the group. Keep in mind that the schizophrenic individual readily misinterprets the reactions of others in a self-referential manner, and readily misconstrues assertion to be aggression against himself. For this reason, among others, schizophrenic patients absolutely require regular private interviews with the therapist in the course of group therapy, to help them integrate their experiences and observations in a realistic way.

Assaying the option of conducting family therapy for the schizophrenic patient is a very individual matter. The therapist must thoroughly acquaint himself with the pattern of the interrelationship between patient and family members involved. The mental health of family members must be appraised. For instance, if the patient's mother is "schizophrenogenic," lacking in capacity for insight, and also psychotic with hostile rejection of the patient, it is unlikely that the relationship between the two is reparable; repeated exposure to the friction of their interaction would simply add fuel to the fire of the patient's low self-esteem, confusion, and anxiety. In such cases, the therapist should encourage avoidance rather than encounter, and aim the patient toward emotional emancipation from any remnant of symbiotic attachment to the destructive parent. On the other hand, if the important members of the patient's family consist of people who are only moderately disturbed themselves, yet are sincerely troubled, warmly concerned, and desirous to resolve the confusion and pathological aspects of their relationship to the patient, a certain amount of time should be allocated for family participation in the therapy. Because the schizophrenic patient suffers an integrative and regulative impairment, the main part of treatment must consist of psychotherapy on an individual basis, however. Intensive dynamically oriented individual psychotherapy is required to resolve the conflicts that stem from the integrative impairment.

With regard to organic therapy, electric convulsive therapy (E.C.T.) is of no value to the nonpsychotically compensated schizophrenic patient, with one exception—when severe depression is the predominant symptom. Whether acute or chronic, if the depression is so severe that the patient is paralyzed to move in therapy, or suicidal, E.C.T. is indicated. This is assuming, of course, that the patient had been hospitalized and received a course of antidepressant medication that failed to remove the depression quickly or adequately.

Keep in mind that depression often occurs secondarily to anxiety. In such cases, when you treat the anxiety with a neuroleptic or psychotropic drug in conjunction with psychotherapy, you will find that the depression very often lifts. However, if the patient continues to remain severely depressed, despite adequate trials of antidepressant drug therapy, E.C.T. is strongly indicated. During the course of E.C.T. and for the following period of several weeks, psychotherapy must be given very gingerly: The treatments will have temporarily robbed the patient of defenses, including past as well as very recent memory, and the patient will require strong support.

Influencing the Transference

Although supportive aspects of therapy begin the moment the patient steps into the therapist's office, actual dynamically oriented psychotherapy commences when the patient has become able to make emotional contact with the therapist and form a transference relationship. From this time on the therapist's role is crucial: In utilizing the transference for actively guiding the patient in the therapeutic process, the therapist is walking a tightrope (Strahl & Lewis, 1972, pp. 753-757).

A patient's attitudes and feelings toward the therapist are an ever-shifting phenomenon and do not progress without occasional turmoil. The schizophrenic patient manifests dysregulation in the transference relationship, as in all interpersonal relationships. The therapist must be on the alert for the tendency to extreme ambivalent swings in the schizophrenic patient, and on the alert for untoward ambivalent transference reactions. Figuratively speaking, the therapist must keep his fingers on the pulse of the patient's attitudes and feelings toward him and toward treatment at all times. These are strong indicators of the patient's level of anxiety; the greater the patient's anxiety, the greater the ambivalence.

Naturally, the phenomenon of ambivalence is present in everyone, changing in context and configuration in different individuals at different times. By analogy, picture a pendulum representing ambivalence reactions in terms of thought, affect, and behavior. The pendulum can swing from one side to the other. Ambivalence swings in a so-called normal individual occur in moderation and are appropriate to the provocative agents. In a neurotic individual sometimes the pendular swings can be rather marked, but are nevertheless explicable and remain in the framework of reality. On the other hand, in schizophrenia, ambivalence quite often swings from one extreme to the other unpredictably and inappropriately to the stimulus. For instance, the patient will feel love for the therapist and behave in a passive, compliant way with regression and magical expectations. Then a seemingly insignificant stimulus triggers such an anxiety reaction that the patient will feel hatred for the therapist, and express aggressive defiance in an irrational struggle for independence. In all this, the schizophrenic individual can react at both extremes almost simultaneously, or swing suddenly from one polar extreme to the other.

In order to temper—or tone down—a schizophrenic patient's massive ambivalent polar swings in response to environmental stimuli, these swings must first be tempered in the transference relationship. Preliminary to this, the therapist must keep constant vigilance with regard to his own countertransference attitudes and feelings toward the patient. This requires introspective candor and objectivity at all times, including occasions when the patient's ambivalence stirs up an ambivalent response in the therapist. Thus fortified with awareness of the patient-therapist transferential interaction, the therapist proceeds to influence the patient's transference, preferably as a preventive measure, rather than allowing the reaction to become full-blown.

In order to enable the patient to maintain a constructive transference without undue ambivalence, the therapist must walk a tightrope in the process of relating to the patient. First of all, he must avoid becoming emotionally too close to the patient and at the same time avoid becoming emotionally too detached. Secondly, he must not be too active in therapy, nor too passive. Thirdly, he must avoid aiming at goals that are too high for the patient; yet he must not set the goals too low.

How to relate to the patient emotionally. We must keep aware that all schizophrenic patients have marked emotional immaturity and, furthermore, they are emotionally unstable (as opposed to being labile), which is an expression of their homeostatic dysregulation. Therefore, you cannot discuss with them emotional material in the same way you would with a neurotic individual. Schizophrenic patients readily misinterpret emotional expressions in other people in a dereistic way. Their emotional perplexity is often profound. Even in simple situations they are unaware of the emotional implications that are quite apparent to "normal" or neurotic individuals. For instance, they will intepret positive emotions in a negative way, and they will exaggerate and distort negative emotions. Therefore, do not allow a patient to become too close to you emotionally.

You avoid this by not getting too close to the patient. In other words, do not be a pal to a lonely patient, or an indulgent loving parent to a rejected patient. Parry the patient's manipulative prying into any aspect of your private life. He may ask you if you are married, where you live, if you like chocolate, and so forth. If you let the patient get too close by divulging personal information about yourself, the patient becomes overly dependent. The patient may secretly evolve love fantasies that will lead to resentment when they are not fulfilled. Feeling helpless, the patient may regress and manipulate you by bringing gifts and flattering you in efforts to gain magical gratifications, in the way that an hysterical neurotic patient often does. In any case, the patient will cease to work in therapy.

Furthermore, if you get emotionally too close, the patient will feel this as an emotional demand that he can't meet and will become anxious or defensive. Giving the patient excessive emotional support can lead the patient to feel you love him but do not understand his real problems—and he desperately wants to be understood! Nevertheless, it is beneficial to keep the patient somewhat dependent upon you emotionally in order to suppress any hostility against you, so that it is easier for him to accept your interpretations.

Another thing about emotional relating: Just as you should not get too close to the patient, do not act too "cool" or distant emotionally. You cannot sit like a Buddha (as some analysts do) and act impassive. If the emotional relationship becomes too distant, the patient feels unsupported and feels that you are making an impossible demand upon him to do the treatment unaided. The schizophrenic is confused about himself and does not know what is expected of him. The patient will also feel that you are rejecting him. He might misinterpret your emotional reserve as coldness, indicating that you consider him a hopeless case, or that you dislike him because he is inferior. Here again, the patient will interpret your detachment as an indication that you do not understand

him. Naturally the patient will then suffer increased feelings of detachment, and mounting anxiety will compound his contact impairment.
In other words, the schizophrenic patient needs to depend on the therapist's emotional support and acceptance, otherwise he becomes increasingly confused about his self-identity. Without emotional support, the
schizophrenic patient feels like a chip of wood floating in a vast stormy
ocean where there is no harbor.

While the therapist is walking the tightrope with regard to emotional interrelating with his patient, he must also be careful not to
express strong positive or negative emotions, because the schizophrenic
individual will tend to interpret them in an all-or-none way. If the
patient receives strong positive emotional support, he is likely to interpret that as an all-consuming demand. On the other hand, he is certain
to interpret any strong negative emotions on the part of the therapist as
total rejection or aggressive intent. In either event, the patient's ambivalence is likely to swing from the pole of depression and withdrawal
to the opposite pole of hostility and aggression. In other words, a patient is likely to be frightened by any strong positive or negative feelings expressed by the therapist and will misinterpret them in an autistic-
dereistic manner.

How to relate to the patient in terms of activity. Here, again, you
are walking a tightrope. You cannot be too passive and you cannot be
too active. To learn how to walk this tightrope is probably the most
important aspect of treatment. You must be far more active than is
usual in treating a neurotic patient who has a well integrated ego based
on reality and is able to free-associate and trace his symptoms back to
their unconscious source. But the schizophrenic patient blocks in such
attempts; he is confused. Therefore, you cannot be a silent auditor.
The patient is unable to integrate associations and organize them in a
realistic way toward realistic ends.

How should you be active in treating the pseudoneurotic schizophrenic patient, as compared to treating a psychoneurotic patient? For
one thing, you have to interfere more intensively with the way in
which the patient organizes his personal life. The patient frequently
needs to be given advice about realities with regard to concrete issues.
You have to define the patient's conflicts for him as he relates them to
you and advise him how to deal with them. You have to explain his
ambivalence to him and how it relates to anxiety and self-doubts. You
have to show the patient how to make simple decisions in specific personal situations. Patients are often very grateful when taught how to
make small decisions—such as which dress to buy, or what to plan for
dinner—despite occasional errors and minor failures.

Furthermore, in treating any patient suffering a masked form of schizophrenia, the therapist must be more active in interpreting environmental happenings as the patient relates them. You have to assay the reality of these happenings for the patient and interpret them in concrete terms: which situations are important, which are unimportant; which to handle, which to avoid; which direction to take at which time, and so forth. Keep in mind that schizophrenic pan-anxiety is especially strong with regard to interpersonal relationships. These people are hypersensitive, and simple social situations often loom up as insurmountable because they feel unable to cope. When the therapist shows him concretely how to cope with simple events in a realistic way, the patient is usually responsive and grateful.

Some psychiatrists try to treat everything—all the symptoms—at once, and this compounds confusion for the patient. Therefore, interpret those symptoms that are the most incapacitating to the patient at the time, and relate the symptoms to anxiety. Show the patient that symptom X is based on anxiety, or that symptom Y is based on anxiety. Indicate that his present task in treatment is to understand the dynamic basis for this particular anxiety.

Although you must be active in treating a nonpsychotically compensated schizophrenic patient, you must be far less active than in treating an overtly psychotic patient. A very active approach cannot do much harm to the overtly psychotic patient: you can interpret anything you like to him because he is decompensated anyway and he will either come out of it or he will not. However, the compensated patient is delicately balanced and if you stir up the embers in his unconscious you can mobilize aggression, mobilize chaotic sexuality, provoke ambivalent swings, aggravate anxiety, and cause the patient to suffer more than before treatment began; the patient may "flip" into an overt psychotic state. Therefore, be less active and less blunt than in treating the overtly psychotic individual. Do not bombard the patient with strong positive or negative interpretations. In fact, do not bombard him with a great many interpretations; that will only confuse and frighten him. And certainly do not flood him with unconscious material. Although some patients may find this fascinating, more fearful patients may compliantly attempt to absorb it and then will panic. Avoid deep interpretations; be leisurely; do not give the patient insights prematurely. Watch the patient's level of anxiety; some are quite allergic to unconscious material.

Early in treatment, active interpretations should not tamper with a patient's overinhibitions. The "superego" is often shaky in the schizophrenic and is loaded with ambivalence. Be careful not to advise moral or ethical values that you think appropriate for the patient. Be careful, on the other hand, not to override conscience patterns by encouraging the patient to practice less self-denial. Keep in mind the problem of schizophrenic dysregulation: A patient will act overinhibited for a time and then will suddenly become underinhibited. Therefore, do not attempt to influence the "superego" in any direction until you have treated the patient for months and know his ambivalence patterns.

Transference problems. Regardless of a therapist's skill in relating to the delicately balanced compensated schizophrenic patient, transference conflicts are bound to develop in the course of treatment. When and how to interpret the transference to the patient when such a conflict arises depends on a number of factors including the dynamic nature of the conflict, the integrative strength and weakness structure in the patient, and the time and circumstances in which the transference conflict becomes evident. As a general rule, interpretation of underlying dynamic mechanisms can be given at a similar time and in a similar manner as when given to neurotic patients, except that in schizophrenia the dynamic mechanisms are peculiar to the disorder and require a different type of interpretation accordingly.

I do not consider it always appropriate to interpret a transference problem directly, as such, whenever it becomes apparent during an interview. Actually, in some patients a problem in the transference may arise in practically every session; if it is continually focused upon by the therapist, the patient may get the idea that the therapist is perhaps slightly paranoid or is overly preoccupied with his own importance in the patient's life. However, direct interpretation is indicated when the transference conflict interferes with the patient's progress in therapy.

Schizophrenic individuals do not tolerate tension and frustration and are likely to regress considerably when under such stress. This can become conspicuous in the transference situation. Sometimes the patient regresses to a compliant and ingratiating passive-dependent state, whereupon he projects his problems onto the environment and behaves as though expecting the therapist to resolve the problems on his behalf. The source of the tension and frustration that triggered the regression should be recognized by the therapist, and the manner in which it affects the transference relationship should be interpreted. This is followed by affording the patient insight into the dynamic factors involved in the conflict, then showing the patient realistic ways whereby he can utilize certain assets to gain desired resolutions.

A patient often projects his own attitudes and feelings onto the therapist. In this instance, it is appropriate to interpret the way in which the underlying dynamic conflicts that are currently disrupting his adaptive efforts have become mirrored, or reflected, in the transference. Here, also, interpretive follow-up consists of pointing out to the patient his realistic assets and the remedial measures at his disposal. In these interpretations, however, it is usually appropriate to aim at the target of the underlying dynamic conflict rather than dwelling at length on the transference per se.

At other times, a patient may project onto the therapist certain attitudes and feelings—usually negative—which he attributes to other authorities in his past or current life. The nature of this projection should be interpreted to the patient; that he is reacting toward the therapist in the same way he reacted toward significant persons in his life, and that he does so because of certain dynamically established patterns based on early conditioning. Here again, this should be followed up by affording the patient insight concerning certain realities regarding the persons involved and what would be the realistic way for him to relate to these persons. Keep in mind that all schizophrenics need to be taught reality concerning interpersonal relationships.

As we shall soon discuss, when giving any interpretation, whether in the context of the transference or otherwise, it is imperative to keep an eagle's eye on the patient's level of self-esteem—which is always low in schizophrenia. When giving interpretations, it is important to remind patients to examine their existing assets. This is an integral part of the process of reeducating patients to understand the reality of the self as well as the environment.

In conclusion, I would like to point out one interesting fact. Schizophrenia is an oscillating disorder. Symptomatology fluctuates; it varies. Symptoms may appear and then fade, as occurs in multiple sclerosis. In schizophrenia there is a strong tendency for many patients to regain their particular capacity for mental homeostasis. We do not understand why, but the tendency for spontaneous remission is rather pronounced. Among nonpsychotically compensated schizophrenic patients who manifest a sudden acute psychotic episode, those whose upheavals occurred following clear-cut precipitating factors will be the most likely to respond with remission, especially when a strong defense of neurotic or other nonpsychotic symptomatology existed prior to the acute episode. These are the best candidates for psychotherapy. For all we know, perhaps the main value of psychotherapy is that it fosters this spontaneous tendency for remission.

CHAPTER 5

Attacking the Target Symptom of Anxiety

There is a vast qualitative difference between the dynamics of the neuroses and schizophrenia. Because therapy with neurotic patients involves unraveling the patient's symptom pattern through dynamic insights into environmentally-determined factors underlying the symptoms, the treatment approach for neurotic patients differs vastly from that for pseudoneurotic schizophrenic patients. Let us briefly review in general the treatment approach appropriate for the neurosis, and then compare it to that appropriate for treating pseudoneurotic and other masked forms of schizophrenia.

Treatment of the neuroses consists mainly of exploring the psychodynamic mechanisms underlying the neurotic symptoms. According to existing theory, the etiology of neurosis lies in external environmental conflicts that occurred during the patient's formative years—usually stress due to excessive parental demands, prohibitions, rejection, and perhaps traumas. These stress factors presumably lead to dynamically determined symptom patterns. Treatment aims at the target of the predominant neurotic symptoms—hysterical, obsessive-compulsive, or other. By means of free association, the patient traces the symptoms back to the etiological conflicts of early childhood that aroused anxiety against which the patient defended himself by means of repression and symptom formation. It is because these neurotic mechanisms are presumed to have an external environmental etiology, and because a neurotic patient is endowed with a well-integrated ego structure, that he is able to trace his symptoms to their origin and to effect a cure. In other words, therapy aims to have the patient focus on his neurotic symptoms in order to analyze the way in which they are linked sequentially to dynamic defense patterns, and thereby to bring to consciousness the repressed ideation and affect connected to the etiological anxiety-producing conflict.

To apply the neurotic psychodynamic formulations in treating pseudoneurotic schizophrenia is definitely improper. First of all, the etiology of the neurotic symptoms in schizophrenia does not rest on external environmental vicissitudes. Secondly, the schizophrenic individual is not endowed with a well-integrated, strong ego "core": He suffers an inherent flaw in his capacity for integration and organization of stimuli; his adaptive potential is inadequate. Therefore, if the therapist decides, "Well, my patient must trace his neurotic symptoms back to their early childhood conflicts," he is guilty of barking up the wrong tree. Even though the neurotic patient's symptoms are seemingly explicable in terms of early environmental conflicts, applying neurotic psychodynamic formulas will not help the patient. The therapist would be steering his patient to peel off the neurotic symptom façade; underlying this thin layer of defense the therapist would be confronted with the "mush" of pan-anxiety. It might take a long time for this to happen, or perhaps not long at all. Nevertheless, if the patient's neurotic defenses are ripped away, one of three things can happen.

For one thing, if the schizophrenic patient's ego integrity is not too markedly impaired, he might defend himself against the massive anxiety fomented by removal of his neurotic defense by shifting to another neurotic symptom. Then the therapist finds himself confronted with the need to rearrange his own dynamic formulations for the patient: Perhaps he had assumed he had an hysteric patient on his hands, and then suddenly he finds the patient is actually an obsessive-compulsive neurotic, or vice versa. He then revises the dynamic formula and treats the patient accordingly, only to find later on that the patient is phobic, or hypochondriacal, and so forth.

A second thing that could happen would be that this nice neurotic patient suddenly goes over into an acute overtly psychotic state, or perhaps a suicidal depression. In other words, once the neurotic façade is removed, the underlying "mush" turns out to be "le bon plastique" and explodes in the therapist's face.

A third eventuality could be that the patient develops strong resistances in therapy: He defends himself in the transference situation. He may come to interviews late, or skip appointments. Or, he may become silent and resentful, or free-associate with a barrage of circumstantiality and inconsequentia. Sooner or later, the patient may quit therapy. Oftentimes such a patient will seek out a charlatan or mystic and get "cured"; he then will most likely telephone the therapist to gleefully inform him of the fact. Meanwhile, if the therapist is unable to admit to his diagnostic and treatment errors, he will mark on his record that the patient was "not motivated," or "uncooperative."

Now, the appropriate way to deal with neurotic symptoms manifested by the pseudoneurotic schizophrenic patient is to show the patient how these neurotic symptoms are linked to an underlying anxiety. Later in treatment when the patient has sufficiently resolved his anxiety, he will no longer require his neurotic symptom defenses and they will subside. Occasionally, however, one encounters a patient who wishes to discuss his neurotic symptoms according to some dynamic theory of neurosis. Such patients should not be contradicted bluntly, because at that time dynamic "insights" may give them a feeling of mastery. On the other hand, if allowed to probe in this manner, patients can become frightened by the so-called insights that emerge; therefore it is important to refocus the patients' attention onto the dynamics appropriate for schizophrenia. For instance, a schizophrenic patient may tell you, "The reason I have an aversion to women is because I hate my mother for rejecting me when I was a child." Now, this might be a good reason for the patient's symptom, but probably it is not the real reason. Instead of replying, "We must trace your attitude about women to your Oedipal conflict," it would be more appropriate to explain, "Probably you have an understandable reason for hating your mother and we will examine it in time," and then guide the patient to explore the symptom in terms of anxiety connected to his confusion about sexuality, or whatever. In any case, it is important to interpret in such a way that the patient's anxiety will become allayed rather than aggravated.

Similarly, when interpreting dreams with a schizophrenic patient, place emphasis on insights that allay the patient's anxiety. For example, if a pseudoneurotic patient tells you, "Last night I dreamed I had sexual intercourse with my mother," you do not reply, "You are fixated on an Oedipal level of psychosexual development," any more than you tell the patient, "My God, that dream is proof you are psychotic." Either intepretation would stir up equally great anxiety. Instead, an appropriate interpretation might be, "Well, the problem is that you feel sexually starved and yet do not feel safe with women; so, in your dream you gratify your normal sex drive with the only woman with whom you feel safe and it happens to be your mother." Be sure to add, "That does not mean that you want sex with your mother, but it simply means that you want sex with a safe object." This is a type of interpretation with which the patient can work. Furthermore, it allays intense anxiety that the patient may experience concerning fleeting incest fantasies with which, of course, he cannot deal.

It must always be kept in mind that the schizophrenic individual reacts with anxiety to stressful stimuli in a much more massive and all-pervasive way than does the neurotic. His inherent integrative deficit cripples him in his adaptive efforts. Thus, he has deep feelings of inferiority; he is very hypersensitive; he misinterprets his environment; he is not realistic. In other words, he is autistic and dereistic.

All things considered, the appropriate method of approach in treating a pseudoneurotic patient consists of interpreting the patient's symptoms according to the dynamics of the integrative impairment. Refer to the dynamic chart (Figure 2-1, p. 22): You begin by exploring the surface dynamic mechanisms with the patient—i.e., the relationship of his neurotic symptoms to an underlying anxiety—and gradually focus the patient's attention on a deeper dynamic layer, giving him insights at a rate at which he can utilize them to learn how to adapt more realistically. External stress factors and conflicts, past and present, should be dealt with for what they are—predisposing or precipitating factors only, *not* etiological ones.

The time to interpret is when the patient is emotionally receptive and able to understand the insight offered. If an interpretation is given too soon, it can mobilize the patient's anxiety and he will show some form of resistance. On the other hand, too much delay in interpreting can cause a patient to feel anxious, helpless, and confused because he has insufficient guidelines with which to proceed. The symptom most distressing to the patient should be focused on in each interview. You cannot interpret all the symptoms presented in each interview; you have to keep your own Gestalt about you. So, you focus on the symptom the patient presents which is the most troublesome to him at the particular time. In one interview the symptom presented may be a manifestation of an inner conflict, and in another interview it might be related to conflicts in interpersonal relationships, and occasionally you must interpret transference conflicts that arise.

Allow the patient to describe his feelings, ideas, and events and do not interrupt his productions until you are able to clearly observe the true meaning of the symptom the patient is describing and whether it belongs in the category of inner, environmental, or transference conflict. Direct your interpretations accordingly. If the patient is blocked, gently draw him forth. If the patient is circumlocutious, interrupt and bring him back to the main issue. The patient will not resent your doing that, and in fact may be quite relieved when helped to find what to focus on, because his Gestalt is confused.

INTERPRETIVE TECHNIQUE IN TREATING MASKED SCHIZOPHRENIA

Now, by referring to our dynamic chart—the "onion layers" if you like—we can observe how to proceed with interpretations. Sometimes, depending upon the problem that the patient presents in the interview, interpretations lead the patient down from the surface of the dynamic "onion" to the anxiety underlying the compensatory symptoms. You may penetrate down one or two layers to whatever level of integrative problem needs to be pointed out to the patient in that particular instance. At other times, interpretations will start from deeper layers and spiral outward to the anxiety that is the outcome of the particular problem the patient is describing at the time.

In the first instance, if the patient's presenting problem is a disturbing neurotic symptom, you point out the meaning of the symptom. Then, you point out that it is based on anxiety, which in turn is based on an inability to cope adequately, compounded by inferiority feelings. In other words, you work down and interpret to the depth at which the patient is able to utilize the insight at that particular period of treatment. In the second instance, if the patient's presenting problem is that of "inferiority feelings," you might point out to him that these feelings arise because he feels unable to cope adequately with his problems, and this causes anxiety, which in turn interferes with his adaptive performance—and so on. It is often helpful to the patient to point out the nature of the dynamic feedback in terms of how anxiety interferes with a person's ability to utilize his potentials.

It now becomes obvious, however, that treatment is much more than merely interpreting the patient's presenting symptom and leaving him to draw conclusions about applying the "insight" to his daily life. The compensated schizophrenic patient, unlike the neurotic, cannot associate freely around superficial insights and gain additional insights for himself, because he does not have a well-integrated sense of self, nor does he have a realistic appreciation of what is going on in his environment. In other words, because of his integrative impairment, the patient does not know what reality is in many, many matters. Thus, he cannot use reality as a guiding light in his attempt to gain further insight on his own. He has to be taught reality over and over in the context of every problem he presents.

Therefore, when the patient presents a very disturbing symptom during an interview, the therapist's interpretations follow along in a certain sequence: He defines for the patient *what* the presenting symptom is in terms of its meaning; *why* the interpretation is given; *how* the symptom evolved; and from *where* the symptom derived. In conclusion, *remedial measures* consist of reeducating the patient to reality with regard to the self, the environment, and interaction between the two. What purpose is served by each step in the interpretive sequence?

Interpreting *what* the symptom is defines for the patient the meaning of the presented symptom. It clarifies the patient's problem to him. And it shows the patient that the therapist understands. However, the patient will not know how to apply the statement for any practical purposes.

The explanation of *why* the interpretation is given consists of pointing out to the patient the concrete ways in which the presented symptom interferes with performance and pleasure in current life. This should be done in such a manner as to indicate to the patient that he will eventually be able to do something about it. But he must be shown.

Interpreting *how* the symptom evolved consists of giving the patient the insight that the symptom is directly connected to anxiety. The patient's focus is directed to the main problem—anxiety—the stem from which other symptoms branch. He then must be guided to explore the basis of his anxiety.

Interpreting from *where* the symptom is derived aims the patient's attention to the dynamic processes underlying the anxiety. He begins to gain insight into the reasons for his anxiety: that he maintains certain unrealistic attitudes. By this time the patient understands more about himself, but he does not feel jubilant because he is at a loss what to do with his new insights. Therefore, interpretations must always conclude with practical remedial measures.

Discussion of *remedial measures* largely consists of reeducating the patient to reality—with regard to himself, the environment, and the processes of their interaction. It is done in the context of the patient's presented symptom. This lesson in reality begins to loosen the patient's rigid, conditioned, unrealistic patterns of thinking, feeling, and reacting. The task of breaking these long-standing habit patterns, concomitant with relearning new patterns based on reality, naturally requires repetition. Over and over again, lessons in reality are reiterated to the patient, each time in the context of currently presented symptoms.

Now, to give an example of how the interpretive sequence can be applied, I will describe a single interview with a pseudoneurotic schizophrenic patient. It is condensed for the purpose of highlighting the general principles of interpretive approach.

The patient is a young married woman who works long hours as a secretary for a demanding boss. Her husband is preoccupied with his business problems and is irritable to his wife and sexually withholding.

One day the patient presented in interview the following serious complaint. "Doctor, I cannot resist eating. It's been going on for weeks. For breakfast, I will have 6 eggs and 6 donuts; for lunch, 8 sandwiches; I will sometimes have 2 dinners; I've gained 16 pounds in the last month. I cannot control myself." (Incidentally, were she psychoneurotic, the dynamics of her compulsive overeating could be formulated in terms of depression with regression to the oral erotic stage, or devouring rage against her demanding boss and depriving husband, or a repressed wish for pregnancy, or a number of other possible psychodynamic configurations. However, this patient is schizophrenic.)

The first interpretation defined for the patient *what* her symptom signified: "You eat compulsively in an attempt to reduce tension and to gain substitute gratification in the face of certain frustrations." This clarified for the patient that her symptoms were tension and frustration. *Why* the interpretation was given then followed: "Your compulsive eating is self-defeating. It does not remove the causes of your tension and frustration, and the weight gain has made you very anxious." The patient was encouraged to describe the current problems in her life that provoked tension and prohibited gratifications. The patient could then see that she must somehow deal with environmental problems, yet she did not know where to start. So, the next interpretation indicated *how* the symptoms (tension and frustration) evolved: "The problems you have described loom as insurmountable because of anxiety. The greater your anxiety, the more you feel inadequate to cope with them." However, the patient cannot reverse this anxiety cycle. She must be informed from *where* the anxiety underlying her symptoms derived: "Your anxiety is largely based on a lack of self-assertion due to lack of self-confidence—and low self-esteem. Do you consider yourself inferior?"

The patient, of course, quickly admitted feelings of inferiority. The feedback was interpreted: "The greater your inferiority feelings, the greater your anxiety, and then the more difficult it is for you to cope with your problems. You try to cope with your tension and frustration by overeating and, of course, this goes right back and increases your inferiority feelings." Adding, "A person cannot function well on an empty self-esteem" cuts the tendency for the patient to blame herself for her symptoms.

Having given the patient insight into some of the reasons for her symptoms, the next step required follow-up interpretations of explicit remedial measures. Discussion of *remedial measures* consisted of a lesson in reality about herself and her environment, and how she might assert herself effectively: "Your inferiority feeling is an attitude of habit more than it is fact." The patient was directed to examine reality in terms of her present assets as well as past achievements. Thereupon, she felt able to view some of her realistic potentials which (at least temporarily) antidoted the intensity of inferiority feelings. When her self-esteem was sufficiently elevated during the interview and her anxiety diminished, she was in a position to view the reality aspects of her environment. In other words, "You are not a helpless pawn to be exploited or rejected by a self-seeking boss and troubled husband. Let us examine ways whereby you can assert yourself and influence people to respect your needs." After considering the realistic opportunities and limitations presented, the patient was able to contemplate taking one or two self-assertive steps to alleviate stress in specific areas of her work life, and to influence her husband for their mutual gratifications.

The above patient, as do a great majority of compensated schizophrenic patients, interpreted environmental situations in a distorted way, compounded by her own ambivalence with regard to herself and those around her. Such patients underestimate people and overestimate people. They underreact and overreact, and at the wrong times. They vacillate between anxiety and rage reactions. All of these things compound their dilemmas. This is why reality must be taught to these patients in just about every interview for the purpose of reeducating them to realistic self-assertion.

The same young patient entered her interview in a panic state one day, saying, "Last night my bowling score was only 70 and *everybody* else in the game did *much* better!" Now, why the panic? (If the patient were psychoneurotic, the panic could be dynamically explained on the basis of an unconscious sibling rivalry, or a fear of failure and punishment from parental authority, or anxiety about sexual impotence, and so forth. However, this patient is schizophrenic.) You point out to the patient *what* the symptom is: "You have overreacted to a minor failure just as though it signifies you are a total failure now and forevermore." This indicates to the patient her actual symptom and that you understand how she feels; however, she does not know how to change her atitude. You can then tell her *why* you give her that interpretation: "Your whole attitude about yourself needs examining because your generalized negative self-esteem robs you of all pleasures." The patient will agree, but she does not know where to go from there. Then you explain *how* the symptom evolved: "Your low self-esteem causes you so much anxiety that you become too tense to perform according to your natural abilities. Whenever you do poorly it is largely on that account." But the patient does not understand the basis for this attitude. From *where* the symptom is derived can be interpreted: "... You have a deep feeling of inferiority—due to a lifelong habit of adding up the poor performance scores in life and ignoring all successes."

Here again, *remedial measures* consist of reeducating the patient to reality in the context of the presented symptom currently under interpretation. With regard to the patient's self: "Success is not an all-or-none affair; you are much more than a 'bowling-score' self." Encourage the patient to explore her positive assets and achievements in various life areas. You can interpret reality about the world of people: "No one is all-perfect; no one is in all ways inferior. Moreover, no one can sustain top performance continually. Incidentally, your bowling score last week was 120, and I wonder if it will be perhaps better or worse next week." Remind the patient that even though her friend Suzy bowls better than she, Suzy can't bake a cake or type technical manuscripts, or whatever.

In conclusion, the interpretive sequence aims to give the patient insight into the anxiety and its dynamics. It culminates in teaching the patient about his or her unrealistic, rigid patterns. Of course when you teach the patient realities in terms of himself and the environment, these realities may be very, very simple to you because you know what is real, but you must not forget that the patient does not. To some extent, he is autistic and dereistic. He may understand what you tell him right away when you point out reality and be very glad to hear about it. However, unrealistic patterns are so conditioned in these patients that reality teaching must be repeated throughout therapy in different ways, in different situations, and in different contexts. Therefore, treatment in schizophrenia is largely a matter of education, and any education requires repetition. When a person has to undo old habit patterns of thinking, feeling, and reacting and learn new ones, it requires even more repetition. Habits are hard to break—we all know that—and symptom habits are very hard to break, and we all know that also.

Part 3

TREATMENT OF BASIC SYMPTOMS

CHAPTER 6

The Low
Self-Esteem
Problem

Schizophrenic individuals suffer greatly from a self-esteem problem. That is certain. Due to their integrative impairment and dysregulation of responses, their thinking, affect, and behavior are quantitatively and qualitatively inappropriate (see Figure 2-1, p. 22). They are confused about themselves and the world; they cannot cope with stimuli in a realistically adaptive manner; they err. It follows that deep feelings of inadequacy blight their self-esteem. Many schizophrenic patients will tell you that they feel somehow different from other people, somehow inferior, but are unable to define the matter. The social environment has kept them aware of their inability to cope in many situations and they have grown acutely sensitive to their failures. These hypersensitive patients harbor negative feelings and attitudes with regard to self, and invariably interpret the reactions of others in a negative way, self-referentially, or with projection. As Hoskins (1946) expressed it, "The schizophrenic personality can be likened to the distorted image of a man seen in an irregularly curved mirror."

The self-esteem conflict culminates in massive pan-anxiety, which, of course, feeds back to the sources of the withered self-esteem—the faulty integrative capacity. Over the years, the self-esteem falls far below the level which the individual's actual potentials would allow, and this is continually aggravated by the anxiety feedback system.

In each schizophrenic patient, self-esteem conflicts vary in pattern depending on which personality components contain significant dysregulation. In just about every interview, some such conflict becomes apparent one way or another. However, the therapist cannot confine interpretations to this one problem in every interview because, of course, other problems will require priority attention from time to time. There is a general rule to follow: Interpret that symptom which is the most disruptive to the patient at the time.

At no time, however, should interpretation aim directly at neurotic or other nonpsychotic symptoms that serve as a defense against anxiety. When the patient describes a troublesome neurotic symptom, the therapist can define that symptom to the patient in terms of its true meaning, or significance, in connection with the existing underlying anxiety. For instance, should a disruptive neurotic symptom clearly point to anxiety connected with the patient's self-esteem problem, it is appropriate to deal with this problem directly. Sometimes interpretation will focus on the problem as it reflects the patient's conflict with regard to the self; at other times, as it reflects the patient's conflict in attempts to make social contact, and occasionally as it is manifested in the transference scene. In any case, keep in mind that the target symptom is anxiety.

In dealing with a presenting symptom indicative of the patient's self-esteem conflict, just as when interpreting any other conflict, the therapist proceeds according to the method we have discussed—a step-by-step exploration of the dynamic processes with the patient. During the course of therapy, the therapist reiterates these interpretations appropriately to the context in which the problem is presented. Thus, the patient is guided toward a gradually increased understanding of the dynamic processes involved (as outlined in Figure 2-1). The schizophrenic patient cannot be simply allowed to free-associate around the symptom in an analytic way as can a neurotic patient. Because of the integrative impairment, the schizophrenic patient becomes increasingly confused and increasingly anxious: verbal productions become tangential, disorganized, and circumlocutious, or the patient becomes blocked. In schizophrenia, the patient's associations must be guided along each analytic step, always culminating with a lesson in reality with regard to the self and the environment.

Thus, an interpretation of the self-esteem conflict first aims to make the patient aware of *what* the presented symptom is by redefining it in terms of the conflict per se. Clarifying the significance of the symptom dispels some of the patient's confusion and, more important, reassures him that you, the therapist, recognize and understand the problem he suffers. The patient is thereby made aware of what to focus upon.

The therapist then clarifies for the patient *why* the interpretation is given by pointing out the particular ways the negative self-esteem disrupts performance or destroys chances for experiencing pleasure in daily life. The patient will then feel motivated to do something about it. However, he will not know just how to go about it. Further guidance is required.

Interpret to the patient *how* the self-esteem problem evolved; that it evolved on the basis of anxiety connected with a great sense of inferiority. Anxiety over an assumed inferiority has caused him to become so hypersensitive in self-criticism that even the slightest flaw in performance becomes exaggerated and looms as a seeming proof of some intrinsic inadequacy. Inferiority feelings, in turn, foment even more anxiety which further compounds the already disproportionately low self-esteem.

Deeper dynamic interpretations may be introduced cautiously when the patient grasps the dynamics thus far explained. You then interpret *where* the self-esteem problem is derived from by pointing to one symptomatic factor underlying the dysregulated responses to environmental stimuli—confusion. Deeper penetration into the dynamic mechanisms is usually contraindicated, because learning that he suffers an ineradicable integrative impairment would frighten a patient into desperation. Teach the patient that any inadequacy to cope in certain situations is largely a matter of confusion—confusion with regard to a sense of self, and confusion concerning ordinary social interactions. Here, again, remind the patient of the feedback mechanism and how it aggravates the anxiety.

Specific areas of confusion need to be defined for the patient many times during the course of therapy. Each time such intepretations are given, it is essential to resolve the patient's confusion with lessons in reality in the context of the presented problem. This *remedial measure* serves to direct the patient's focus to corrective positive realities about his self. It is reeducational for the patient, and actually the most important step in the entire interpretive sequence. Autism and dereism are basic to schizophrenia, and, throughout the course of treatment, every patient requires repeated instructions and guidance in order to learn reality with regard to the self and the social environment.

The importance of educating the patient to reality can be understood by way of the following analogies. The phenomenon of color blindness is based on a relative lack of retinal cones; the symptomatology in schizophrenia is based on a relative impairment of integrative ability. As yet, there are no cures for color blindness, and there is no cure for schizophrenia. However, the color blind person can be taught the relative significance, for instance, of red and green colors in a specific context—such as the fact that on a traffic signal the red light is the one above and the green light is under it. Similarly, the schizophrenic individual can be taught the relative significance of positive and negative attributes in a specific context—such as the fact that certain potentials and assets are apparent in one area and not in another.

Interpretive techniques vary among therapists, naturally. Each therapist maintains his own personality style and his own preferred approach. Furthermore, one therapist's view of a patient's crucial presenting symptom will vary slightly from the point of view held by another therapist. Therefore, the 3 examples I will now give outlining the interpretive approach are intended only as an indication of the general principles involved. The material in the 3 examples presented shall, by necessity, consist of a condensation of more than one treatment session, for the purpose of elucidating the main concept contained in each step of the interpretive series. You will also note that sometimes interpretations zig-zag back and forth between the outer and deeper dynamic layers because, of course, symptom feedback operates from each layer and interpretations aim to show the patient their dynamic relationships.

The examples deal with the interpretive approach for each of 3 conflictual self-esteem situations: the patient's self-esteem conflict (1) with regard to the self; (2) in relation to the social environment; and (3) in the transference situation.

The Self-Esteem Conflict with Regard to the Self

Mrs. H. is a 26-year-old part-time accountant. She has been married 4 years but is infertile, and in her case infertility is a vegetative defense mechanism against stressors that is also observed in many other mammalian species. She is dysplastic in build, but petite, graceful, and very pretty. Her symptoms include pan-anxiety with an inability to experience pleasure in any sphere of life; low tolerance for tension and frustration, and great feelings of physical, social, and sexual inadequacy. Neurotic defense symptoms consist of obsessive-compulsive perfectionism (she is an excellent CPA and a meticulous housekeeper) and hysterical devaluation of her self-image with histrionic exaggeration of her physical flaws. The diagnosis is pseudoneurotic schizophrenia.

At the onset of one interview she presented the following problem: "My body is ugly, ugly, UGLY! I hate myself for it." When asked to explain what is so ugly, she exclaimed, "My legs are so fat and grotesque that I'm embarrassed walking down the street." She flatly denied having any attractive physical attributes. In her usual habit of generalizing from the particular, she added, "I'm ugly; I'm stupid; I'm hateful!"

What symptom should be interpreted? Her exaggerated and distorted negative concept of her legs and body image? No, because she would argue the issue in the need to maintain her neurotic defense. The obsessive preoccupation with her hysterically distorted body image served as a receptacle for pan-anxiety. *What* the symptom is was translated to her in terms of its meaning: "You measure your total self only in terms of the negative, in an all-or-none way, and on the basis of a single physical trait." *Why* this interpretation? "Preoccupation with self-criticism for an assumed inferiority makes you feel continually unhappy." *How* did the symptom evolve? "We must explore the source of the anxiety that is connected with your great feelings of inferiority." The patient replied that the anxiety is due to the fact that, as she views it, "total inferiority is indeed a fact." From *where* is the symptom derived? "I don't think 'inferiority' is the appropriate label for yourself. You actually are suffering with confusion about your body image, and about who and what you are as a person." The patient was in agreement.

The *remedial measures* consisted of engaging the patient in the task of exploring the reality about her self: "You have a negative misconcept of yourself in all aspects. This all-or-none attitude is not in the realm of reality. You are neither beautiful nor ugly; neither a genius nor stupid," and so forth. Teaching the patient reality involved encouraging her to focus on the positive as well as the negative side of the ledger of self-evaluation. She was enticed to enumerate a few of her many past and current successes, no matter how minor. She was given a lesson in proper Gestalt by asking her to relate which qualities in a person she considers important and which unimportant. The patient was asked what she values in friends, and "tricked" (if you like) into admitting that she, herself, possesses many of the valued attributes she mentioned. She was reminded that her friends also have areas of inferiority; that all people have positive as well as negative attributes.

For example, I asked the patient, "Do you judge others in terms of their physical flaws? Do you demand of your friends that they be perfect? Who do you know who is perfect?" At this point, the patient conceded, "No, my best friend is bright and has a good disposition. . . ." And then she laughingly remarked, "You know, she weighs about 200 pounds and you should just see the amusing contrast between her and her small poodle." Having left herself wide open for it, she was given another interpretation, namely: "It is your responsibility to judge yourself as fairly as you judge her, rather than in a totally negative way." The therapist also reiterated: "My role is to help you see yourself realistically; I shall be honest in appraising you, and your role is to learn honest self-appraisal."

In the course of therapy, discussions such as those summarized above served as brief, concise lessons aimed to reeducate the patient to realistic self-observation and self-evaluation. In different sessions and in various contexts, remedial interpretations were proffered, over and over again, and the patient's rigid grip on her negative self-appraisal became increasingly lessened.

The Self-Esteem Conflict in Relation to the Social Environment

The patient, Dr. B., is a 43-year-old single male. He is a highly talented physicist. He appears ectomorphic in build, tense, verbose, and ingratiatingly polite in manner. He has had a series of brief sexual affairs during recent years, prior to which he had a history of voyeurism that was resolved during earlier therapy. Presenting symptoms included compulsive work habits and an inability to sustain social relationships. He complained of inexplicable episodes of acute depression, and a consuming anxiety in anticipation of social ostracism with loss of his research post. He rationalized that the anxiety was in relation to his current sexual affairs and possible disclosure of past voyeurism, as well as professional jealousy of his fellow scientists. Diagnosis is that of pseudoneurotic schizophrenia with obsessive-compulsive defense mechanisms.

One day he presented the following complaint in interview: "Today I encountered the director of research in the company cafeteria and he didn't speak to me. He's down on me. Perhaps he has heard some gossip about me. I fear my colleagues all know about my love affairs, and perhaps have heard about my past sexual problem." (Note how readily inferiority feelings and guilty fear foment self-referential thinking and paranoid projection.)

Should interpretation at this point focus on the paranoid ideation, the sexual acting out, the dynamics of voyeurism, the competitive anxiety, or what? None of those lines of interpretation would hit at the most disruptive symptom presented, namely, the patient's negative self-evaluation, which gave rise to anxiety in interrelating with his professional environment. *What* the disruptive symptom is was defined for him as follows: "You expect punishment and rejection because you consider yourself an inferior, 'dirty sex pervert.'"

Why the interpretation? "You must know that these obsessive preoccupations interfere with your concentration in your work, as well as your objectivity concerning interpersonal relationships." The patient agreed.

How the symptom evolved was interpreted as follows: "We must explore the derivation of the anxiety. It is connected with strong feelings of inferiority." The patient exclaimed that his past sexual problem deserved no badge of superiority, and then launched into his usual elaborate discourses concerning his past and present social as well as sexual indiscretions.

From *where* the problem evolved was then mentioned, namely, that much of his feeling of inferiority is on spurious grounds; that actually the problem is one of certain confusion about himself in the area of interpersonal relationships. With the aim of encouraging him to explore this confusion, he was commended on his past achievement, namely, that of resolving his voyeurism through insight, and reminded that similarly he will be able to resolve his confusion about himself pertaining to interpersonal relationships. Interpretations about reality were in order.

Remedial measures consisted of pointing out to the patient a series of simple realities about the self and its influence on the environment, which this schizophrenic, although a brilliant man, had never perceived. In preface to this, his unrealistic all-or-none attitude about himself and others was questioned, "Do you assume you are indecent and inferior to others? Do you assume all other people are decent and superior to you?" He was reminded that everyone has personality problems, sometimes including sexual transgressions; that no one is a paragon of superiority in all things any more than anyone is completely inferior to others. In teaching the patient proper Gestalt, he was reminded of the relative importance and unimportance of matters when it comes to evaluation of the positive and negative attributes of others. For example, "The director hired you for your scientific abilities; he cannot concern himself with nonprofessional irrelevancies such as the status of an employee's private affairs that in no way conflict with professional responsibilities."

Further remedial interpretations focused on the patient's negative self-esteem as reflected in his previous day's encounter with the director: the reality of this simple encounter was clarified. "If the director failed to greet you in the cafeteria, quite likely it was because he was preoccupied with selecting his lunch, or with some personal problem—having nothing to do with you—which caused him to be momentarily impervious to his surroundings. This happens to you and to all of us from time to time." The interpretation was followed by an insight singularly appropriate for a great many schizophrenic patients: "You will admit, Dr. B., that when someone reacts in a positive way with a personal compliment about you, you either dismiss it as invalid, or doubt the person's sincerity, or fear it is a joke. Yet, you are quick to interpret any negative reaction as a personal affront, often erroneously, due to your assumption of inferiority. When such situations arise in the future, check your reactions for bias on your part; be honest with yourself, and correct your reactions with logic."

For Dr. B., such interpretations required many repetitions before he began to apply them and alter his self-evaluation. But eventually he loosened the hold on the lifelong automatic negative attitudes about himself, and thereupon moved in a position to become gradually re-conditioned to self-esteem reality in his social interactions. He increasingly recognized and enjoyed his high reputation for brilliance as a physicist, and fears of rejection for social-sexual "indiscretions" disappeared.

The Self-Esteem Conflict
Manifested in the Transference

Richard is a handsome, 19-year-old, single male, whose only measure of positive self-esteem centers around narcissistic pride in his powerful athletic build, which he augments with ritualistic body-building exercise. He dropped out of high school during his senior year, soon after reaching the goal of becoming captain of the soccer team. He had a compulsive need to exercise daily, nevertheless, and his main symptoms center around the fear that following exercising his sweat could quite probably be causing him to give off an offensive body odor. He presented that fear as the excuse for withdrawing from the soccer team, then from school and social contacts. History discloses that he had always been troubled with shyness. The one sustained close friendship in childhood dissolved during early adolescence following a brief period of sexual "fooling around" with a girl to whom both boys were attracted. Although Richard was not rejected by her, he nevertheless assumed himself competitively inferior to his "aggressive" friend.

The diagnosis is that of pseudoneurotic schizophrenia; obsessive-compulsive traits and hypochondriacal fear of body odor are the predominant symptoms of defense against anxiety. (It is important to note that he denied having any olfactory perception of his own body odor, either when alone or in social contacts. It was not an olfactory delusion, such as develops in overtly psychotic schizophrenia and which is refractory to psychotherapeutic influence.) The fear of body odor was a symbolically concretized representation of his fear that his total personality "stinks." This obsessive fear, however, failed to adequately absorb the pan-anxiety, some of which was connected with the guilt-laden sexual drive initially aroused by his sexual acting out with a girl earlier in adolescence. But it did enable Richard to avoid the tremendous anxiety related to his social contact impairment.

During the first two weeks of treatment, Richard was tense and anxious. He was courteous but spoke tersely and only in response to questions, always avoiding eye contact with the therapist. (Incidentally, it is important that the therapist takes care not to "assault" such a patient by gazing directly at him during an interview.) Mellaril® was prescribed to provide some relief from the anxiety.

At one point early in the course of treatment, Richard abruptly exclaimed, "You're wasting your time, Doc. Treatment won't help me." When asked to explain, he replied, "You must know by now I haven't got what it takes. I see no reason why you're so nice to me other than because you're paid." Naturally, a schizophrenic patient who views himself negatively readily assumes all others will view him negatively, and Richard carried this attitude into the transference. He resisted therapy due to self-distrust, and distrust of the therapist's seeming acceptance of him. Interpretation first aimed to reduce the patient's resistance to therapy.

What the symptom consisted of was defined in the transference context: "You don't like yourself and you assume I don't like you." Richard nodded in agreement. *Why* the interpretation? "Treatment is blocked by your fear that I will reject you if you relate your feelings." He was told that a great many patients similarly distrust a therapist's real acceptance for the same reason he does. Then he was asked, "Should you go to a surgeon with the symptoms of appendicitis, would the surgeon reject you for describing your pain? Similarly, here, the more you clue me in about your painful feelings, the better I can understand the cause and determine how you can rid yourself of the pain."

How the patient's negative self-esteem evolved was suggested: "Your negative feelings about yourself are connected with anxiety—and fear of 'sweating it out' in treatment is one part of this anxiety. To you it seems like 'Catch-22': you dare come here to resolve anxiety conflicts only to find that contact with me stirs up more anxiety. I admire you for your 'guts.'" The patient admitted that it takes "guts" to come, just as it does to sit down at evening dinner with his family and their friends. He related at length how he has to "sweat it out," moment-by-moment, and asked the therapist, "I actually sweat with anxiety—be honest with me; do you notice if I smell bad now?" He was given an honest answer and then commended for connecting the sweating with the anxiety. At the end of the session he was reassured that with continued exploration of the basis for the anxiety, it could be resolved.

The patient continued keeping his appointments and became increasingly able to relate a variety of anxiety conflicts he experienced. He expressed concern to know the basis for these anxiety conflicts. *Where* the anxiety was derived from was interpreted in the context of his negative self-esteem: "Your anxiety experiences all seem to stem from feelings of inferiority. Everyone has valid reasons to feel inferior in some respects, but you harbor many misconceptions about yourself, which have led to unrealistic reasons for feeling inferior. These we shall explore—and resolve, in time."

Further interpretations were given appropriately in the context of his contact impairment when Richard described his clumsy responses in social encounters. The therapist explained, "I can see that these indications of apparent inferiority stem from the confusion you have as to exactly who you, as a personality, are. This further confuses you with regard to other people—how they think, feel, and why they react the way they do. Naturally, this impairs your ability to relate to them, and you find it so anxiety-provoking that you withdraw, quite understandably." To facilitate Richard's understanding of this, it was stated in an empathic metaphor: "It is as though you have been living in a foreign country where strange people speak a strange language. In our relationship, now, you can use me as an interpreter: I shall translate for you the meaning of your own feelings and reactions, and at the same time unravel the confusion you have in social contacts by translating their nature."

Over the months that followed, the patient utilized the therapist as a reflecting mirror for the process of reeducation to an increasingly realistic self-image. *Remedial measures* included insights into various aspects of reality with regard to the self and the evaluation of others. His all-or-none attitudes became modified by reeducation to the realization that extremes of inferiority and superiority, acceptance and rejection, do not exist in reality.

Over the 2-year period of treatment, Richard became sufficiently reconditioned to open the door to social contacts—gingerly at first, but with increasing success in furthering his reality testing in a modest way. The obsessive fear of being an unacceptable "stinker" dissolved. Although the "cure" was orthopedic and residual experiences of shyness and withdrawal protected him from the anxiety that a close attachment to a girl would provoke, he was at least able to form tenuous sexual and social relationships and no longer suffered the chronic pain of loneliness and depression.

The above outlined interpretive procedures for dealing with the self-esteem problem exemplified in the types of conflicts presented here are only intended to indicate the general principle to follow. Each therapist must employ his own style when giving a patient these sequential interpretations, and appropriate interpretations vary with each patient according to presenting therapeutic needs. The target symptom is always the anxiety responsible for the disruptive symptom presented by the patient—in our present discussion, the patient's misconcepts of self. The underlying dynamic mechanisms are gradually traced, step by step, during the course of treatment. And with each step along the way, interpretations culminate with a lesson in reality aimed to correct the patient's distorted self-image—whether manifested in connection with the self, in reaction to the social environment, or in the transference.

Finally, there is another very important fact that requires consideration. Interpreting positive realities to correct a misconcept of self in many cases must be done very cautiously and gradually. Schizophrenic patients often remain deaf and blind to positive insights concerning themselves and often resist accepting these realities for a long time. There are several reasons for this. First of all, schizophrenic patients have been conditioned over the years to regard themselves as inferior human beings. Reconditioning them to reality requires a great deal of repetition in order to loosen the patients' hold on this lifelong habit of negative self-evaluation.

Secondly, schizophrenic patients are hypersensitive and will usually reject positive suggestions and compliments due to their distrust in the therapist's honesty or understanding. This is one reason why it is preferable to entice patients to do their own probing and discover their positive attributes as much as is possible. Even then, schizophrenic individuals have difficulty in learning from past experiences and require interpretations to explore the underlying basis for this.

It is also a fact that schizophrenic patients, like small children, will automatically regard compliments from others as implied demands that they must perform accordingly—and, of course, to perfection. Such a patient will not verbalize this directly because it is only a vague feeling, but may mention, "Doc, when you just said that about me I started to feel depressed," or, "I feel a little angry now." Patients will continue to defend themselves by rejecting positive insights until they are better able to accept the fact that, in reality, adequacy of performance, or relating to others, is never a matter of total success or total failure.

You will invariably find, therefore, that until their anxiety is reduced by means of a gradual increment of remedial interpretation, schizophrenic patients actually need to feel inadequate—and will struggle to maintain this attitude. Feeling inferior serves to justify their symptomatic avoidance of anxiety-provoking environmental contacts. Therefore, whenever a positive insight is rejected, the therapist must quickly interpret to the patient that the compliment is not to be regarded as a demand, but simply a tool he may want to use to his advantage at some future time.

It does not take much experience for an intuitive therapist to measure the timing and dosage of positive insight that a patient is able to assimilate without experiencing "emotional indigestion" and resistance to therapy. The fact remains, however, that schizophrenic patients must be regularly encouraged in the task of recognizing the positive side of their self-esteem ledger in order to counteract their habitual preoccupation with "ego" deficits. They need to learn that realistic self-criticism must always involve assaying existing positive as well as existing negative attributes. A soldier cannot march on an empty stomach; neither can an individual progress in therapy, or in life, on an empty reservoir of self-esteem.

CHAPTER 7

Thinking Disorders in Schizophrenia

The basic thinking disorders in schizophrenia vary in pattern with each schizophrenic individual. Furthermore, each individual manifests different amounts of thinking disorder. In masked schizophrenic patients it may be rather obvious clinically, but in the majority of these patients the manifestations of the thinking disorder are subtle; sometimes they are so subtle that it requires thorough examination over a considerable period of time before the symptoms are discerned. The fact remains, some amount of inability to deal with intellectual concepts properly is always present in schizophrenia, even though it may be hidden from view by compensatory defense or other symptoms; the snake may be very small and concealed by tall grass, but it is there.

The basic thinking disorder in schizophrenia can be defined according to its two main aspects: Fragmentation of thinking, which Bleuler referred to as loosening of associations; and impairment of concept formation, or categorical impairment. One aspect is not usually observed without its entanglement with the other. The etiology is as yet unexplained, but both phenomena are actually outgrowths of the same basic impairment of integration and organization. The basic thinking disorder is unique to schizophrenia, and probably its only pathognomonic sign. Therefore, its recognition is important for making diagnosis, and very important for ascertaining the treatment approach appropriate to the dynamics involved.

For exploration into the probable roots of the basic schizophrenic thinking disorder we refer to Hoch's theory of the dynamics of schizophrenia—schematized in our "onion layers" chart (Figure 2-1)—and apply it in terms of psychophysiological (mental) phenomena. Our assumption is that in the deep dynamic layer there exists some peculiar faulty screening of afferent stimuli: Percepts are received that are inappropriate and those that are appropriate to receive may be ignored, or they may be jumbled up with inappropriate percepts, or at times the majority of percepts may be either ignored or received regardless of their relative values. This is followed by faulty integration of percepts: There is an inability to fuse percept parts into a realistically meaningful whole. Based on that, faulty organization of percepts is bound to result: Meaningful whole percepts are not available to be fused to form a realistically meaningful concept. These all involve content as well as process. The natural outcome of the dynamic sequence is dysregulation of psychophysiological functioning manifested in terms of fragmentation of thinking and impaired concept formation.

Because we are talking about the deeper dynamic layers in the chart, we must first define what is meant by integration and what is meant by organization on the psychophysiological, or thinking, level of behavior. Integration is the process of combining sensations (percepts) that realistically belong together. Organization is the process of combining interdependent percepts into a meaningful conceptual whole. As an analogy: if you perceive a paper with letters on it, you might accept through the screening process "n" and "o" and "w" and in integrating these percepts you arrive at a meaningful whole of the word "now" or "own" or "won." The schizophrenic, on the other hand, might not perceive them at all, or might fuse them in a sequence "wno" or "onw," which in English would be rather incoherent. Meanwhile, other afferent stimuli are being cortically received through the screening. For example, these new percepts can be integrated to arrive at the word "act." The schizophrenic might also fail to accept or integrate the percept parts "a," "c" and "t" at all, or might fuse these, along with the former three percepts, inappropriately, i.e., he would not integrate the two groups of percepts into meaningful whole words. Therefore, because these whole percepts would not be available, the schizophrenic would be unable to organize the interdependent percepts (each having a special function or relation to the whole) into a systematized, meaningful conceptual whole. To continue the analogy: instead of simply arriving at the concept "act now," or "now act," for instance, the schizophrenic might conclude with a disorganized jumble such as "wnoc ta," or perhaps use correctly integrated words but organize them to form "won act," which perhaps only another schizophrenic could accept as a meaningful concept.

FRAGMENTATION OF THINKING

Now, fragmentation of thinking implies an absence of a goal-idea, because the individual is unable to put concepts together in meaningful logical sequence. Impaired concept formation further implies that the individual puts the concepts together but the sequence is illogical and he arrives at an erroneous goal-idea. Naturally, fragmented thinking is always involved to some extent in augmenting the existing impairment of concept formation.

Fragmentation of thinking and impairment of concept formation vary in degree and configuration among schizophrenic individuals. In some cases the clinical signs are subtle and difficult to discern; in other cases they are obvious—sometimes glaringly so—and very disruptive to the patient's life. When the signs are seemingly absent, you may have to examine the patient over a period of many weeks before discerning any. It is the snake concealed in the grass, which can be found. Once in a while, however, you encounter a so-called normal person who very occasionally manifests a sign of fragmentation or concept disorder— especially if the person has had a few drinks, or is tired, or is distracted. It could be an accidental coincidence. Nevertheless, should this subtle display occur again and again, you must then appreciate that it most likely indicates schizophrenia.

Fragmentation of thinking is clinically manifested by either jumbled-up sequences of thought or by mental blocking. In the first instance, the person rambles on and on, in a scattered and incoherent manner, and any leading goal-idea is absent or soon lost. Results of this are sometimes the paralogic or "derailed" logic observed in the pseudo-philosophizing of educated intelligent schizophrenics. It could be that many a student has received a Ph.D. degree when submitting a thesis containing jumbled thoughts with goal-ideas so lost in the shuffle of inappropriate connections that the professor could not understand the "brilliant" logical sequences and therefore concluded that the content was intellectually far above his head.

Sometimes fragmentation is observed during the period of fact-finding. The patient relates material in a vague, unorganized manner with illogical sequence, circumstantiality, and perseveration on inconsequentia. Or, the patient becomes blocked and is unable to express himself except with terse answers to questions that should evoke elaboration.

When beginning therapy with a patient, I often employ a diagnostic "gimmick": I ask the patient to submit at the next interview two written accounts: on one page a life history written in his own words, and on another page descriptions of relatives and other important persons in his life. It is surprising how often this discloses fragmented thinking and concept disorders. A law-student patient handed me a 14-page life history but forgot to write anything concerning people in his life. Most of his life history account described in detail the games he played with peers at the age of 10—and that was about it. This disclosed a great deal about him, diagnostically.

When such a patient rambles on during the fact-finding period of treatment, with perseveration on an inconsequential theme and derailment from any goal-idea, he must be interrupted and told what the symptom is. The therapist can state, "You are describing a brief period in your life, which may be important, but I do not get the all-over picture," and then ask specific questions aimed to indicate to the patient a more realistic Gestalt of his life. The patient usually does not object to these interruptions and questions because he is made aware of his need to be given "structure" and "direction" in his thinking. (This is far different from interrupting patients who perseverate on the topic of current painful symptoms.)

In response to a request for a written account of her life and the people in it, a young lady patient demonstrated fragmented thinking in terms of intellectual blocking. The referring doctor had described her as a brilliant creative writer, which led me to expect an hysterical self-dramatization or a similarly engaging production. Yet, in all earnestness, the patient submitted a half-page history consisting of a chronological list of events: date of birth; age when she started school; date of college graduation; and job procurements. The so-called description of persons in her life consisted of a list giving the names and ages of her grandparents, parents, and siblings. When asked how she felt about any of the people mentioned, she replied that she could think of nothing important to say. As it turned out, she was a creative writer who had never gotten around to finding anything important to write.

A markedly blocked patient needs to be drawn forth by means of directed questions, and a realistic goal-idea must be defined. However, it is obvious that the intelligent woman just mentioned was blocked even more by pan-anxiety than by her thinking disorders, and treatment first aimed at the anxiety symptoms. Actually, when anxiety was considerably alleviated, the young lady spoke somewhat fluently, although her confusion regarding important versus unimportant issues remained, and treatment then focused on teaching her reality in that context.

Fragmentation of thinking is clearly portrayed in the following account of a 40-year-old male newspaper editorial writer. He came to treatment with the complaint, "I can't meet deadlines; I spend two days doing what should take two hours." When asked to describe the problem more fully, the content of his response was the following: "Well, you see, I can't work at home because my wife keeps interrupting, and I can't work in the town library because, in the first place, you have to be a jobless bum to frequent a library, and also I need to smoke when I work, and during the morning I like to go to the coffee shop and get coffee in containers." (He described the coffee shop and the amount of sugar he likes in his coffee.) "I smoke cigars, you see, and there is a certain brand I like but they are expensive and hard to find. In the afternoons, I don't drink coffee, though, but I do drink beer because it relaxes me and I can write better." (He described the pub he frequents and the persons he encounters there.) "My wife complains about my cigar and beer expenses but she doesn't understand. She spends too much on clothes, you see, because she competes with the women at her club. And I tell her she doesn't spend enough time at home caring for our little girl Susan-Ann, and, frankly, if it weren't for Susan-Ann I would divorce my wife. . . ."

The patient was interrupted and reminded of his presented problem —the goal-idea that he had completely lost. He then described the difficulty he had concentrating on his work, and admitted to confusion in attempts to organize his articles, adding, "The boss says they are 'too wordy,' but I can't shorten them because I don't like to delete some of my good ideas. The boss isn't very bright, either, because he doesn't always understand what I write, or else he doesn't read carefully and grasp my ideas. . . ." Actually, this man's fragmentation of thinking had been recently aggravated by his boss's threatening to fire him. The patient's coffee ingestion to keep alert, cigar smoking to ease tension, and beer drinking to allay anxiety were self-defeating oral habits of increasing necessity to this desperate man.

What was the most disruptive presenting symptom and how should theapy deal with it? The most urgent symptom was his fragmented thinking insofar as it threatened his job. Anxiety was the main factor augmenting the thinking disorder. The connection between the writing block and the anxiety was pointed out to the patient. Yet, diminishing anxiety with medication would require the patient to forego his beer-drinking habit. He agreed to that requirement in order to receive the prescribed medication—10 minutes after the first oral dose was given him in liquid form during the therapeutic session. A few practical directives were offered to guide him in establishing a favorable working milieu. Subsequent interviews focused on how his thinking problem evolved in connection with anxiety, tension, and mild agitated depression. The derivation of the thinking disorder was interpreted in a constructive way; that he is hypersensitive to all external stimuli; that

anxiety connected with inferiority feelings requires him to project blame
for his poor concentration and mental confusion; and that he truly has
high intelligence despite his difficulties in organizing his ideas. Remedial
measures consisted mainly of teaching this writer the very simple reality necessity of outlining his ideas into appropriate thought sequence
before writing them. In other words, the Gestalt reality of "following
the main goal-idea to conclusion" was reviewed with him in different
ways and at different times in each interview. To use an old-fashioned
phrase, the patient borrowed the doctor's ego with regard to work habit
in order to break an unrealistic habit pattern (fortunately only recently
formed) and establish a realistic action pattern of organized thinking.
Thinking disorders other than fragmentation were dealt with effectively in the course of therapy but, of course, they were not completely
resolved. However, due to extraordinary patience on the part of the
writer's boss, he retained his job.

IMPAIRMENT OF CONCEPT FORMATION

Impairment of concept formation is largely manifested by three in-
termeshing types of categorical impairment: (1) faulty connection of
concepts; (2) confusion and misinterpretation of what should be accepted as concrete or abstract; and (3) confusion and misinterpretation
of elements of the Gestalt. Again, it must be realized that these thinking
disorders in schizophrenia are sometimes so slight that they are difficult
to discern. The patient's logical reasoning may be only minimally impaired, or may even be quite logical but contain a line of reasoning
inappropriate to the situation with which the person is dealing.

Faulty connection of concepts refers to a line of reasoning based on
an inappropriate premise: dissimilar things are connected on the basis
of only a single common feature, or apparently similar things are connected which have no appropriate common denominator.

Some years ago I hired a housekeeper; she was intelligent and well
educated. One morning I asked her to clean my office bookshelves, dust
the 600-odd books and replace them, please. Now, how those books
could be organized when replaced on the shelves is open to several
logical alternatives: She could have used subject categories such as basic
science, psychiatry, history, art, and so forth; or, they could be organized alphabetically according to titles or authors. Of course, one
could speculate about further logical alternatives, such as color or—I
don't know—perhaps some other criteria. Anyhow, that evening my
housekeeper was eager to delight me with her achievement: On each

shelf the tallest books were placed in the center and the shorter books arranged on either side according to graduated order of height. The top shelves contained the thinnest tall and short books and the thickest were on the bottom shelf. The whole arrangement resembled a veritable monument of Romanesque architecture with its graduated levels of columns. Being rather pedantic, I yielded to the urge to reorganize the books according to their former subject and author category positions so that I could locate each one without spending time playing "treasure hunt." I thereby "disordered" her quite logical arrangement. Was the criterion for organized thinking an indication of schizophrenia on my part, or the housekeeper's? Not necessarily that of either. Both contained good logic and both followed through with valid thought sequence to an intended goal. However, the housekeeper—intelligent and educated—followed a line of reasoning to an inappropriate goal. The books were primarily valued for reading purposes, not for decoration. The housekeeper had connected dissimilar things (books with dissimilar subject matter) which had only a single common feature (size). So, I suspected she was schizophrenic and later on it was verified, interestingly enough, by her expounding to me on the topic of the intellectual inferiority of people having brown eyes.

Actually, sorting objects or concepts by connecting them in an innovative manner that is clearly inappropriate to an obvious or usual line of reasoning is not always incorrect, nor is it necessarily illogical. However, it usually indicates a faulty connection of concepts, insofar as the basic premise is one that is "private" to the individual. It is observed in schizophrenia, or in the uneducated, in mentally deficient people, or in children, i.e., it can occur in individuals who do not perceive the "obvious" order of things in their environment. Occasionally discoveries are made by scientists who organize a group of factors in such an innovative way, in that they perceive some order in things that ordinary people overlook. It points toward schizophrenia nonetheless, and this unusual type of thinking behavior should alert the psychiatrist to look for other clues of distorted concept formation. The treatment approach focuses the patient's attention on the issue of inappropriate and appropriate lines of reasoning, and their adaptive value, with regard to the particular situation confronting the patient.

Confusion and misinterpretation of what should be accepted as concrete or abstract are commonly manifested in schizophrenia. Concrete matters will be treated as abstractions in some situations, and abstractions will be treated as literal concrete facts in others. An example of the former is the patient who insists that the painter, Van Gogh, is a coward because many of his pictures contain a great amount of yellow pigment. Misinterpreting the concrete (the use of the color yellow) as an abstract concept (cowardice) is clearly schizophrenic thinking. An example of concretization is the man who had read a Bible directive (Matthew 6: 6), "Enter into thy closet, and when thou has shut thy door, pray to thy Father...," whereupon he routinely entered his clothes closet each day and shouted out prayers to God. Misinterpreting the Biblical use of such abstract concepts (to closet one's mind off from distractions and to lift up one's level of thought) as literal commands is indicative of schizophrenic thinking—but not in all cases. The psychiatrist must know his patient's cultural and religious indoctrinations before pronouncing these productions indicative of schizophrenia. Perhaps the man who prayed in his closet had Fundamentalist religious indoctrination and was conditioned to literal interpretation of every statement in the Bible. In such case, his behavior fits into the norm of his society and is not a sign of personal pathology. Incidentally, it must also be kept in mind that children below the ages of 9 or 10 normally do not deal with abstractions reliably, nor do so-called primitive peoples in illiterate societies. They normally tend to treat abstractions in a concrete manner.

In other words, treating the concrete as abstract, or vice versa, indicates a conceptual thinking disorder when it is a "private" experience, but not if it is a "public" belief or a manifestation of primary process thinking in children. This is why it is important when treating a patient for the psychiatrist to familiarize himself with his patient's cultural background, just as he takes into consideration the age of a child patient. No experienced psychiatrist would assume his patient was schizophrenic if the patient told him that Catholic priests turn wine into the blood of Christ during the Mass. No psychiatrist would assume a 4-year-old child was schizophrenic because, having been hurt by a doctor who injected him from a syringe drawn from his black bag, showed fear of the plumber who subsequently came to the house carrying a black bag. However, if the child was asked to draw a picture depicting the concept, "two heads are better than one," and drew a picture of a person having two heads, *that* would indicate the child is schizophrenic, because it is illogical and bizarre, it is not culturally prefaced, and is not primary process reasoning on the basis of any realistic experience the child has had.

For comic relief, let us look at a myth that has gone down through the centuries and see how primary process thinking along with concretization of symbols can be woven into a concept pleasing to a child: Rabbits are symbolic of fertility. Eggs are equated with fertility. The Spring Equinox signifies fertility of the ground. Therefore, at Easter time (the Equinox) "Easter rabbits lay eggs."

Confusion and Misinterpretation
of Elements of the Gestalt

Disturbance of Gestalt is usually manifested in schizophrenic individuals to some extent, in one or another way. There are two main elements involved. For one, the schizophrenic is sometimes unable to differentiate parts from the whole. Moreover, there is an inability to fuse the conceptual parts of a matter into a realistic and meaningful whole. For example, there is the patient who regards her whole body image as ugly on the basis of a distorted and exaggerated concept that her legs are ugly.

Another Gestalt problem in schizophrenia is the person's difficulty in differentiating between that which is foreground and that which is background in terms of concept and meaning. For example, there is the famous ambiguous figure (Rubin, 1921). Normally, one perceives either two face silhouettes, or one perceives the outline of a vase—but they are not both perceived simultaneously. The eye can switch from one percept to the other. Normally, the perception selected is appropriate to the person's idea situation: the student of people will tend to perceive the faces; the student of archeology will tend to perceive the Greek vase. In either case, the object perceived can be elaborated in the mind of the viewer; the eyes and mouth filled in for the faces; and certain designs applied to the vase. The schizophrenic person, however, comes up with an inappropriate Gestalt, or with no recognition of foreground and background. Due to faulty screening and impairment in integrating and organizing percepts, thinking can be fragmented and essential elements of the faces or the vase omitted, or confusion with contamination of the two images can occur.

In schizophrenia, therefore, the individual manifests some distortion of reality "landscape" formation in thinking. Confusion and misinterpretation of what is important or unimportant occurs and the person becomes bogged down with heterogeneous details. The appropriate are combined with the inappropriate, and the significant with insignificant concepts. An example of this would be the schizophrenic patient who judges a man on the basis of his title, social position, handsome face, money, or any one of these factors alone, rather than establishing priority judgment in terms of personality, character, kindness, or other qualities pertinent in interpersonal relationships. Here again, the patient's cultural indoctrination of values must be known by the psychiatrist, because every culture has its particular burdens of prejudice that are accepted as the norm by those within each cultural group. However, if a patient tells you he does not like Mr. Smith because he has droopy eyelids like Uncle Joe who was unkind to him, and you find that your patient personally arrives at the conclusion that Mr. Smith is therefore an unkind person, you are dealing with a patient whose thinking disorder includes a disturbed Gestalt. Usually, as in this case, it is in connection with emotionally charged thinking, which we shall discuss later.

In treating a patient who misinterprets and confuses the important and the unimportant and arrives at an illogical picture of a situation, one is reminded of an old fable. The young mouse is attracted to a cat: it is soft, purrs, is beautiful, and therefore it is "good." The little mouse is afraid of the hen: it has a sharp beak, cackles, is ugly, and therefore it is "evil." But the "good" hen cackles to warn the little mouse that the "evil" cat eats mice. Silly though it may seem, we sometimes must teach our patients which simple elements in life are relatively "good" and "evil" in terms of reality and adaptive significance.

Fragmentation of thinking and impairment of concept formation are intermeshed in most cases, and treatment aims to teach the patient reality by focusing on the aspects of these thinking disorders most disturbing to the patient. This varies according to the patient's productions during any given interview. The what, why, how, and where questions are answered by interpreting the dynamics of the disturbed thinking disorder presented by the patient. However, the most important interpretation in this sequence is the remedial measure. The thinking disorders must be corrected, in a supportive manner, by explicit lessons in logical and realistic thinking, with regard to process and content of thought.

One more important point: The affect connected to the fragmented thinking and illogical categorical reasoning must always be evaluated in each interview. Whenever the patient's thinking disorder so disrupts his life functioning that a surge of great anxiety is the result, then teaching the patient how to remedy his faulty thinking serves to lessen the patient's anxiety. On the other hand, whenever the patient's anxiety or any marked affect so disrupts his life functioning that an aggravation of the thinking disorder is the result, then the affect problem must be dealt with first in the therapeutic approach. Obviously, a therapist is unlikely to influence a patient's thinking disorder when the patient is preoccupied with strong emotional distress.

CHAPTER 8

Emotionally Charged Thinking Disorders

The human organism functions as a unit of interacting processes on all neural levels and so, naturally, thought behavior cannot be divorced from emotional, vegetative, or other levels of behavior. For instance, "pure" thought process is not devoid of emotional influence—with the possible exception of concentrating to solve a purely mathematical problem. However, emotional factors do not explain the existence of schizophrenic thought disorders, nor are thought disorders caused by emotional factors. Nevertheless, the basic thinking disorders in schizophrenia, fragmentation and impairment of concept formation, are always influenced by some amount of affectivity. A patient's affective state often serves to quantitatively augment the clinical manifestations of the existing thinking disorder. Actually, there is a feedback of meshed interplay in response to every stimulus: emotional dysregulation and thought dysregulation add fuel to each other's fire. These interactions are followed by emotional as well as intellectual regression. The following example demonstrates the phenomena.

A shy young lady, a college student, has a certain idea. She thinks one of her professors is the most attractive man imaginable. The idea becomes emotionally charged because the student is socially and sexually frustrated; she feels lonely and yearns to be loved. Then another stimulus arrives: The professor "gives" her an "A" grade for some work she did. She perceives this in a peculiar way. To her, it gains more connotation than simply that of a grade earned for achievement. To the student it means that the professor loves her; that he loves her and expects to invite her to his apartment. Then, additional proof of this evolves in her mind, due to select hypermnesis of irrelevant and unimportant percepts. The added proof rests on the fact that sometimes he smiles at her in class, and sometimes he wears a certain nice suit "just to please" her. There is amnesia for the relevant facts that he smiles at all his students and attires himself in accordance with the weather. Relevancies are lost, such as the fact that the professor's cordiality and attire bore no significant relationship to his teaching role.

This is an example of how the student's emotions were bound in with and influenced her thinking responses to select stimuli. The basic thinking disorders in the student were augmented by their emotional charge. It is an example of wishful, magical thinking that deviated away from reality and became involved in fantasy.

Emotionally charged thinking in schizophrenia can be defined according to two categories: complex-bound thinking and autistic-dereistic thinking. Here again, these phenomena are usually intermeshed, but for treatment purposes each must be recognized for what it is.

Complex-bound thinking means that an idea becomes charged with emotional content. Both the idea and the emotion bound with it then determine how stimuli are perceived. In the framework of the particular emotional complex, a stimulus will be perceived in a fragmented and distorted way. Then, a certain amount of regression takes place in the patient's thinking, which causes a disability in the selection of past experiences appropriate to the immediate thought synthesis. It often involves hypermnesis of irrelevant and unimportant experiences and amnesia for certain relevant and important experiences. For instance, a schizophrenic person who has just been told he is stupid while facing an ordinary task will react with anxiety and count the times he thinks he failed in the past, while quite forgetting his realistic abilities and past successes. Schizophrenic patients have a penchant for thinking in negative terms especially, and blinding themselves to the positive, which is one reason why repetition in reeducating them to reality is imperative.

Autistic-dereistic thinking is subjective, or self-involved thinking that veers away from reality. An emotional charge aggravates the existing schizophrenic thinking disorder, and ideation becomes self-referential and illogical. It becomes "wish-thinking" or "fear-thinking," whereby positive or negative ideation becomes confused with, or interrelated with, fantasy. In the first instance, a friendly gesture can be misinterpreted as a total love-commitment. In the second instance, a friendly smile can be misinterpreted as a sarcastic gesture of scorn. Thinking becomes contaminated by the emotional charge of a need, or a fear, and objectivity is lost. The individual thereby regresses emotionally and his autism becomes more manifest. He also regresses intellectually to the more archaic, infantile mode of "magical" thinking, which compounds his basic intellectual impairment. The question is often asked: Is autistic-dereistic thinking based on withdrawal from reality? Probably the converse is true—that withdrawal from reality is prefaced on the autism and dereistic thinking which, in turn, is prefaced on fragmentation of the mental process.

Autistic-dereistic thinking resembles primary process thinking, but it is not the same, because fragmentation occurs and there is conceptual distortion in autistic-dereistic thinking. For instance, the patient is confused between fantasy and fact, between the concrete and the abstract, the foreground and background of relevancies, and so forth. This you do not observe in a healthy child. A small child thinks in concrete terms and his primary process reasoning may lead him to erroneous conclusions, but the logical process is not impaired: his logic is valid on the basis of his limited life experiences and neurological immaturity.

There is, naturally, a developmental sequence in a maturing individual's concepts of a sense of self and the world around him, and this throws light on the differences between archaic thinking of a child and that of the schizophrenic. A normal one-year-old who learns to walk will exclaim, "I walk"; his self-image at that time is "a walking-self." A normal 5-year-old will wield a toy gun and exclaim, "I am a soldier" or "I am a cop." However, when his self-image is questioned he will reply, "Not really." He may be annoyed that you interrupt his pleasurable "pretend," but he will know that it is only pretend, that he is not really a soldier or a cop. A schizophrenic 5-year-old, however, might wield his toy gun and exclaim, "I am a soldier," or whatever, and in the process of play will actually drift into believing it for the time. Similarly, an adult schizophrenic tends to assume, "I am intelligent" or "I am stupid" on the basis of his performance at the moment, or his wishes or fears of the moment. When under emotional stress, he will judge his self according to emotions provoked by the immediate situation in which he finds himself—and that is infantile, magical thinking.

Incidentally, occasionally there are individuals who under great emotional stress will defend themselves from intense pan-anxiety by suddenly endorsing, hook, line, and sinker, some fanatical religious dogma. They will believe the symbols utilized in the dogma to be concrete, literal truths. When such a religious conversion occurs in a schizophrenic patient, it is a poor idea to simply try to reeducate the patient to realistic thinking. In the first place you probably would not be able to budge him, and in the second place if you did so you would do the patient the disservice of returning him to his former state of unbearable anxiety. Treatment should leave this symptom alone, provided the dereistic thinking serves a useful adaptive purpose for the patient. In fact there are times when the psychiatrist wishes his patients would develop a built-in "opiate" such as religious conversion—but it cannot even be suggested to a patient; it has to emerge spontaneously from within.

The reason each and every person thinks and feels any particular way with regard to himself and the environment is because it serves some adaptive purpose, realistic or otherwise. We perceive what we want to perceive; we believe what we want to believe. Emotions influence our thinking, and vice versa, in practically everything we do. Prejudices exist in every culture. In the United States, for instance, the president of a huge corporation is regarded by some cultural segments as superior to his factory worker, and in other cultural segments the opposite interpretation is considered valid—the "good" worker is oppressed by the "evil" boss. The symbol becomes the thing and because thinking is emotionally charged is it accepted without much question within the different cultural factions. Although social prejudices are ubiquitous and certainly not confined to schizophrenic people, the schizophrenic will not only adopt these cultural prejudices but will incorporate them into his thinking in a magnified and distorted way to suit his emotional needs. Or, he will conceive his own personal prejudices according to his particular emotional needs, wishes or fears, and they become a "private" matter in the framework of his complex-bound and autistic-dereistic thinking (and the seed of potential delusion). In other words, on the basis of his intrinsic thinking disorders and emotional dysregulation, emotionally charged faulty concepts compound the basic disorder in his thinking. Emotional and intellectual regression then lead to primary process type thinking, with its repression of certain observations and experiences and overvaluation of others.

The symptoms of complex-bound and autistic-dereistic thinking are sometimes very vivid even in the masked schizophrenic individual. Many of these symptoms, and the treatment approach in dealing with them, can be viewed in the following example.

Mr. W. is a brilliant young executive in an accounting firm. He was reared in a well-educated, cultured upper middle-class Jewish family. In appearance he is dark-complexioned, meticulous, and conservative in his attire. He is serious and unsmiling in demeanor. He entered "analysis" because of pan-anxiety ineffectively controlled by obsessive-compulsive habit patterns. He was distressed that his wife was "the victim of social slander" and he did not know how to cope in her defense.

Years ago Mr. W. had anglicized his Jewish name and veered away from social contact with Jews: He was strongly anti-Semitic. He perceives Jews as aggressive, "money-mad," ethically and sexually im-moral, and therefore inferior to so-called Christians. Mr. W.'s father is a retired banker, now philanthropically active, and his mother, an obese woman who dresses ornately with heavy jewelry and makeup, is an accomplished musician. To Mr. W., both parents exemplify the "inferior Jew," despite their being culturally and morally exemplary: he is ashamed of them.

Mr. W. married a blonde, blue-eyed, slender and petite Anglo-Saxon Catholic whom he nicknamed "Angel." He dissuaded her from wearing jewels or makeup and prefers her to wear British tweeds a size too large. She is socially active but has few cultural or intellectual interests. Past history of pelvic inflammatory disease rendered her in-fertile, a fact that Mr. W. denies admitting to himself; he hopes to become a father. When his wife suggested adopting his orphaned niece, Mr. W. objected on the grounds that because the baby's parents were both Jewish "the child would not be happy in our surroundings."

What is the appropriate diagnosis? Mr. W. manifests obsessive-compulsive as well as hysterical neurotic symptoms. He is a compulsive worker and is obsessed with factual perfection in his daily life. Hysteri-cal symptoms of wish-thinking are meshed with obsessive ideation. He presented himself as a "superior" gentile in a continually acted-out drama, Stanislavsky modified, with his "angel" wife filling the leading supportive role. This wide spectrum of neurotic symptoms serves as defense against an all-pervasive anxiety based on Mr. W.'s deep-rooted inferiority feelings. The marked impairment of conceptual thinking involved in his pan-neurotic defense symptoms indicates a diagnosis of schizophrenia.

The dynamic configuration can be outlined as follows: Mr. W.'s feelings of inferiority derive from a basic deficit in ability to integrate and organize thought processes and affect in a realistic way, leading to dysregulation of responses to stimuli, especially in the intellectual realm. His symptoms evolve out of his attempts to explain and resolve his anxiety-provoking inadequacy feelings, but he does so in an un-realistic way, prefaced on his conceptual thinking disorder. He con-fuses abstract with concrete issues, namely, "I am inferior; I am a Jew; therefore I am inferior because I am a Jew." The symbol becomes the thing. Gestalt disturbance is involved in this: the concept of "Jew" becomes an important symbol of inferiority and is in the foreground, while abstract concepts of his personality and character are relegated to the background and their realistic importance escapes his appraisal. In other words, he judges himself negatively entirely because he is a Jew and is amnestic concerning his realistic positive attributes, which should be valued.

Strong emotional charge is present and his thinking is complex-bound. He develops scorn for all Jews and feelings of admiration for all gentiles. Thus, his inferiority feelings can only be resolved by ceasing to view himself a Jew. This requires dereistic wish-thinking: "I wish to be superior; gentiles are superior; therefore I wish to be gentile." He changes his name and adopts the superficial style and social traits that to him symbolize the gentile. He consolidates his position by marrying a gentile who has, in a symbolic and superficial sense, style and appearance antithetical to those of his Jewish mother. There follows an amnesis for the important "inferior" traits in his wife and a hypermnesis for her unimportant "superior" traits. By this time in his autistic-dereistic thinking, Mr. W. feels secure in impressing the environment that he *is* a gentile. But he is not delusional and knows he is not: a continuing undercurrent of inferiority feelings and anxiety requires him to maintain his neurotic facade. Fantasy is confused with reality in his thinking.

After a few weeks of psychotherapy, Mr. W. exposited about his wife's problems; that jealous acquaintances gossip about a sexual affair she is presumed to have with a neighbor and that it is whispered that she also receives money from her lover. Mr. W. flatly denied the validity of accumulating evidence substantiating the gossip. His denial continued to function in a particular incident: One evening Mr. W. returned from his office earlier than usual and found his wife in bed with the man in question. He felt stunned, and as he was backing out of the bedroom his wife shouted at him in aggressive defense that she and the man were not engaged in sexual activity and, "If you believe what your eyes tell you more than you believe what I tell you, I shall leave you forever!"

In interview, Mr. W. was tense and anxious, and with great feeling explained how much he depended on his wife socially; that if she left him he would feel his whole life shattered. He was firmly convinced of her innocence and had even apologized to her for having upset her by his arrival on the scene. He did not know what to do now.

What do we see here? First, the symbol is the thing, augmented by strong wish-need. Second, the wish leads him to "logically" reason her behavior to be innocent. Third, he is amnestic to all evidence to the contrary. Last and mainly, exposure to reality shook his defenses and fomented paralyzing anxiety.

Treatment approach should aim at the most disruptive symptom related in the interview. In this case, what is the presented symptom requiring interpretation? It must be kept in mind that Mr. W.'s faulty conceptualization is emotionally charged. His self-esteem is supported by autism and dereism. His complex-bound anti-Semitic ideation that he can resolve inferiority feelings by passing for a gentile is a defense that cannot be tampered with. For so long as he can convincingly affect a gentile self-image to the environment by means of appearance and behavior, and for so long as he is supported by the symbolic token of "superiority" represented in his wife, he is able to bolster his self-esteem. Therefore, he cannot afford to accept any evidence of her "inferiority" and must defend himself against its reality by a mechanism of massive denial.

However, the time arrived when his wife threatened rejection and disrupted his delicate neurotic façade of defense against anxiety—that thin line of defense against destruction of his dereistic self-image. Without therapeutic intervention at this crucial time, Mr. W. would have become overwhelmed by anxiety. He would have to attempt construction of some other defense. Perhaps he would promote his neurotic denial mechanism to the level of a delusion that his wife is a victim of planned persecution, or that Jews were plotting against him, or some such conviction. On the other hand, perhaps he would actually perceive the stark reality of his wife's "inferiority" and sexual betrayal and react with either severe depression or homicidal rage against the fallen "angel."

His wife's threat of rejection provoked tremendous anxiety in Mr. W. and therapeutic intervention in that context was urgently required. Thus, the most disruptive symptom presented at the interview in question was the panic that the love object on whom he was so dependent might reject him and thereby destroy his illusions. This appears to be the appropriate target for immediate interpretation.

The presented symptom was interpreted as meaning, "You believe what you want to believe about your wife, don't you? And her self-compromising behavior has thrown you into panicky confusion." The patient added that he also believes what she wants him to believe about her. Agreed; and then it was mentioned why the symptom is important to recognize: "That is why you apologized to her, but she was the one to apologize. You are so afraid of her rejection that you shoulder the responsibility for her behavior. This could be a threat to your marriage." Mr. W. appeared surprised. How the symptom under interpretation evolved was suggested: "I think your great anxiety that she will leave you has existed for a long time. You believe she is superior to you and have anxiety in assuming she is hard to hold. For some reason you seem in awe of your wife." The patient admitted that is so. From where is this derived? "You are dependent on your wife. For some reason you feel inferior to her. We must explore that." The first step is taken: Mr. W. is afforded insight into the fact that his present anxiety is rooted in long-standing inferiority feelings. At that point, remedial measures focused only on the anxiety and inferiority symptom complex in a realistically supportive way. The emotional dependency-need for his wife had to be explored and resolved before the symptoms connected with his complex-bound thinking and magical thinking could be interpreted and influenced.

In subsequent interviews, rhetorical interpretations first aimed to reeducate Mr. W. to a realistic self-esteem appraisal. For instance, "What do you feel about yourself as a *person*?...*Are* you inferior to your wife, to your friends?...Let us examine the facts," and so forth. Once his self-esteem became higher in the evolutionary scale of vertebrates, his categorical impairment was focused upon: "You *deserve* a good wife, but, logically speaking, that doesn't *make* a wife good." Considerably further in treatment, he became able to come to grips with his faulty connection of "inferiority" with Jewishness: The important qualities of his parents came under casual discussion and reality was there interpreted: "*Are* Jews inferior to gentiles...always?" And, "You have already come to realize that you are not inferior to your wife even though you are a Jew. . . ." Further discussions led him to insights for separating symbol and fact and realistically judging himself and others on the basis of value merit rather than by labels.

Simultaneously, throughout the interviews, Mr. W. became reeducated to an awareness that all-or-none attitudes with regard to anything, including ethnic groups, social groups, and individuals, are not in the realm of reality; that no single group and no individual is superior or inferior to another group or individual in all respects. The goal in therapy was reached when Mr. W. gained realistic self-esteem and functioned in interpersonal relationships with adequately realistic judgment evaluations of those with whom he relates. It was an "orthopedic" cure.

In conclusion, reeducating the schizophrenic patient to reality is very often conducted seemingly on the level of teaching a child how to read a primer. Because he has an autistic-dereistic personality, the schizophrenic patient is usually so immature emotionally and in his thinking that he is unable to perceive even the simplest realities about himself and the environment. Commonplace reality issues that are quite obvious to us must be interpreted to the schizophrenic and are often received as surprising revelations. He needs to "borrow" the therapist's integrated "ego" to serve as a mirror of reality. In this process the reeducation requires repetition because the patient's crippling anxiety is long-standing due to conditioned unrealistic attitudes that have led to "habit patterns" of dysregulated behavior in many spheres of his life.

CHAPTER 9

Emotional Dysregulation

Autism on the emotional level is the counterpart of dereism on the intellectual level of functioning. Autism and dereism are basic phenomena in schizophrenia; these primary symptoms are present to some extent in all schizophrenic individuals and are often obvious in those who are well compensated. Thought and affect go hand-in-hand, the one dynamically intermeshed with the other. This autistic-dereistic behavior is one of the manifestations of homeostatic dysregulation, all of which stems from the essential schizophrenic integrative and organizational impairment.

The autistic-dereistic personality is one who is shy, introverted, emotionally shut-in, and withdrawn. The person suffers some amount of complex-bound thinking and illogical "wish" and "fear" thinking. Unable to cope with life events in a realistic and regulative way, such a personality harbors deep-rooted feelings of inferiority and inadequacy. This, coupled with great sensitivity, foments a low tolerance for tension and frustrations and, of course, pan-anxiety and ambivalence. Feedback always occurs, which compounds the autism and dereism.

In order to understand how and why pan-anxiety is fomented by emotional dysregulation in the schizophrenic person, we shall discuss the two main interrelated components of the emotional disorder: Autism (the emotional counterpart of subjective, dereistic thinking), per se, characterized by emotional withdrawal and hypersensitivity; and emotional "incoordination" (the emotional aspect of "intrapsychic ataxia"), characterized by disturbance of modulation of affect, inappropriateness of affective responses, and inappropriate timing of

103

these responses. Schizophrenic emotional responses to stimuli can be described as reactions that are "too much, too soon" alternating with "too little, too late"; also, the wrong emotion can be expressed in the wrong direction at the wrong time, or in the right direction at the wrong time. The entire phenomenon is unpredictable even in response to the same stimuli.

Autism

Autism indicates that feelings are directed inward, or introverted. The individuals are withdrawn emotionally from people and surrounding events. However, despite a bland demeanor, autistic persons usually experience inner turmoil. They also suffer great hypersensitivity. Their emotional reactions to people and events are subjective; they interpret every happening in reference to themselves. Actually, this self-referential misinterpretation of what goes on is usually in terms of the negative. Due to great feelings of inferiority, autistic people are always on guard against slights, rejection, and hurt. Naturally, they overlook positive reactions from the environment and usually have great difficulty accepting kindness or a compliment. All this augments their awful feelings of loneliness, tension, frustration, and anxiety, which compounds the autistic emotional withdrawal.

Self-preoccupation is characteristic of an autistic person: he is "narcissistic"; he is emotionally infantile. Such a person will perhaps stare at himself in the mirror for hours, scrutinizing his bodily flaws. He distrusts every step he takes when people are around because he assumes all eyes are on him, and in such a tense and anxious state he is as likely as not to stumble downstairs. He is preoccupied with self-evaluation: "Should I feel confident or not?" or "Am I attractive or repugnant to other people?"—in a typically all-or-none way. The autistic individual will readily judge himself by other people's reactions to him, also in an all-or-none way. In fact, even a stranger on the street is afforded the role of a judgmental authority of his worth. It is as though the schizophrenic person carries around a little set of scales on which he weighs his worth in terms of what he construes to be the reactions of other people toward him.

The autism in these people is not always obvious to the untrained eye. There are the occasional "pseudo-extroverts"—people who are able to camouflage their inability to relate emotionally by giving a superficial appearance of relating well. These are the "super-salesmen" who are the "life of the party." They impress people socially as being happy and friendly, and no one is aware that actually they are cold, calculating, and unfeeling toward others, although sometimes you can see it in their eyes. Underneath his compensatory extroverted behavior, which conceals his inability to make true emotional contact, the pseudo-extrovert harbors very great anxiety. He will go home following a social event and lie awake brooding, "Should I have said 'thus-and-so'?" or "Was I too aggressive...?" and so forth. He usually suffers an "emotional hangover," worrying that he did everything wrong and is unacceptable, despite any realistic evidence to the contrary. The majority of autistic individuals, however, manifest shy and withdrawn behavior.

The primary target symptom in treating withdrawn or pseudo-extroverted patients is, of course, the massive anxiety and feelings of hypersensitivity, which cause them to misinterpret people's reactions in a self-referential way. The hypersensitivity diminishes and the ability to make emotional contact with people increases as anxiety is reduced and the patient's self-esteem is elevated.

Empathy is indeed present in the masked schizophrenic patient, but it is paradoxical. (Do not be misled by many texts which state that anhedonia exists in the schizophrenic. Even Rado's (1960) hypothesis that schizophrenia is based on an inherent pleasure sensory defect rooted in the thalamus is not substantiated. Anhedonia only develops in deteriorating schizophrenic patients.) Actually, masked schizophrenic persons are seething with emotions. Their empathy is good in one sense and poor in another, but empathy exists nonetheless. Their empathy is good insofar as negative feelings are involved: Schizophrenic individuals can easily identify with the suffering of others because this is their experience. Their empathy is also good in their ability to experience strong affect in the context of magical wish ideations. For instance, they can feel great joy or sorrow when involved in a daydream, or attending a stage drama. On the other hand, empathy is poor insofar as positive feelings are concerned: It is difficult for most schizophrenics to identify with the joys and pleasures experienced by others because such have not been their personal experience. In analogy, if you are color-blind it is rather difficult for you to empathize with a person who is experiencing the pleasure of viewing a vivid sunrise.

It is also important to realize that the ability of the schizophrenic individual to experience love, in an adult sense, is poor. He can only experience a dependency form of love, because he is emotionally immature. Emotional maturity with feelings of self-worth and inner security are prerequisites for experiencing outgoing love for another person—other than in the magical wish context such as a fantasied love for a movie star. In therapy, many of these patients express great lament that they are unable to feel love for someone, and they feel guilty for an inability to return some other person's love. Interpreta-

tions should first focus on the symptoms of pan-anxiety, which naturally block the ability to experience love and other positive emotions. This
should be traced to the patient's deep-rooted feelings of inferiority and
unworthiness; the patient must gradually be taught self-reality. The
patient needs reassurance that the potential capacity for love is indeed
present; that "You are able to love others when you learn to feel
worthy of love."

It is interesting that the schizophrenic patient's ability to empathize
with others where negative feelings are concerned occasionally is observed on hospital wards. A patient can surprise you with the observation, "Doctor, Mrs. X. is extremely upset this morning; when you interviewed her, did she tell you she wants to kill herself, or someone
else?" Such a patient knows all about the negative feelings of others;
the patient has been there. Sometimes a patient can give you an elaborate description of how another patient feels, and can even interpret it
for you. The patient can understand symbolisms expressed by other
patients. Patients can be empathically protective of each other due to
mutual feelings of hostility, anxiety, uncertainty, and hypersensitivity.
In other words, schizophrenic patients have emotional insights into the
feelings of others that pertain to their own ego, and here the empathy
can be amazing—much better than ours. Yet, in terms of positive feelings, the schizophrenic will miss very simple and obvious emotional
reactions. They manifest a tender-versus-tactless syndrome—in other
words, alternately acting with warm hypersensitivity to the feelings of
others, and then with cold indifference—which often leads to difficulties with their environment and augments the great sense of failure
these individuals all feel.

The inability of the schizophrenic to externalize feelings is also an
aspect of emotional autism. A patient will tell you, "I have strong feelings but am unable to express them; I'm afraid." And you may observe
that this patient behaves in a calm, contented, bland way, despite an
inner boiling cauldron of tension and anxiety.

Contact impairment evolves out of the autistic individual's anxiety
and hypersensitivity. A patient will state, "I don't know how I am expected to respond to people so I shut my feelings in." Or, "Every time I
try to express my feelings to people they either drift away, or they try to
get too close to me so I must back away." Autistic people desperately
want to be accepted, to "belong" socially. However, they remain inexorably lonely. When they do establish contact, the contact quickly
breaks down because the patient does not know how to cope with it
emotionally. Very few autistic people have the hysterical ability to
play-act as does the pseudo-extrovert. Treatment should unravel their
deep feelings of confusion.

Emotional Incoordination

Emotional incoordination, or dysregulation of emotional behavior in relating to the environment, is interwoven with autism. The self-oriented schizophrenic individual is in conflict as to when, to what extent, and in what way it is appropriate to show positive or negative feelings. There are quantitative and qualitative aspects to the inappropriate affect behavior in schizophrenia.

Inappropriate modulation of affect is very commonly observed. Quantitatively, the schizophrenic overestimates emotional situations and he underestimates them. He will sometimes overreact in situations requiring slight or moderate emotional responses. For instance, a patient will state, "I was furious when Mr. X. kept tapping the table during the conference, so I resigned in protest." At another time the same patient will underreact when moderate or marked emotional reactions are indicated. The patient will state, "I didn't feel gratitude when Mr. Y. accepted my [cherished] plans at the conference."

Many times the affect shown by a patient is qualitatively inappropriate to the situation confronting him. There is some confusion in his mind as to whether positive feelings or negative feelings are appropriate for a situation. Positive feelings are usually more difficult for schizophrenics to feel or express. Sometimes, however, positive feelings surge up in the wrong situations. When told by his best friend that the friend's mother just died, one patient blurted out, "I'm so glad because she was old and irritable." Another patient burst into laughter because of his aunt's description of how her son died by falling down an elevator shaft because, ". . . her description seemed so very funny"; yet such a patient can at times be highly empathic and sympathetic to suffering in others. Schizophrenic individuals also show negative feelings in the wrong situations. A sensitive and autistic person can go through an entire wedding reception feeling sad or angry while everyone else expresses happiness, due to a personal inability to comprehend why marriage is of significant worth.

There is also the problem of timing of emotional reactions in schizophrenia. Timing is often peculiarly inappropriate; it can be delayed, or it can be too sudden, in response to situations. The autistic individual, like the proverbial centipede counting its feet, seemingly asks himself, "Should I express my feelings now or later?" Or he will react impetuously due to delay in judgmental thinking. Thus, the individual's emotional expressions are sometimes too soon and at other times too late. For instance, if a man's wife informs him of the emotionally laden fact that she is pregnant and he immediately replies, "Get an abortion," the timing of his emotional response might be as inappropriate as dead silence on his part would be.

Thus, with regard to dysregulation of emotional responses, one encounters the syndrome of too much, too soon alternating with too little, too late, and also the syndrome in which the patient reacts with the wrong emotion in the wrong direction at the wrong time, and all variations of these patterns. Due to continual anxiety, and due to a low tolerance for tension and frustration, the schizophrenic individual's emotional reactions are unpredictable. Reactions can differ even in response to the same stimulus at different times. Actually, emotional dysregulation is always present to some extent and when any of its aspects is a disruptive symptom presented by the patient in interview, it must be dealt with directly.

As therapists we are dealing with nonpsychotically compensated schizophrenia, and "compensation" is the patient's tenuous game of defense against pan-anxiety, which the therapist must respect. Adler (1917) taught us about compensation in the context of "organ inferiority," and so-called normal people compensate for their areas of personality deficits in their style of living. For instance, an individual having an obsessive-compulsive personality style can be exceedingly considerate of another person's feelings by compensating for his own "reserved" affect with the use of intellect to instruct himself in what the appropriate emotional reactions should be. Those of us who are not schizophrenic automatically compensate one way or another quite well and thereby are able to adapt with emotional responses appropriate to the confronting situations. The style and competence in this varies, depending somewhat on our background experience and somewhat on our basic personality organization—hysterical, obsessive-compulsive, or whatever.

Schizophrenic individuals, however, suffer varying amounts of dereism and autism. Depending on which type of disorder is the more predominant in a particular patient, therapy aims to teach the masked schizophrenic patient how to employ the strength in one area to compensate for the weakness in the other. In other words, in the course of therapy the patient with relatively slight thinking disorders is enabled to employ his intellect in a compensatory way to influence the modulation, appropriateness, and timing of emotional reactions in daily life. The reverse procedure is of course applicable if the patient's thinking disorder predominates over emotional dysregulation. Due to the fact that emotions and thinking are always intermeshed and have a reciprocity of influence, the therapist must know his patient well. When a patient relates a problem with emotionally charged ideation, the therapist must know which of the two functions—emotional or intellectual—is basically the better integrated and regulated one in the patient.

If the patient's thinking disorder is greater than the emotional dysregulation, the thinking disorder is likely to be the disruptive element in the symptoms presented by the patient; therefore, interpretations must first aim at the thinking disorder. After this disruptive force has become moderated in treatment, interpretations can shift to deal with problems of emotional dysregulation.

On the other hand, if the patient's emotional dysregulation is greater than the existing thinking disorder, it is often the more disruptive component of the symptoms presented. Interpretations follow in their usual sequence. The therapist interprets what the symptom is, the way in which it operates, and from where it is derived. The patient's attention is focused on appropriate ideation, which will serve to compensate for the problematic emotional deficits. Of course, the patient must be taught how to effect this. The patient is taught how the emotional dysregulation influences thinking and how to apply his thinking to correct the emotional dysregulation. For this, the patient must be reeducated to reality with regard to appropriate emotional responses to particular stimuli in the context of the problem presented and then in a general sense.

I would like to outline a case in point to clarify the interpretive procedure. The patient is a young masked schizophrenic lady who arrived for the interview in tears, sobbing, "I am so very depressed that I want to kill myself." When asked why, she explained, "Last evening my pocketbook was stolen in a restaurant and it contained $20, all my makeup and a full pack of cigarettes," adding, "I'm such a fool! How could I be so stupid as to leave my pocketbook on a chair for even a moment?"

The patient was obviously distraught and her intense emotional reactions to the theft required immediate interpretation. However, the patient's total personality must first be understood. Did the patient emotionally overreact, or did she simply displace emotions from another area that would have realistically warranted the quantity of emotion she displayed? Perhaps the theft had symbolic meaning for her: loss of power, loss of sexual integrity, loss of financial security, or something else. If a strong undertow of anxiety existed in one of those symbolic areas, interpretation should aim accordingly, and the symptom should be defined: "You are panicky because the theft aroused a feeling of helplessness," or whatever. However, this patient was known to suffer from exaggerated emotional reactions to all kinds of events, regardless of their actual or symbolic importance or unimportance. In this instance, emotional overreaction was the most disruptive symptom the patient presented. In fact, at least two dysregulative emotional reactions were apparent:

acute suicidal "depression," and the reaction of anger against herself.

Before interpreting the anger reaction, dealing with the patient's intolerance for tension seemed indicated because that was what gave rise to her suicidal ideation. Moreover, the patient could not be very receptive to interpretations of her other presented symptoms until the level of tension was lessened. Therefore, she was reassured that she did *not* feel depressed; that she felt disconsolate; that she would feel all right immediately if the pocketbook and its contents were returned to her. (Incidentally, if you allow the hypersensitive schizophrenic patient to assume the existence of a symptom that is not present, it is likely to be incorporated into an existing symptom complex. Your patient in treatment has enough problems to deal with without accumulating those that do not exist.)

When the patient felt calmer and was receptive to additional interpretations, her presented symptom of emotional dysregulation was defined: "You are reacting to a very minor theft as though it were more important than life itself." And, "I mention this because the incident seems to paralyze you with such agony of preoccupation that it interfered with your ability to function today at all." How the symptom evolved was suggested: "Tension and anxiety are largely responsible for your emotional overreacting in situations. You seemingly blame the theft on foolishness and inadequacy on your part." To which the patient responded with a torrent of self-criticism. Her feelings of inferiority and distrust of her judgment were discussed and its sources touched upon in terms of a general sense of confusion and feelings of failure for not reacting to situations appropriately.

Subsequent interpretations focused on remedial measures, teaching the patient reality in terms of the importance of the theft event and what it signified about her so-called inadequacy, and then reeducating her with regard to the nature of an appropriate emotional reaction. The patient's intellectual compensatory ability was put to use as a correctional tool for her emotional dysregulatory responses. The patient tacitly "borrowed" the therapist's objectivity.

The importance of the theft event shrank to a suitable size when it was compared to serious theft situations that might occur, in which a person's life savings or irreplaceable valuables are taken; in which a person gets hurt or even killed by the thief, and so forth. Borrowing the therapist's feelings of, "I'm so glad you are alive and well," the patient could agree. With regard to the patient's feelings of inadequacy, the patient borrowed the therapist's objective view: "A great many people get robbed due to momentary carelessness; if that signifies you are a fool, join the club with the rest of us human beings." Here again, the schizophrenic all-or-none attitude—with its generalized assumption that people belong in one of two categories, superior or inferior, and that there is nothing in between—needs correction. The patient continually needs reminding that, "No one is perfect; no one is totally inferior...," and so forth.

When the patient had corrected her emotional responses by moderating their intensity to fit the "tragedy," she was commended on her intelligent arrival at a proper perspective. Her self-esteem was reinforced by encouragement to recount a few relatively severe adversities in her past life to which she had responded emotionally with calmness and presence of mind. This remedial measure is *very* important! It serves to antidote the patient's sense of failure. In the process, the therapist is often capitalizing on the fact that many schizophrenic patients have indeed responded to past severe adversities with surprising emotional control, sometimes due to emotional underreaction. Incidentally, it is interesting that sometimes the therapist cannot bring any of the patient's successes or assets to his own mind; perhaps he has focused attention for so long on the patient's pathology. Yet, when required to draw on them, the therapist suddenly "discovers" that quite a long list of the patient's positive assets wells up from his subconscious mind at just the right time. You will have many such experiences in treating patients. On such an occasion both the patient and the therapist feel a surge of optimism by the end of the interview. Do not forget that schizophrenic patients easily sense the therapist's mood, and this can be beneficial in treatment.

To return to the patient under discussion, when her anxiety surrounding the presented disruptive emotional overreactions to the theft was allayed and her self-esteem became elevated to a rather appropriate level, she ceased feeling disconsolate and felt "normal, like other people." The success in working through her particular experience of emotional dysregulation was filed in her own mental filing cabinet and in the therapist's for future reference.

Obviously, it takes a great deal more than an occasional lesson in reality to "cure" a schizophrenic's long-conditioned pattern of emotional dysregulation. Other incidences are bound to occur whereby the patient will again overreact to relatively minor "tragic" events, or will surprisingly underreact to them, or will react at an inappropriate time, or with an inappropriate affect. Continued "doses" of reality with regard to appropriate emotional regulatory responses to various life situations are necessary to effect reconditioning of a patient's emotional reaction patterns. Here again, the therapist draws on the patient's areas of relative integrative strength to compensate for the particular area of integrative weakness manifested in the patient's currently disruptive symptom presented.

CHAPTER 10

Chaotic Concepts
of Sexuality

The organization of sexuality is disrupted in schizophrenia in a manner different from that occurring in nonschizophrenic psychosexual disorders. Actually, sexuality in schizophrenia is characterized by chaotic disorganization. There tends to be bewilderment about male and female anatomical differences. Hypothesized "stages" of psychosexual development are not clearly delineated, and confusion exists about oral, anal, and genital functions. So-called pregenital drives tend to be jumbled up along with homosexual and heterosexual genital drives and sometimes all these fragments coexist in an unorganized manner. Sexual preoccupations on an autoerotic or anal level, or homosexual and heterosexual tendencies, may all be present simultaneously.

Furthermore, there tends to be confusion between sexual and nonsexual matters. All kinds of nonsexual functions and experiences may be eroticized, and at the same time sexual functions are often desexualized. Marked sado-masochism is usually linked with sexuality. Or, the concept of pleasurable satisfaction may be altogether negated or repudiated. Sexuality is viewed with fascination, being regarded as dirty, dangerous, mysterious, and yet as a solution for all problems.

Thus, polymorphous perverse manifestations are rather characteristic of schizophrenic patients. Their manifestations vary in extent and configuration with each individual. They are clinically blatant in some masked schizophrenic patients, yet in others are subtle and clinically difficult to discern.

Treatment of disordered sexuality, or of any other symptom, is conducted in accordance with the dynamics specific for the diagnostic category in which the symptom developed. Therefore, accurate diagnosis of the patient is extremely important. Diagnosis cannot always be determined on the basis of an individual's sexual symptomatology, however. Many forms of sexual pathology can develop in the diagnostic framework of social and neurotic disorders, as well as in schizophrenia.

It is of concern to psychiatrists that diagnosis can sometimes be overlooked when an actual symptom of a sexual disorder is strongly influenced by the social environment, and especially when the symptom is accepted as a social "norm." In such case, the social attitude tends to conceal the pathology of the patient's sexual attitude. Diagnosis can also be confused by the influence of environmental stress factors. Stress plays an important role in the development of symptom pictures, and sexual symptomatology often first becomes apparent when an individual is under acute or chronic stress. In such cases the symptoms are simply precipitated by the stress, but are not caused by it, even though they may appear to have no other basis. Current social climate, as well as the patient's social background, may influence the clinical picture of a patient's sexual disorder but not be the causative factor, and the treatment of choice is determined by the patient's diagnosis.

A great many patients suffer from more than one diagnostic disorder. In such case, the therapist must recognize the diagnostic complexity and aim treatment primarily at that disorder most basically responsible for the patient's symptomatology. For instance, if a patient's sexual symptoms are bound in with social stress factors as well as neurotic conflicts, all these factors must be taken into account when determining which ones are primarily responsible for the evolution of the sexual conflict. However, if the patient also suffers from schizophrenia, the schizodynamic factors are undoubtedly more basic than the others and require priority focus in therapy. In other words, some amount of sexual disorganization exists in schizophrenia and therapy must aim primarily to reduce this internal source of stress. In such cases, any social and neurotic factors that exist merely play a role in coloring the symptom picture. Their influence is only superimposed on the inherent schizophrenic dynamic process and requires therapeutic attention accordingly.

In dynamic terms, the concept of sexuality is fragmented in schizophrenia. Schizophrenic individuals show impairment of sexual integration and organization, just as they show this impairment on intellectual, emotional, sensorimotor, or autonomic levels. Chaotic concepts of sexuality in schizophrenia derive from inherent integrative impairment, in which a leading order of fusion of the fragments of percepts into a conceptual whole is somehow lacking with regard to body integrity. Confusion evolves concerning the concept of body image in toto—maleness and femaleness, their sexual structures, and their functional roles. Confusion also exists regarding concepts of organization of body parts and their structure and function.

In schizophrenia, the peculiar tendency to confuse sexual and non-sexual stimuli also stems from the basic inability to properly integrate and organize sensations perceived. The individual tends to confuse sexual with nonsexual inner need-tensions, and the individual tends to confuse sexual with nonsexual stimuli from the social environment. Thus, sexual stimuli are often desexualized, and nonsexual stimuli are sexualized in a peculiar way.

It follows that confusion about the sexual self and confusion about sexuality in relationship to the social environment warps the schizo-phrenic individual's sexual attitudes and feelings and adversely influ-ences his sexual behavior. This is an influential dynamic factor in the schizophrenic dysregulation of sexual responses to internal and external stimuli. This dysregulation is manifested by the myriad symptoms of perversions. The extent of these symptoms, however, depends mainly on the existing level and configuration of the schizophrenic disintegra-tive disorder in the individual.

Although a large number of schizophrenic patients are crippled by sexual confusion, many are relatively well integrated in their sexuality and actually practice a seemingly normal sex life. The disintegrative tendency is always present in schizophrenia nonetheless, and if you do not question your patients, the existence of their sexual pathology may easily be overlooked. Perversions and aberrant social-sexual attitudes are sometimes restricted to the patient's fantasy life. On the other hand, many patients indeed act out their symptoms but fail to mention this to the therapist: Some patients feel too anxious and guilty about their sex-ual behavior, and others may assume it normal and experience such minimal anxiety that the topic is omitted from their agenda in thera-peutic sessions. Therefore, it is important to investigate the patient's sexual attitudes, feelings, and functioning. Often you will be amazed at the perversions and misconcepts of sexuality a patient will describe when questioned.

Polymorphous perversions appearing in schizophrenia may include exhibitionism, voyeurism, fetishes, a variety of sado-masochistic "ritu-als," and many other sexual strivings involved in masturbatory, homo-sexual, and heterosexual activities. Multiple perversions may be pres-ent simultaneously or may be present singly and shift. Oral and anal elements are confused very often with the vaginal. The uninformed girl reared in a sexually inhibiting society might fear that a man's kiss will impregnate her, but in our sophisticated society an intelligent individual harboring such a fear is most likely schizophrenic. Confusion of fragmented drives can result in the sado-masochistic concept of the vagina as a bloody wound, or as a "vagina dentata." The latter confusion may, paradoxically, drive the schizophrenic male to avoid vaginal intercourse in favor of oral sex.

In body image confusion, the stomach is likely to be equated with the uterus: this is observed in children's primary process reasoning due to misinformation when a mother explains "a baby grows in the stomach," or when some joker tells a child, "If you eat the orange seed, a tree will grow in your stomach." But the confusion in schizophrenia is based on inherently impaired fusion of percepts and concepts.

It has been hypothesized that in the "collective unconscious" the paired glands, such as the thyroid, breasts, ovaries, and testicles, are somehow equated. However, these structures are confused on the conscious level and in a bizarre way in overt schizophrenia, as is sometimes depicted in patients' art productions. In masked schizophrenia, the tendency is nonetheless there. In any case, confusion of nonsexual and sexual body components contributes to the development of sexual perversions, many of which have special significance to the schizophrenic patient and can be interpreted in treatment.

Interestingly enough, when the penis is equated with the head in the unconscious, sexual potency is often equated with intellectual power, and this is sometimes an important observation in masked schizophrenia. Years ago a middle-aged man, a brilliant creative scientist, was referred to me by his internist because of the following problem. The patient suffered malignant hypertension and was told by a team of doctors that in order to survive he must undergo sympathectomy. My role was to prepare the patient for acceptance of this procedure. It soon became apparent to me that the patient suffered pseudoneurotic schizophrenia. In the initial interview he exclaimed in a state of rage, "No one is going to tamper with *my* brain!" I explained to him the facts: that sympathectomy is lumbar surgery and it does not involve the brain; that, although the surgery might obviate a penile erection, it would most likely restore his health including the full use of his mental powers. Educational data concerning sexual anatomy and physiology, and repeated answers to repeated questions on the subject from the patient were required to assure him the surgery would not render him intellectually "impotent."

For the patient suffering from a chaotic concept of sexuality, the sexual symptomatology is compounded by a great deal of anxiety. Hypochondriasis is very likely to center around sexuality. The hypersensitive schizophrenic who is preoccupied with concern about bodily integrity readily misinterprets sexual structures, sensations, and responses as indicative of bodily malconstruction and malfunctioning. For example, a young male patient who suffered masturbatory guilt expressed the fear he had cancer of the scrotum. Evidence? He happened to observe the normal fold on his scrotum for the first time. Guilty fear connected with masturbation or any other sexual activity can give rise to multiple and shifting hypochondriacal ideations. Fear of castration, disintegration, or disease emerge in connection with sexual activities that should normally be experienced as pleasurable.

The confusion and anxiety connected with sexuality are, of course, accompanied by ambivalence. The schizophrenic patient experiences simultaneous conflicting attitudes about sex. The power of the sexual drive renders sex a desired pleasure, and at the same time many schizophrenic patients confuse sexual assertion with destructive aggression. They harbor the fear that sexual behavior can be self-destructive, destructive to the sex object, or can led to destruction by the sex object. It is understandable that sado-masochism can be much more marked in schizophrenia than in the neuroses. And, unlike the neurotic, the schizophrenic individual is able to alternate from sadism to masochism rather than sustaining one or the other sexual pattern.

It is no small wonder that with all the great anxiety and ambivalence connected with sexuality, the normal ability to experience sex as pleasurable is so frequently lacking in schizophrenia. Schizophrenic individuals often shift from the use of one perversion to another in desperate attempts to gain some sexual pleasure and a gratifying relief from tension and frustration. They will attempt every perversion in the books or not in the books, simultaneously or in sequence. Many schizophrenic patients will tell you that they are dependent upon their perversions; that they cannot become sexually aroused without employing certain perversions; that "straight" sex leaves them cold, and impotent or frigid, as the gender case may be. In this respect, you might say, a sadistic person is not cruel, but kind—to a masochistic person. Actually, each is dependent on the other's perversion for sexual gratification. Whatever the sexual perversion, acting it out serves as an attempt to override some of the anxiety connected with sex. Sometimes the perversion is seemingly a symbolic representation of a particular dynamic conflict. In any case, treatment aims to connect for the patient the perversion with existing sexual anxiety conflicts.

During treatment, interpretations aim at the disruptive sexual symptom presented by the patient. Abnormal attitudes, feelings, and behavior must be defined as such and their evolution and derivation interpreted in dynamic terms. Connecting the dynamic relationship of the symptoms to the underlying anxiety is the initial interpretive step. For example, sexual impotence is an extremely prevalent symptom, and interpreting the way in which anxiety normally renders a person impotent might be done very simply through analogy: "A mating lion in the jungle cannot sustain an erection when he hears the hunters' drums: anxiety blocks performance and pleasure." Or: "Two people engaged in sexual intercourse will lose sexual arousal when they hear a loud knock on the door: anxiety intrudes." In schizophrenia, much of a patient's sexual anxiety stems from chaotic concepts of sexuality, and interpretation aims to replace misconcepts with realistic concepts. Here again, patients tend to sustain confusion between assertion and aggression in sexual as in all other areas and require repeated interpretations to clarify the difference.

Lessons in sexual reality are given to the patient step by step, over and over again during the course of treatment. Anatomical and physiological facts about various aspects of sexuality must be explained in terms understandable to the patient. Keep in mind that reeducating a person with regard to sexual facts may not take long, but undoing years—perhaps many decades—of conditioned pathological attitudes and patterns of sexual behavior often requires long perseverance on the part of the therapist and strong motivation on the patient's part.

Only when able to resolve the sexual confusion in the patient's mind and diminish his anxiety concerning sexuality are you able to influence the patient to even consider reality-testing with aim to achieve normal sexual gratification. There are exceptions in schizophrenia, of course, because some schizophrenics will take a 180° turn, in their inimitable ambivalent way, and to their surprise as well as yours will suddenly adopt a comparatively normal sexual performance pattern. At any rate, in therapy every step of progress serves to chip away at the great feeling of inferiority felt so acutely by all sexually crippled patients.

The general approach in treating schizophrenic patients suffering from any perversion is applicable in dealing with a sexual symptom very prevalent in our society today—so-called homosexuality. As has been mentioned, the sexual life of the schizophrenic can contain a vast number of sexual deviations, and homosexuality is merely one. Despite an increasing trend to accept homosexuality as a social "norm," the fact remains that it is a perversion symptom. It is neither an entity nor a disorder in itself: It is a symptom. Probably there is an inherent proneness to the development of this symptom in certain people (Kallmann, 1952) that can be potentiated by a number of environmental influences. However, the dynamics of the symptom are to be appraised along with other symptoms in the framework of the neurotic, psychotic, or other disorder in which it appears.

The symptom of homosexuality can be coincidental, but unrelated, to a disorder. For instance, a person can suffer from tuberculosis and homosexuality, or cancer and homosexuality, with no direct relationship between the disorder and the homosexual symptom. Whenever a hypochondriacal schizophrenic patient complains of homosexuality and tries to connect it with an entirely unrelated existing disorder, it gives you a clear opportunity to exemplify for the patient how confusion about body integrity becomes connected with anxiety and leads to ideas that sexuality causes disease or destruction.

Homosexual symptomatology can occur in response to environmental influences—often in connection with certain early conditioning factors, or with a milieu conducive to its social acceptance. Provided the environmental influences are predominant and the schizophrenic patient's integrative impairment is minimal, treatment of the symptom can focus considerable attention on the environmental factors and in a supportive way reeducate the patient to sexual-social biological reality.

Although homosexual symptomatology can also develop as a part of an existing dynamic pattern in a psychiatric disorder, it is never basic to the disorder, nor is it the cause. When it is a part of the psychodynamic configuration in a neurosis, that is one thing. But when it is a part of the dynamic configuration in schizophrenia, that is an entirely different dynamic issue requiring an entirely different therapeutic approach—which is why diagnosis is so important. In schizophrenia, the dynamic basis for so-called homosexuality is not primarily external environmental influences, but is primarily the influence of the inherent schizophrenic integrative impairment. What therapists, and also schizophrenic patients, sometimes interpret to be homosexual symptoms actually are not: they are only fragments among other fragments of confused concepts of sexuality manifested in schizophrenia—all based on integrative impairment.

In this connection, male and female structures and roles are often misconstrued by schizophrenic individuals. In some patients this confusion foments acute anxiety. Psychoanalysts sometimes refer to this as "homosexual panic" and treat it as indicative of homosexuality, from which label the patient may never become emancipated. Schizophrenic patients are easily influenced to believe themselves homosexual, especially when the belief is supported by homosexual fantasies. Usually, however, the sexual fantasies manifest a sexual identity confusion. An example of this is depicted in a masturbation fantasy of a young male schizophrenic patient who entered treatment complaining that great anxiety blocked him from attempting sexual contact with either men or women. He described the fantasy as follows. "As I stimulate myself sexually I imagine myself a member of a harem, a lovely woman: I am being forcibly raped. When I get an erection it indicates I have been impregnated. When I reach climax, I fantasy that I am giving birth to a baby." The patient assumed himself homosexual. He was not: his problem was far more complex. Due to fragmented concepts of sexuality this patient suffered confusion about total body structure as well as the functional roles of male and female components.

It is an important observation that a great many schizophrenic patients who present themselves as "homosexual" actually engage in both heterosexual and homosexual activity. As some patients label it, they are "AC-DC." Obviously, this is not true homosexuality. These patients may describe their homosexual experiences, a week later describe sexual acts with someone of the opposite sex, and later on may tell you they like to have sexual relations with children or dogs. Any and every perversion described can also be contained in such a patient's fantasies. If these facts are not divulged in therapy, the therapist may perhaps assume his patient suffers no sexual problem other than perhaps occasional bouts of homosexual behavior in massage parlors. Unless questioned by the therapist, many patients will not describe their sexual fantasies and actions, and will even omit telling their dreams of incest, sexual violence and mutilation, and so forth.

The point is that the "AC-DC" syndrome in schizophrenia is a manifestation of an underlying chaotic confusion concerning sexuality. It is not even so-called pseudohomosexuality. Incidentally, this confusion syndrome certainly must not be ascribed to individuals—including many sailors, prisoners, adolescents confined in boarding schools, and so forth—who engage in sexual activity with someone of the same sex entirely on the basis of lack of opportunity for heterosexual contact. Such individuals will fantasy that they are performing sexually with someone of the opposite sex and, upon gaining the opportunity, will invariably do so.

Whether schizophrenic patients manifest homosexuality or other sexual symptoms, therapeutic interpretations should deal with the most disruptive symptom presented. Yet many patients are not significantly troubled by their aberrant sexual way of life. Provided such a patient's sexual attitude and behavior is also not troublesome to the environment, why disrupt the patient by focusing on those symptoms at that time? It is appropriate to focus on the sexual aberrance when the patient's motivation to resolve a sexual conflict is expressed and recognized to be consistently strong, and when ambivalence is insignificant.

Actually, one encounters a growing number of patients who are relatively satisfied with, and even profess to be proud of, their homosexual way of life. There are also patients who only occasionally complain that the symptom is disruptive to their lives and at other times indicate that their homosexuality affords significant sexual pleasure. These ambivalent patients are not clearly motivated to have their sexual deviance influenced in treatment. In such cases it is usually contraindicated to directly tamper with these patients' homosexual adjustment, particularly if it affords them some gratifying social adjustment and it is viewed as a cultural "norm." However, a large number of schizophrenic patients are extremely unhappy with their homosexual symptoms and consider them very disruptive to their lives for a variety of reasons. When they express clear and strong motivation to "change," treatment should aim accordingly.

Occasionally one encounters schizophrenic patients who do not discuss in therapy their sexual activity because they convince themselves there actually is nothing to relate. For some of these patients, sexual contact with people would arouse intolerable anxiety for many possible dynamic reasons, and so they attempt to relieve sexual tension and frustration by means of masturbation: It is a safe way out, even when accompanied by guilty fear of damaging effects. One also encounters patients who avow to having a satisfactory heterosexual adjustment. It is important to realize, however, that even here the schizophrenic individual's sexual functioning is not necessarily normal. Very often they remain emotionally detached from the sexual partner, and intercourse is performed simply as a masturbatory act with accompanying fantasies that can be quite bizarre. In other words, the sex object is used for orgastic purposes only, because the patient is unable to attain or sustain an affective bond with the sexual partner.

Incidentally, despite current social attitudes about sexual liberation, patients are encountered who are seemingly well able to repress all sexual ideation and feelings; they have nothing to discuss in therapy about sex, and are not disturbed by their lack of sexual drive. If such patients are schizophrenic and their apparently asexual adjustment has always served them a relatively anxiety-free social adaptation, what should be the treatment approach? It might here be suggested that the embers in the unconscious need not be stirred up. These patients maintain repressions for good dynamic reasons: They avoid an intolerable anxiety connected with sexuality. In treating schizophrenia, we aim for an orthopedic cure, and repression for many patients serves as a curative agent.

On the other hand, certain sexually inhibited patients are able to probe into their sexuality, and sometimes when they uncover a lot of sexual confusion are even able to resolve it sufficiently in treatment and begin to function sexually. However, one often then finds that the patient will begin to fail in one or another area of adaptation. By analogy it is the old story of the partially deflated rubber ball which dents at one area, and when that section is forced out a dent then appears at another area of the ball. For example, I once interviewed a young salesman who in 2 years of previous psychoanalysis had been "cured" of his massive sexual inhibition. And now he resumed treatment because ever since attaining an active sex life, he found his talent as a salesman completely dissolved. As he expressed it, "I once could sell an air conditioner to an Eskimo; now I would be unable to sell a bottle of liquor to an alcoholic."

The dynamics of this phenomenon in schizophrenia can be speculated on in terms of a shift in compensatory defenses against pananxiety. It is also usually related to all-or-none ambivalence, in which the schizophrenic individual will excel in one area and completely withdraw from another, being somehow unable to succeed with moderation in all major life areas of functioning at the same time. Within the area of sexuality, the therapeutic process may lead a patient to discard one sexual symptom only to shift to some other symptom of pansexuality. Thus, when tampering with a schizophrenic patient's defenses by focusing on problems in a single area, it need be realized that the structure of the patient's anxiety and ambivalence can mobilize a symptom shift to some other nonpsychotic defense against pan-anxiety.

The procedure for treating schizophrenic patients suffering from sexual pathology follows along the line of interpreting the dynamics of any other disruptive symptom. First, the symptom is delineated for the patient. For instance, let us assume the patient presents the complaint, "Doctor, I am a homosexual!" The therapist clarifies for the patient, "You are not *a* homosexual; homosexuality is a symptom, nothing more." The patient feels hopeful when realizing he is not "a homosexual" anymore than he could be "a depression" or "a foot fetishist" or "a sadist." In other words, by rectifying the patient's misconception of his sexual self and liberating him from the idea that homosexuality is a basic entity, or an indelible personality trait, or some physiological malformation, he is able to realize his condition is curable.

When the symptom's meaning has been clarified for the patient, the evolution of the sexual symptomatology can be interpreted in its relationship to underlying anxiety. Provoking influences from the social environment on the patient's sexual orientation that transpired in the patient's childhood or adolescent sexual life must be dealt with cautiously. You can understand that the sensitive and confused schizophrenic person can well have been an easy target for influences from the social environment on the development of his sexual symptoms, ranging from early parental conditioning to current social attitudes. Psychodynamic probing into seemingly neurotogenic factors, however, does not aim toward the source of the sexual problem in the schizophrenic individual. Probing deeply into existing neurotic dynamic mechanisms risks the possibility of stirring up repressed conflicts—Oedipal, incestual, fantasies of mutilation or annihilation or other—that would provoke overwhelming anxiety. However, general insights into environmental influences upon present symptomatology, such as presenting an overview of current sexual attitudes and behavior existing in the patient's society, serves to lessen the feelings of personal inferiority suffered by a great many homosexual patients. All patients need reassurance that they are not alone in suffering any symptom, sexual or other.

For the vast majority of compensated schizophrenic patients, naturally, the environmental factors play only a contributory role in the evolution of their sexual symptoms. Interpretations regarding the derivation of the symptoms focus mainly on the schizodynamic mechanisms that led to sexual confusion. Step by step, these are explored to the depth at which the patient is able to emotionally deal with them at each point in treatment.

Remedial measures aim to reeducate the patient to specific aspects of sexual reality—sexual anatomy and physiology as well as sexual behavior in the social context. The ways in which stress with its anxiety and rage reactions influence sexual interpersonal relationships are also discussed, in time. It is appropriate to reassure the patient that, "We are all living in a stressful environment, and everybody living under tension, anxiety, and frustration is prone to develop symptoms, including those involving sex." Whenever possible, influence the patient to maneuver away from certain environmental pressures, including sexual pressures coming from social contacts with those of the same sex—provided, of course, that the patient is motivated to attain a heterosexual adjustment.

In one sense, you can be quite optimistic in treating patients who are confused about sexuality in that you are dealing with concrete matters: anatomical facts; physiological facts. It is often relatively easy for schizophrenic individuals to comprehend the concrete, provided you explain phenomena concisely and simply. Patients usually respond well to this, especially if you are didactic, and able to draw diagrams of sexual organs. In such ways, their fears based on misconceptions diminish—provided they are not too blocked by anxiety to learn the data in the first place. One of my patients successfully profited from just one such lesson in sexuality, much to his wife's delight. On the other hand, another pseudoneurotic patient reacted to the same type lesson as though I was talking a strange language and drawing Martian symbols. He assured me he understood, yet his confusion and fears remained.

This clearly indicates that reeducation entails a long process of loosening up of a patient's decades of pathological conditioning. And, unfortunately, it must be admitted that reconditioning is sometimes very difficult, or seemingly impossible, to accomplish in many patients.

One further point is important to emphasize. The therapist must always keep in mind that the sexual symptoms are not the only symptoms suffered by the patient: Sexual attitudes reflect and are reflected by a patient's interpersonal relationships. A patient cannot benefit from sexual reeducation unless it can be applied, and no patient is able to apply it when suffering marked anxiety in social relationships. Perhaps such a patient will attempt to relate sexually but will remain emotionally detached, or perhaps the anxiety will interfere with sexual performance. In treatment, therefore, sexual conflicts and social conflicts must both be dealt with before the patient becomes successful in any social and sexual efforts to reality-test.

Now to discuss the peculiar phenomenon in schizophrenia whereby there is confusion between the sexual and the nonsexual in reaction to inner need-tensions and external stimuli. Nonsexual situations are frequently sexualized, and sexual situations are desexualized in a schizophrenic patient's thinking, sensations, and reactions.

When such a phenomenon occurs in so-called normal or neurotic individuals, it is due to some predominant need-tension of the moment, which motivates the person to interpret and respond to an environmental stimulus in the context of his needs. For instance, any sexually frustrated person can be expected to attribute sexual connotations in response to nonsexual stimuli. These sexualizing (or desexualizing) responses are orderly; they are specific to the existing need-tension, and serve some normal or neurotic adaptive purpose.

In schizophrenia, however, the sexualizing or desexualizing processes appear on a very different dynamic basis. These processes are usually not orderly, but chaotic. Furthermore, it is not reliant on any specific need-tension because in schizophrenia there is a confused mixture of existing need-tensions, no one of which is reliably predominant. The schizophrenic individual is anxious, tense, and frustrated in so many areas at the same time that a variety of sexual and nonsexual need-tensions accumulate. They are present simultaneously; they are jumbled together; they form no leading order. Any semblance of goal direction is unpredictable and often inappropriate. For instance, a schizophrenic person might misinterpret a social approach as a sexual demand, and respond with hostile rejection, or with sadistic sexual aggression.

An example of sexualized or desexualized reponses in normal or neurotic, as compared to schizophrenic, persons can be illustrated as follows. A nonschizophrenic man eating at a restaurant is asked by the attractive waitress, "Sir, would you like cherry pie for dessert?" (In some social quarters the mention of "cherry pie" is a code solicitation by waitresses who moonlight as prostitutes.) Now, if this man's predominant need-tension is an alimentary appetite, he will interpret the waitress's question literally and order the pie or some other dessert. However, if a sexual need-tension is predominant, he will probably ask the price of "cherry pie" and set a date for sex with the waitress.

A schizophrenic man, however, might interpret the same question from the waitress as an aggressive intrusion on his right to make his own decisions, or an insinuation that he has a "dirty mind," or whatever. This perceptual confusion can result in a paradoxical sequence of responses in his efforts to organize his various need-tensions. And any existing sexual need-tension is likely to become contaminated by fusion with nonsexual need-tensions.

Along with the fact that need-tensions are jumbled up in schizophrenic patients, the sexual drive itself is not perceived purely as a drive leading to pursuit of a sex object with pleasure gratification as the goal. The sexual drive is especially likely to be contaminated with aggressive drives and fears. Thus, any act of aggression from the environment can be interpreted in the sexual context. Due to the confusion of assertion with aggression, even friendly overtures can be interpreted as acts of aggressive sexual provocation. Conversely, a sexual assertion can be desexualized by a schizophrenic individual and perceived as simply a social intent or, very likely, as a hostile assault. There is a paranoid tinge here.

The fusion of sexual need-tension with other need-tensions in schizophrenia frequently leads to sexual pursuits largely for the purpose of attaining nonsexual gratifications. For instance, an individual may perform sexually but the sexual performance is employed as a concretized symbol of a drive for much-desired power, social popularity, competitive superiority, and so forth. Thus, sex can be utilized to resolve a number of nonsexual conflicts, or as an attempt to gain compensation for failures in nonsexual areas. Of course, this phenomenon is also observed in nonschizophrenic individuals and in fact is a very prevalent cultural phenomenon—exemplified in the "machismo" criteria endorsed by poverty-stricken peoples for whom life affords no power gratification other than sex, nor material property other than children. However, in schizophrenia this phenomenon is illogical and often goes to ludicrous extremes. I recall an obsessive-compulsive schizophrenic male patient who, in an effort to reassure himself of his general competence as a man in all ways, drove himself to have intercourse with a woman—a prostitute, any kind of woman—every night of the year. He experienced absolutely no pleasure in the sexual performance; it was a perfunctory task. A single night's failure in this threw the patient into great anxiety because, as do so many schizophrenics, he obsessively judged his total self on the basis of day-to-day performance of a single act.

In schizophrenia, the inability to form and sustain affective relationships with other people is a very prevalent problem, as we have so often discussed. Many schizophrenic patients who are frustrated in their social relationships often employ sexual intercourse as a substitute for social acceptance and love. Moreover, many of these patients will relate sexually in an attempt to bridge the emotional gap they suffer, hoping through sexual contact to become able to form an affective bond. They tend to interpret the sexual response from the sex objects as an indication of acceptance and love. They will persist in this illusion. Employing sexual contact does not usually lead to emotional contact, but for a number of schizophrenics this is their only means for sustaining a social relationship. Many of these people, however, continue to suffer from loneliness, tension, anxiety, and social frustration.

When treating a patient who confuses the sexual and the nonsexual, explore the patient's greatest areas of frustration and try to unscramble the existing need-tensions. Then determine which tensions and frustrations appear the most disruptive to the patient's life at the time. Define the significance of the patient's symptom—the confusion concerning sexual and nonsexual situations—in whatever context presented by the patient in interview. Clarify for the patient the way in which the symptom disrupts his life and how it evolved, perhaps in connection with sexual anxiety and social conflicts. Afford the patient insight into the confusion concerning specific needs and motivations, both sexual and nonsexual, and how these conflicts derive from inferiority feelings, sexual misconceptions, unrealistic expectations from the environment, and so forth. Of course, the most important part of the interpretive procedure consists of reeducating the patient to reality with regard to sexual and nonsexual need-tensions. This includes teaching the patient the concept of the direct pleasure of sex, as opposed to using sex to gain some nonsexual goal—all in the context of the patient's presented problem.

Rectifying the state of confusion about sexuality regarding body structure and function and clarifying to schizophrenic patients the role of sexuality in normal interpersonal relationships is often a major therapeutic task. Affording reassuring insights into that which is actually normal about their own sexuality relieves some of the patient's generalized feelings of inferiority. In consequence, elevation of their self-esteem hopefully frees them to profit from their gained insights by testing reality and learning to function sexually in an increasingly gratifying and adaptive way.

In conclusion, it is quite obvious from our discussion that treatment aimed at resolving a patient's chaotic concept of sexuality per se is not sufficient. Sexual conflicts are intermeshed with self-esteem conflicts and very often with conflicts in interpersonal relationships, and these phenomena must be dealt with concomitantly in therapy. Sexual behavior is normally a social twosome activity. Resolution of a patient's sexual confusion and ambivalence diminishes tension and anxiety and may elevate his self-esteem considerably, but it does not necessarily guarantee that the patient will thereupon function with sexual adequacy in interpersonal relationships. And how can a patient who, for instance, suffers a great deal of anxiety in relating to people profit much from sex education if he remains unable to attain or sustain any human relationship! Treatment of a patient suffering with sexual confusion must very often include concomitant treatment for a lifelong self-esteem problem, as well as treatment for varying amounts of social anxiety.

When a patient presents one or another aspect of an existing sexual conflict in any interview, the conflict must be dealt with in the context in which it is presented by the patient—a self-esteem conflict, social conflict, or both. Conversely, you would not expect a patient to effect a sexual adjustment simply by resolving his anxieties about relating to people, to the exclusion of resolving existing sexual conflicts. No problem presented by a patient exists in isolation: It is always enmeshed with other problems. The therapist must keep his finger on the pulse of the patient's life in each area when dealing with any symptom presented in therapeutic sessions.

Part 4

TREATMENT OF AMBIVALENCE PATTERNS

CHAPTER 11

All-or-None Reactions

Ambivalence is defined as the simultaneous attraction and repulsion of oppositional forces. Oppositions are ever present: There can be no north without south, east without west. There can be no light without darkness, life without death, no concept of good without a concept of evil, or of a god without a devil. From the universe of galaxies down to submolecular particles there is seemingly cosmos rather than chaos: balancing processes of positive and negative forces occur in simultaneous and continual interaction. Actually, the interaction of oppositional forces is essential for all life processes on all physiological levels.

In psychiatry, ambivalence is defined as bipolarity; the co-existence of opposite ideational and emotional attitudes and reactions toward a given object or situation. This bipolarity is an ever present phenomenon in life. Only in death, for example, do electrical impulses in the brain cease their bipolar vacillations, and, in fact, the human organism's death can only thereby be defined as such.

Jung's concepts of the complementary and compensatory forces of the "subjective" and "objective psyche" (Jung, 1917) more than imply the ambivalence dichotomy in the functions of the human mind. "Animus" and "anima" are biological oppositions; right and left are also biological oppositions (Jung, 1939). It is interesting that in practically all cultures, "right" is symbolically associated with the male and "left" with the female. Moreover, from ancient times the term "dexter" has signified "fitting"; and "sinister," or left, has borne the connotation of "unlucky" or "evil." In certain old Chinese provinces, curiously enough, left-handed women were considered unlucky, presaging ill-fortune for a marriage, and such unfortunate women were reared with efforts to conceal their "unfitting" sinister quality. Perhaps these ancient attitudes served to support the speculation that so-called male dominance observed in mammalian species has biological roots.

The phenomenon of ambivalence permeates interpersonal relationships in the daily life of everyone. Take, for example, the love-hate dichotomy: To varying degrees, these oppositional emotions exist in every social relationship, regardless which side of the affect coin is uppermost at any given time. While experiencing love for a person, one suppresses or represses resentment feelings. Conversely, when one feels strong dislike for a person, that person's existing assets tend to be forgotten. Actually, ambivalence operates on all physiological levels, ranging from the psychological to the vegetative and skeletomuscular. Provided the individual is healthy and enjoys adequate homeostatic regulation, ambivalence phenomena operate smoothly and are not drawn to the individual's attention.

On the psychophysiological level in schizophrenia, however, ambivalence conflicts can be so massive that often on the basis of ambivalence alone one can correctly arrive at the diagnosis of schizophrenia. Dysregulation of responses to stimuli are both quantitative and qualitative, often manifested by polar swings—the all-or-none policy of the schizophrenic.

The dynamic mechanisms outlined in Figure 2-1 (p. 22) contribute to our understanding of the derivation and evolution of the extreme and maladaptive ambivalence in schizophrenia. As hypothesized, the ability to integrate and organize percepts is impaired, and this impairment leads to homeostatic dysregulation of responses to internal and external stimuli. Responses to stimuli are not properly "braked." The phenomenon of ambivalence is set in motion on this deep dynamic level. Due to inadequate regulatory "braking," psychomotor reactions tend to swing to polar extremes. The "intrapsychic ataxia" that develops is manifested by underreactions and overreactions, erroneously timed and adversely directed. The patient makes errors of omission and errors of commission to the extreme, and in an attempt to rectify matters is likely to react to an opposite extreme. Consequently, through the feedback mechanism, the ambivalence aggravates the manifestations of basic integrative impairment and further renders the confused individual unable to equilibrate reactions to stimuli in an adaptive manner.

Many schizophrenic patients are painfully aware that their daily functioning is riddled with "mistakes," but often they lack insight into the strong role played by the factor of ambivalent reactions. They suffer a sense of failure, inferiority, unacceptability, and isolation. They will often tell you, "I am different from other people; something is wrong in whatever I do and I can't explain it."

With ambivalence and feelings of inadequacy, pan-anxiety is inevitable. It is particularly prominent concerning interpersonal relationships. These individuals maintain a childlike dependency upon the environment, and at the same time feel unacceptable and live in anticipatory fear of rejection and hurt. Thus, they become autistically hypersensitive: They act on guard—like a cornered fox—and negatively misinterpret all environmental stimuli in a self-referential way. This defensive quality serves to further aggravate ambivalent swings from fear and passive withdrawal to anger and aggressiveness toward what appears to them as a threatening environment.

The anxious schizophrenic individual also suffers great tension and feelings of frustration in more than one area of life, including the sexual, social, and occupational areas. Tension and anxiety lower his tolerance for coping with even mild frustrations; this triggers impulsive reactions and further aggravates the ambivalence dysregulation. A dynamic feedback is in motion, all along the line, all the way back to the basic impairment of regulatory functioning and thus further adversely affecting the individual's integrative ability.

Augmented by the feedback processes over the years, certain ambivalent patterns become conditioned in the schizophrenic individual. In order to reverse such conditioning, the therapist must recognize and focus attention on the dynamic structure of each patient's predominant ambivalence patterns and the levels on which they operate. Schizophrenic individuals manifest varying amounts of conditioned ambivalent dysregulation on each level of functioning. Listen to the patient's presented complaint. Listen for evidence of thinking disorder, emotional dysregulation, and action dysregulation. Often, in the framework of one or more of these levels of functioning, you can perceive the ambivalence aspect of a presented problem. If the ambivalence aspect is the most disruptive symptom at the time, then this should be the focus for immediate interpretation.

On the thought level, a patient usually displays poor judgment: He will overestimate situations and people, or underestimate them in terms of what is strong or weak, important or unimportant, good or bad, success or failure—in an all-or-none manner. The schizophrenic person's self-evaluation is also unrealistic; he has a penchant for exaggerating personal negative attributes.

In connection with poor judgment, the schizophrenic individual usually manifests ambivalent extremes and inappropriateness of affect regarding situations and people. Ideations are frequently endowed with fanatic emotionality, from which the individual can suddenly take a 180° turn of attitude. Or, the schizophrenic can adhere rigidly to an emotional stance regardless of the rationale for change. In relating to people, he will experience intense love feelings, and can feel hatred with equal intensity, often on the basis of erroneous assumptions or trivial criteria. Affect can swing from one extreme to another suddenly and unpredictably, or perseverate at one or the other pole. Some amount of sado-masochism is usually involved in the affective relationships, wavering with the amount of conflict present regarding the dependence-independence struggle or any dominance-submission anxiety. Thus, the individual can swing from love with passive-dependency to anger and rebellion, back and forth, triggered by an anxiety provoked at the time.

Ambivalent behavior in schizophrenia is very often conspicuous. Reactions to situations and people are inappropriate in terms of quantity: The schizophrenic individual will overreact and will underreact, and sometimes will perseverate in either or switch suddenly and unpredictably. Reactions are inappropriate in direction: The individual will move back, when going forward would be appropriate, and forward instead of moving back. Often the individual is aggressive, when passivity would be appropriate, or passive instead of aggressive. These inappropriate reactions often involve errors of timing: The individual will act in the wrong way at the right time, or in the right way at the wrong time. It is also a matter of reacting too much, too soon or too little, too late. The word "moderation" is not in the schizophrenic's vocabulary.

Some patients manifest ambivalence dysregulation on all psychological levels—thought, affect, and behavior. It can be conspicuous in one or more areas of functioning, and is often seemingly in the framework of neurotic or other compensatory defense mechanisms. Even though an ambivalence conflict appears in the setting of a neurotic defense, such as obsessive-compulsive symptomatology, interpretations should aim at the dynamics of the ambivalence rather than at the dynamics of the neurotic symptom. This dysregulation is basic to schizophrenia: It is not a defense symptom against anxiety but rather an expression of very disruptive anxiety and it dynamically operates as an effort on the part of the patient to cope with the confusion connected to the anxiety.

There are many possible patterns of ambivalence that can become conditioned into a patient's personality configuration over the years. This applies to neurotic individuals also, but in schizophrenia the ambivalent dysregulation is much more massive than that observed in the neuroses, and an all-or-none reaction tendency is clearly observed. There are any number of ambivalence patterns that can develop in an individual. To name a few important patterns of conflict, there is the passive-aggressive, the dominant-submissive, the success-failure, the struggle between independence and dependency, and a number of subsidiary patterns connected with each. Of course, categorizing ambivalence conflicts into such groupings is to some extent arbitrary insofar as they are not manifested in pure form. Patterns overlap; a predominant pattern interacts with relatively subordinate patterns in an individual. And they all involve the patient's anxiety structure stemming from the great self-esteem problem.

The passive-aggressive ambivalence struggle is a basic biological ambivalence phenomenon. Actually, the aggressive struggle for dominance hierarchy serves social survival insofar as the maintenance, or acquisition, of territory is essential to the survival needs of a mammalian social group: Bands of males cooperate together in waging "war" on would-be intruders. Nietzsche recognized the phenomenon of conspecific aggression to be an innate drive in man; he viewed the warrior as an "uberman," or superman, with the admonition, "Ye shall love peace as a means to new wars—and the short peace more than the long" (Nietzsche 1905, p. 74).

We can all fairly well agree that the history of man is the story of territorial and social hierarchy power struggles and, as Nietzsche seemed to imply, a continuum of warfare interspersed with occasional accidents of peace. Of course, in treating the schizophrenic, pointing up such a philosophy is not conducive to resolving the patient's view of the world as hostile—especially if the patient has been conditioned to such a view in the war-torn rice paddies of Vietnam or the ghetto of the South Bronx. Nevertheless, even schizophrenic individuals reared in a relatively delightful environment tend to be anxious and fearful of others, with a kill-or-be-killed outlook on the world. The fact remains that aggressive behavior and passive behavior are basic adaptive maneuvers in the human animal. It is simply the basic biological rage or fear response, with fight or flight reaction, of the animal confronted with danger. But in the schizophrenic these reactions occur in a dysregulated and maladaptive way. Here, ambivalent behavior is magnified by the fact that schizophrenic people live in an internal climate of fear and therefore misinterpret external stimuli as threatening.

In response to anxiety-provoking stimuli, schizophrenic individuals tend to react with extreme passivity, or with impulsive aggression, or will vacillate from one extreme to the other unpredictably, or perseverate at one polar extreme. The pattern of stubborn defiance alternating with passive compliance is quite prevalent in schizophrenia. The reactions are often quite maladaptive: The timing is off, the degree of reaction is off, and the direction is beyond reality boundaries. Many schizophrenic individuals are confused: They do not know when they should be passive, assertive, or aggressive, nor to what extent they should react.

Incidentally, confusion between assertion and aggression is extremely common in schizophrenia and is important to deal with in therapy. Many patients misinterpret another person's assertive advance as an act of hostility. Also, patients often obsessively brood over an act of their self-assertion toward somebody, fearing they have antagonized or hurt that person. Even highly intelligent patients continue confusing assertion and aggression, despite repeated reminders of the qualitative difference. You are obliged to clarify this in therapy on many occasions, perhaps with a concrete analogy, or a metaphor. For instance, you might need to explain to the patient, "If you enter the office and greet me with a handshake you are assertive; but if you greet me with a karate chop then you are aggressive." In any case, the content of the interpretation should be tailored to the patient's style of comprehension as well as to the circumstances surrounding the confusion.

To return to the passive-aggressive ambivalence conflict, the following example of a disruptive conflict presented by a patient in an interview might best illustrate how this pattern can intermesh with subsidiary ambivalence patterns, and how it can be dealt with in therapy.

The patient, a 30-year-old unmarried woman suffering from a pseudoneurotic form of schizophrenia, was referred for consultation due to an intractible anxiety and her urgent request to be "locked in a mental sanitarium." The patient appeared 10 years younger than her age; she was petite, pretty, coy, and manifested an inappropriate smile while expressing her disruptive conflict. Under pressure of speech, she expressed an obsessive preoccupation about an "error" she compulsively made in relating to a boyfriend on two occasions, which resulted in his ceasing to date her. They had been dating casually for about a year prior to her first "error." When asked to describe this problem, she related the following story of what had transpired a year ago during the summer.

"My boyfriend, Jay, is a handsome lifeguard." [That was the extent of her ability to describe his personality.] "I had not seen him for two weeks. I sat with my friends on the beach near Jay's lifeguard stand. I desperately hoped he would see me but was very careful not to glance in his direction. Out of the corner of my eye I saw him coming toward me, and I was so anxious for fear my eagerness would show that I pretended I didn't notice him. He asked me for a date. I avoided looking at him and told him I had another date for that night, which was not true. Then he walked away! I desperately wanted to chase after him but was afraid I would throw my arms around him and make such a fool of myself that he would reject me. So I forced myself to remain sitting on the sand and laugh and act happy with my friends so that Jay wouldn't know how terrible I felt. That was a year ago. Since then I have been unable to get this whole incident out of my mind; my daydreams about Jay are haunted by it. I think I know how I should have reacted at the time but don't know why I couldn't do it. And then 6 months ago Jay phoned me for a New Year's Eve date. I was so scared of sounding nervous and eager that I refused. I told him I had another date, which I didn't. By doing that I think he got the wrong message, because I haven't heard from him since."

The patient, smiling through her tears, continued, "Now summer is coming again. The reason why I am seeing you, Doctor, is this: I want to quit my job so that I can spend all my time on the beach near Jay. But I'm afraid if I do that he will think I am too aggressive and reject me. Yet I am so afraid I will be unable to resist the temptation to do this that I beg you, please put me in a mental sanitarium for the summer. Please lock me up so I won't see Jay and get rejected. If that happened I'd kill myself, really I'd kill myself!"

The dynamics of the ambivalence are clear-cut in this patient. One can observe the powerful role played by anxiety in her dysregulative passive-aggressive behavior. Due to accumulation of sexual tension and frustration, this very hypersensitive patient endowed Jay's moderate assertion with life-or-death import. With the accompanying anxiety, she reacted impulsively in an all-or-none way, but opposite in direction to that which normally would have gained her gratification. She was regressed to the level of a child who might impulsively respond to smiles from a little boy whom she secretly adores by kicking him in the shins. In other words, fear of overreacting with positive self-assertion caused her to overreact in a negative way with passive-aggressive withdrawal. The extreme polar response was quantitatively and qualitatively completely inappropriate to the mild and direct stimulus.

Finally, obsessive fear of an irresistible impulse to "aggressively" throw herself at Jay in ambivalent conflict with fear of the consequences provoked such intolerable tension that, once again, she reacted with extreme withdrawal—seeking hospitalization to protect herself from acting out in her ambivalence struggle.

The patient had been referred for consultation. During the single interview, therefore, interpretations simply aimed to reduce the intensity of the patient's anxiety and bolster her self-confidence for continuing treatment with her therapist. Her symptom was defined for her, namely, the all-out reaction in the opposite direction from that which would have been appropriate to the stimulus. A succinct lesson in reality stressed that life is not an all-or-none proposition. She was reassured that she suffers an anxiety conflict that can be resolved with psychotherapy, and that feelings of desperation will subside when she becomes less tense. In this context she was emphatically informed that hospitalization is not necessary because she is not "crazy" and therefore will not lose control by throwing herself at Jay. Incidentally, for suggestible patients such a disguised command from authority often lowers the patient's tension level to below the "boiling point" and forestalls impulsive acting out. The therapist thus buys time until the medication takes effect and psychotherapy begins to unravel some of the anxiety- and tension-provoking conflicts.

Medication was prescribed for the young woman. Upon resuming treatment, her therapist aimed interpretations at the problems the patient presented. Her areas of strength—especially her high intelligence, empathic quality, and insight capacity—were brought into play. The therapist pushed her to explore her potentials; he drew the patient forth, which served to antidote the anxiety structured on her great feelings of inferiority and failure. The dynamics interpreted to the patient over a series of interviews are here outlined below in condensed form.

The symptom was delineated: "When Jay steps forward to accept you, your impulse to move toward him is so intense it scares you. Instead of moving in the right direction moderately, you move in the wrong direction excessively." The patient agreed.

"Why do I tell you this? Because you convey the wrong message strongly, in fear of conveying the right message too strongly, and this pattern of overcompensating is self-defeating."

"How did this symptom evolve? It evolves out of anxiety, including an anticipatory fear of rejection. You are tense and frustrated in your need for love, but when opportunity arises, anxiety disrupts your judgment and you overcompensate: *You* do the rejecting to allay anticipatory fear of being rejected."

"From where is this symptom derived? It is difficult for you to feel acceptable to Jay or anybody else for as long as you judge yourself completely unacceptable. And you do so judge yourself. You have deep feelings of inadequacy; of inferiority. This has made you very shy and caused you difficulties in relating to people. This has increased your lack of self-confidence and has rendered you very hypersensitive, always in anticipation of failure. Thus, every minor stimulus looms up as all-important to you, and every little response on your part you view as all-important to other people. It is easy to understand, then, why you wish to be locked up for protection from your 'errors.'"

During the therapeutic session, of course, lessons in reality aimed to modify the patient's all-or-none attitudes about herself and to moderate her reactions to the environment. Her main task in therapy was to resolve her conflict about inferiority, and the task required intellectual honesty in examining her realistic assets to counterbalance her exaggerated and negatively distorted self-image. In other words, her task was to resolve the self-esteem conflict, around which anxiety had mounted, culminating in her ambivalence struggle. Thus, her therapist proceeded with appropriate remedial measures. First he said, "So that you can repair matters, let's examine the reality of the situation when Jay asserted himself toward you. Jay simply asked you out on dates, that's all. Were these events of life-or-death import? Due to your anxiety they seemed all-important and you responded accordingly." Here, the patient also received her first lesson in how to differentiate between "assertion" and "aggression."

"Now let's examine the reality about your self. Your exaggerated sense of inferiority has you too blinded by anxiety to see your true self. If you are so inferior, why is it that Jay, and others you have mentioned, are obviously attracted to you? Why? What *are* some of your assets?" The patient was quite blocked on the topic. She had to be approached from a different angle.

"Anxiety has made you hypersensitive about your negative qualities, and insensitive to the positive. You are an honest person, and self-honesty requires you to count your positive qualities as diligently as you count the negative. The more you view yourself in a positive light, and balance the scale, the less anxiety you will suffer and the better you can regulate your life for attaining gratifications." Once the patient was encouraged to enumerate her assets, the therapist filled in further for her, but gingerly. Occasionally a small negative criticism was slipped in, which served to emphasize his candor and honesty.

Incidentally, it is important to anticipate that because the self-esteem in most schizophrenic patients is so low, they are quick to reject a therapist's positive assessments, announcing they never trust compliments; that people lie. The therapist must act first by stating, "I know it is difficult for you to accept compliments; you think I'm lying to you." Jumping the gun, as it were, swings the patient's ambivalence and she will believe your compliment; she will believe it temporarily. Repetition, of course, is an essential part of reeducation: The patient has to be reminded of her assets and past successes in different contexts at different times during therapy. Often the therapist must proceed slowly, however, because many schizophrenic patients need to feel inadequate as protection against demands and expectations for success, and must first resolve their all-or-none concept of success versus failure.

The therapist gave the patient a lesson in the reality of life: That nothing in life is all-or-none; that no one is perfectly superior nor totally inferior; that everyone experiences anxiety because nobody possesses complete self-confidence. Regarding her ambivalence and acting-out, she was reminded that, "Everybody makes mistakes every day, especially when anxious. You are not alone in this; you cannot rightly assume everybody behaves flawlessly except you." It is always important to repeatedly instruct schizophrenic patients regarding the extent to which everybody resembles everybody else in possessing certain assets and deficits of personality or performance. This diminishes the feelings of isolation schizophrenic individuals suffer in their assumptions of uniqueness for their inferiority.

Because the patient was obsessed with fear of rejection for specific "mistakes," the interpretation was tailored to the situation. The patient was asked, "Do you judge your friends so extremely harshly for every minor error? Is this realistic?" It was then suggested, "Friends who are worth much, such as Jay, surely will give you opportunities to remedy little mistakes." At the same time the obvious "remedy" was reviewed: That when someone is assertive toward her he considers her acceptable; that a safe response on her part is self-assertion toward him—in moderation appropriate to the situation. Her aggressive withdrawal was not the appropriate response to Jay's assertiveness.

Over a period of many months, the patient gradually replaced the disruptive ambivalence pattern of negative withdrawal in response to positive stimuli with adaptive moderated self-assertion in appropriate response from others toward her. Incidentally (and typically schizophrenic), upon regaining Jay's interest in her, she immediately lost interest in him. Soon thereafter she developed a relationship with another man and was able to reciprocate affection in a relatively mature manner, especially because he did not venture too close in his demands.

In the patient described, the passive-aggressive conflict appeared bound to her self-esteem conflict predominantly. Although the self-esteem problem must always be dealt with in schizophrenia, at times during therapy the passive-aggressive struggle appears more directly connected with other symptoms or other ambivalence conflicts. It often directly connects with anxiety about an inability to sustain interpersonal relationships. For instance, there is the schizophrenic individual who pursued a love-object persistently with a strong desire to marry, yet when the wedding day arrived ended up in Chicago, 600 miles away, and telegraphed that the engagement was canceled.

Another individual may manifest passive-aggressive ambivalence perhaps involving a strong desire for success in conflict with a fear of his own "aggression," causing the person to alternately strive "aggressively" toward a goal and, when called upon to perform, withdraw and passively accept what he feared was an imminent failure. I observed a startling example of this during my first week in medical school. One of my classmates, a shy, withdrawn fellow, suddenly rushed from the anatomy laboratory, packed his belongings and disappeared from the city. He left a note for the anatomy professor in which he stated a fear that he could not withstand the competition. In more prolonged and subtle ways, major strivings of many patients are repeatedly thwarted by this process of doing-and-undoing polar ambivalent behavior, but in most cases this behavior is rationalized by means of denial and projection.

The passive-aggressive ambivalence phenomenon is often bound with the love-hate ambivalence. In an all-or-none manner, the dependent schizophrenic individual who manifests protracted passive compliance due to fear of rejection by the love-object or an authority, will swing over and manifest aggressive defiance because of accumulated rage against the authority for controlling him in one way or another. This pattern ties in with the ontogenetic independence-dependence struggle and, of course, the dominance-submission conflict so ubiquitous among social animals.

Dealing with the schizophrenic patient's ambivalence conflicts is probably the major task of therapy. Treatment is directed at the ambivalence pattern that gives the patient the most serious trouble. Know your patient well. Know in which areas your patient suffers the most dysregulation, and in which areas the least. It is just as important to know the patient's ambivalence structure as it is to know his anxiety structure: The two go hand in hand. Knowing these phenomena, you then can deal with the patient's ambivalence symptoms in the framework of the schizodynamics (see Figure 2-1, our "onion" chart, p. 22). The therapeutic task is to afford the patient insight into the inappropriate quantity and quality of the ambivalence pattern; the ways in which it disrupts his life adaptation, and what he can do to influence this.

Naturally, attempts to deal with an ambivalence conflict as an isolated symptom are futile. It is inexorably bound in with pan-anxiety, tension, frustration, and their many related symptoms. All symptoms aggravate, and are aggravated by, the ambivalence and must be dealt with concomitantly. In other words, the target symptom of the ambivalence must be interpreted in relation to specific anxiety symptoms and the situations in which they evolved.

When interpreting the dynamics of the ambivalence conflict, as when interpreting any symptom, the therapist interprets at the pace at which the patient is able to cope with insights. It is important not to bombard the patient with interpretations aimed at the deeper dynamic layers early in the course of treatment. You do not want to frighten the patient. Furthermore, the patient cannot emotionally deal with a barrage of interpretive information in one session. You do not want to confuse the patient. Closely watch the patient's level of self-esteem. This, of course, is influenced greatly by the remedial measures that must culminate every dynamic interpretation of symptoms.

The goal of treatment is to recondition the patient: The patient must learn to moderate his ambivalent reactions down from extremes to an appropriate "reality range." By dealing with accompanying symptoms, the patient must learn to qualitatively modify his ambivalence reactions for adaptation in a variety of life situations. If the patient's ambivalence pattern is characterized by perseveration of reactions at one or another polar extreme, the anxiety, rage, or other symptoms that account for this perseveration must be dealt with directly, of course. Occasionally you will encounter a patient who perseverates at one polar extreme to a degree dangerous to himself or others, in which case it is imperative to know how to swing the patient's ambivalence; to mobilize the patient toward security. This strategy is especially indicated, for instance, when a patient is suicidal or homicidal and adamantly refuses hospitalization. We shall discuss this in Chapter 17.

It should be emphasized that the self-esteem conflict underlies all anxiety and ambivalence conflicts in all schizophrenic patients and must be dealt with, directly or obliquely, throughout the course of therapy. Suffering from deep-rooted feelings of inadequacy, the schizophrenic individual is fearful and tends to view everyday life as a survival struggle in a hostile world: In many respects he exists in a continually fluctuating state of emergency. Primitive fight or flight reactions, namely, rage and fear, are readily provoked in schizophrenia. Thus, the basic biological ambivalence struggles operating in the service of self-survival of all animals—aggression versus passivity, and dominance versus submission—tend to operate in an all-or-none and maladaptive manner in schizophrenia.

CHAPTER 12

The Dependence-
Independence Conflict

Along the evolutionary scale, the higher the neural development of a species, the longer the developmental journey from infantile dependence to adult independent functioning. Of course, a state of absolute independence is impossible to attain because every animal must depend upon a supportive environment and on members of its kind for individual and species survival. Viewing the individual alone, the whole is dependent on its component parts, and interacting parts are dependent on the whole with ambivalent fluctuations that never cease motion—except in death.

Normally, when confronted with stimuli an individual reacts in an adaptive manner, independently. He is even able to cope independently in response to certain amounts of stress-provoking stimuli. However, stimuli perceived as nonstressful to one individual may provoke a stress reaction in another. Naturally, an individual suffering inherent integrative impairment is more prone to experience quite commonplace stimuli as stressful than are nonschizophrenic individuals, and, furthermore, is less able to independently cope with these stimuli in an adaptive manner.

When under stress, it is normal to experience anxiety. Anxiety serves as a signal of emergency; it mobilizes the individual to temporarily resolve existing ambivalence in order to decisively cope with a confronting problem. However, when a stressful situation exceeds the individual's ability to cope by means of independent decisive action, anxiety becomes a disruptive force that overrides adaptive efforts. The individual regresses, perhaps only temporarily, to an immature level of dependency adaptation. The degree and pattern of regression varies with the nature of the anxiety-provoking stress, and also with the individual's inherent integrative potential and background conditioning.

The schizophrenic individual is handicapped in terms of integrative potential and, therefore, is prone to react with disintegrative anxiety when under stress. Instead of mobilizing adaptive responses in the individual, the anxiety mobilizes greater dysregulation and heightens existing ambivalence processes. The ensuing regression increases dependency and further aggravates the dependence-independence conflict.

Regression renders schizophrenic individuals childlike, yet, unlike normal children, the level of immaturity is "spotty": It is not consistent with any developmental age level nor in keeping with past life experiences, the schizophrenic pan-anxiety having interfered with the ability to appropriately learn through experience. Thus, the ambivalent schizophrenic will react to environmental circumstances with an undue dependency as well as a stubborn stance for independence.

As has been mentioned, everybody harbors a number of ambivalence patterns, one of which will overlap others to become predominant at any given time in response to immediate stimuli. Nevertheless, an individual's basic personality organization and early environmental conditioning lead to the formation of certain conditioned ambivalence patterns, which become predominant character traits in the individual. (For instance, some people are habitually ambivalent in matters of petty decision-making, yet others experience no such difficulty but spend their lives vacillating between fear of success and fear of failure.)

In schizophrenia, the dependence-independence ambivalence pattern is always manifest, even when overlaid with other conditioned and predominant patterns. And simultaneous manifestations of the two oppositional components in these overlapping patterns are often conspicuous, due to poorly regulated mechanisms of suppression and repression in schizophrenia. For instance, in the framework of the dependence-independence conflict, one can often clearly observe the compliance-defiance struggle with the patient's feelings of love in conscious conflict with feelings of hate.

Actually, the dependent schizophrenic individual is bound to manifest strong ambivalent attitudes toward a protective and supportive "love-object" authority. On the one hand, he loves certain persons on whom he feels he can depend and on the other hand he resents the same persons for being tacit reminders of his inadequacies and inability to cope without support. Thus, the individual will show acceptance of the love-object, and also will show rejection; he will feel warmly and try to get close, then will become angry and withdraw or become aggressive. He seeks help, then rejects help; he is compliant, then unpredictably defiant. At times he acts submissive, yet again struggles for dominance. Masochistic ingratiation alternates with sadistic aggression. The patient may perseverate at one or the other extreme, or will swing from one pole to the opposite; you do not know how the ball is going to bounce. Because these reactions are often unexpected and inappropriate, it is often quite difficult to empathize with the patient, which complicates the difficult therapeutic task.

Despert (1947) described this phenomenon in children and in schizophrenic adolescents. I might add that one also observes a similar dependence-independence struggle operating in nonschizophrenic adolescents when relating to authority. For instance, an adolescent son will ask, "Dad, may I borrow your car?" and will angrily reject responsibility connected with the privilege, such as paying for the fuel. In schizophrenia, however, the ambivalent dependence-independence struggle continues long past childhood and adolescence, and is often carried to a marked extreme because a dynamic feedback of pan-anxiety augments the existing dysregulation.

Concerning the dynamics underlying the dependence-independence conflict, its evolution can be traced through the ideas and feelings that such a patient is likely to express. For example, a series of comments by a patient, if arranged in sequence from deep to superficial dynamic levels, could express the following:

"I am unable to cope with even simple everyday situations; I become confused and anxious."

"I feel very inadequate and unacceptable, because I know I don't make the right decisions and I don't perform the right way."

"I feel inferior to everyone around me. It appears to me that everyone else performs well."

"I must depend on someone stronger than I to make decisions for me; to do things for me; to protect me."

After a period of time, the following comments are made:

"The person on whom I depend [for help or protection] is a constant reminder to me that I am inadequate; that I am inferior."

"I hate this person because I have to go to him [or her] to do these things for me."

Finally, the patient expresses anger and rebellious defiance and, of course, feels at the same time unworthy, with great guilty fear of rejection. His lowered self-esteem and anxiety, connected to anticipated rejection, thus increases the dependency needs and the patient swings back to the former pole. Again, warm affect is felt toward authority; again, feelings of resentment are suppressed or repressed; he again becomes passive, dependent, submissive, and compliant. The vicious circle is completed. The schizophrenic individual alternates thus between compliance and defiance; between dependency and rebellious struggle for independence.

There is the patient who repeatedly asks his wife which tie he should wear with his suit each morning, and when she makes the decision for him he accuses her of "bad taste" and invariably selects a different tie. And there is the woman patient who cannot decide what to plan for dinner, therefore plans no dinner and must ask her husband to take her to a restaurant. Because she is unable to decide which restaurant she prefers, her husband decides; she later complains that he made a terrible choice. Here you observe that schizophrenic individuals, due to lack of self-confidence, can have great difficulty making independent decisions even in very minor matters. They will underreact and then overreact as they vacillate between passive dependency and defiance, with resentment toward the person on whom they must depend.

The following example of a schizophrenic patient suffering from the dependence-independence conflict gives clues for therapeutically dealing with the problem. The patient is a girl in her late teens who complained in interview about her most recent conflict with her mother, announcing, "Mother made me furious yesterday. She meddled in my affairs, was bossy, and humiliated me in front of other people!" The patient continued to condemn her mother in broad general terms out of any situational context. When interrupted and pinned down to describe what specifically had triggered her anger, she explained:

"I confided in mother that I am having a love affair with Jack and am scared I will become pregnant. Then mother got me into the car and drove me to the Planned Parenthood clinic, where the doctor asked me a lot of questions which were none of his business, and then he examined me and gave me 'the Pill.' I felt like a fool! Mother had humiliated me by taking me to the doctor and he, too, was bossy. They are trying to run my life for me and I resent it and I won't give them the satisfaction of taking the Pill. . . ."

When asked what she thought her mother should have done in response to her expressed fear of pregnancy, the patient replied, "I don't know, but it is the *way* she did it that irritates me. She's always telling me, 'Do this' and 'Do that,' pushing me around." Interpretations were given to the patient somewhat as follows:

What the patient's complaint symptomatized: "Well, first you seek your mother's help and then you turn around and resent her for giving it." To this, the patient again replied that she resents being "pushed around."

Why her symptom was interpreted: "This conflictual relationship with your mother continually disrupts your life in a great many situations, not only yesterday's; let us see how you can resolve it."

How the symptom evolved was interpreted: "You continue to rely upon your mother's judgment in matters wherein you lack sufficient confidence in your own judgment." In addition, the following points were made. Feeling hypersensitive about having to depend on her mother enabled her to sense the undercurrent of her mother's love-resentment ambivalence toward her. Hypersensitivity also led her to misinterpret her mother's assertions on her behalf as aggressive interference. It served as a reminder of her inadequacy to cope independently and this hurt to her pride aroused anger with defensive rationalization and defiance. Empathy for her feelings was expressed: "Your mother's actions made you feel like a dependent little girl, and that is an awful feeling, quite humiliating! I can understand why you are angry!"

From *where* the symptom evolved was interpreted to the patient in connection with her deep-rooted feelings of inadequacy and inferiority. The underlying confusion and dysregulation were not probed at this time, but emphasis was placed on her undue lack of self-confidence as the basis for her dependence-independence conflict in relationship with her mother.

The fact that she sought contraceptive advice in the first place was a show of good judgment, which was used as one *remedial measure* to realistically elevate her self-confidence.

First of all, however, the therapist validly sided with the patient concerning the conflict with her mother. She was told that her position was defensible insofar as her mother should have discussed ways and means whereby the patient could plan her own action regarding contraception, rather than "pushing her around." This served to support the patient's self-esteem. Secondly, her mother was defended, also, for having respected the patient's love affair as well as her wish to be protected from incurring pregnancy. This served to diminish the patient's anger and maladaptive defiance. Interpretations ran somewhat as follows:

"You are not so inferior and inadequate to cope as you assume yourself to be. You deserve self-confidence because you demonstrated mature judgment and foresight in seeking contraception and in seeking the help of an experienced person. Secondly, your mother obviously respected your having a love affair and respected your judgment regarding contraception. She meant to cooperate and help you carry out your wishes, but her behavior was awkward; it made you feel that she took the whole matter out of your hands." It was then casually mentioned to the patient: "All mothers tend to get overanxious, even when their offspring are fully mature and competent, and your mother behaved in a typically overanxious way; that's the way mothers are. When you stop to think about it, that's *her* problem, isn't it? But the main thing is that *you* mastered the situation; you attained your purpose; you got your contraceptives."

Here, a lesson in reality concludes the interpretations: Dependence and independence are relative matters, and their reciprocity is one of life's realities. In other words, remind such a patient that no competent person is completely independent nor dependent; that on many occasions we are able to act on our own and on other occasions it is appropriate to rely on some other person; that to depend is not necessarily indicative of inadequacy but often a practical temporary means to attain a goal. Whenever opportunity arises, you can also point out to a patient that the person on whom she or he depends for something often, in turn, has need to depend on the patient for one thing or another. It is always enhancing to any patient's self-esteem to feel needed by other people. Patients yearn for proof of some self-importance.

THE AMBIVALENCE CONFLICT IN THE TRANSFERENCE RELATIONSHIP

The dependence-independence conflict, natually, always develops in the transference relationship. Every masked schizophrenic patient manifests ambivalence conflict in therapy, sooner or later, directly or indirectly. In dynamic terms, its development progresses as follows. The patient enters treatment because he is suffering; he becomes dependent on the therapist to help him. In a short time he develops a love-attachment to the therapist because, as is also observed in a dependent child, it is automatic to love the person on whom one relies for relief from pain. Thus, the patient forms a nice positive transference and relates to the therapist seemingly in a cooperative manner. As a cure is not quickly forthcoming, the patient becomes anxious and begins to regress to increasingly immature levels of dependency. The therapist is unconsciously viewed as the omnipotent authority who, provided he loves the patient, will magically supply security and pleasure in life. The increasingly dependent patient unconsciously shifts his efforts from the therapeutic task to the aim of winning the therapist's love. Ingratiation may include hysterical seduction tactics or compulsive intellectualizing to impress the therapist. This can continue for months on end.

Sooner or later, as the patient senses that no anticipated magical cure is forthcoming, he begins to resent the therapist. Manifestations of passive dependency and infantile compliance become increasingly punctuated by signs of anger and defiance, perhaps eventually with a bursting forth of threats to reject the therapist and the therapy. The greater the childlike love-dependency on the therapist, the stronger is likely to become the patient's resentment and defiance.

There is an additional major dynamic basis for the development of ambivalence in the transference in schizophrenia. We understand why it is that patients are dependent on certain persons in their lives and how it is connected to feelings of inferiority and inadequacy to cope. And we understand why it is that patients resent the authority on whom they depend. These same dynamic processes underlie the ambivalent dependence-independence struggle in the transference relationship. The schizophrenic patient resents the therapist for reasons identical to those that cause him to resent any authority on whom he feels he must depend. Understandably, the patient resents the therapist because the very fact that he needs treatment points up to him his glaring inadequacies. And, having to discuss his disruptive problems with the therapist serves as a continual reminder of his failures and inferiority.

Thus, the schizophrenic patient loves the therapist and is compliant, and at the same time the patient resents the therapist and becomes defiant. Due to anxiety-proneness and deep-rooted dysregulation of responses to stimuli, the ambivalence coin can flip over from love to hate; from passive dependence to passive resistance or aggressive defiance—all quite unexpectedly at times.

In the process of influencing a patient's transference therapeutically, the importance of the countertransference cannot be overly stressed. All therapists experience ambivalence in relating to their patients, and we need to examine the reality level of these attitudes and feelings quite often throughout the course of therapy for each patient. When countertransference is realistic, it can be utilized beneficially insofar as the therapist mirrors reality for the patient. However, when a patient's transference is unrealistic and childlike, it tends to provoke unrealistic countertransference responses—especially when the therapist suffers frustrations and troubles in his life, or some neurotic conflict. Then, the therapist's countertransference reactions can be damaging to the patient and even invalidate a therapeutic process. It is necessary for the therapist to keep on the alert regarding his own conflicts to avoid having them impinge on those of the patient.

Of course, a certain degree of positive transference, as well as a controlled empathic countertransference, is required to enable a constructive patient-therapist relationship for the therapeutic task. But the quality and extent of the patient's positive transference must be recognized and appraised continually throughout the course of therapy and never allowed to become so intense that the patient becomes markedly regressed and increasingly dependent, invariably developing hostile resistance resulting in cessation of cooperation in the therapeutic process. By keeping alert to the patient's current self-esteem conflicts, the therapist is often able to foresee such ambivalent upheavals in the transference and, preferably, prevent their extreme occurrence. Nevertheless, at one time or another, anger and resentment toward the therapist emerges in the course of therapy and the patient expresses these negative feelings perhaps indirectly and in disguised form, or directly.

The patient who manifests a strong positive transference will eventually express the negative side of the transference in some way. However, by appraising the intensity of the patient's positive dependency transferential feelings, the therapist can often find occasions to interpret them dynamically and thereby diminish the intensity of the ambivalence conflict. Interpretation can be direct or indirect. One indirect technique often used in classical analysis consists of emotionally withholding and thus goading the patient into conscious awareness of resenting the therapist for "doing nothing." In treating schizophrenic patients, the direct approach is less anxiety-provoking and can constructively afford the patient ego enhancing insights, as we shall now briefly discuss.

Should a patient express strong positive transference feelings and do so more than rarely, interpretation of the symptom is indicated. When a patient compliments or praises the therapist for something or other, that is all very nice to hear, especially if the patient is grossly incorrect in his judgment, but it cannot be assumed that the patient's motivations are simply altruistic. The patient may be sincere and unaware of ingratiation intent, but the fact remains that the patient's praise announces underlying dependency expectations from the therapist. Remedial interpretations aim to elevate the patient's self-esteem and confidence in his own abilities to progress in therapy, thus decreasing dependency strivings and focusing the patient's efforts back to the task of therapy.

So, when a patient gives you praise and credit for resolving a particular conflict, it signifies a request for you to resolve further conflicts. In response, you do not sit silently and stare at the patient; you do not smugly agree with him; nor do you reply, "Flattery will get you nowhere." You interpret appropriately by stating, "You solved your problem; it is never I who can work these things through and act for you." You then review with the patient the ways in which he utilized his abilities to effect the progress mentioned. The patient is thereby encouraged to rely further on his own resources and is directed away from dependency expectations.

Here is another instance: When a patient of the opposite sex tells you how wonderful you are; that you are handsome, brilliant, kind, and so forth, such seductive behavior clearly manifests strong dependency expectations. Neurotic as well as schizophrenic patients will express eroticized transference feelings, but in schizophrenia the boundary between reality and fantasy is often so hazy that the patient's protestations of love are sometimes extreme and bizarre. Here, especially, the therapist must be fully in command of the existing countertransference in order to deal with the patient's transference therapeutically, rather than accepting it on its face value. Thereupon, interpretations aim to increase the patient's self-esteem, decrease the dependency expectations, and thus dissolve the love-fantasies—all the while taking great care not to hurt the patient's pride. You do not, under any circumstances, treat the patient's pronouncement of love lightly: No matter how ludicrous and unrealistic it appears to you, the patient takes the matter very seriously. The love pronouncement signals great dependency needs and the need for reassurance that the patient is acceptable. You do not want to reject the patient on the matter of acceptability.

For instance, if you are a male therapist and a woman patient announces she is in love with you, your task is to raise her self-confidence in order to lessen her dependency cravings. This enables you to moderate the intensity of her positive transference and desexualize it at the same time. You indicate to her that, yes, indeed you consider her attractive, and then you go on to explain that your relationship with her is very special; that your professional purpose is to help her resolve conflicts which now interfere with her power to achieve independent gratifications in life; that romancing with her would destroy the professional relationship and halt her progress, and because of your great respect and esteem for her you will not thus betray her, and so forth. By thus showing acceptance, such a lesson in reality is usually very acceptable to the patient: Her self-confidence is elevated, her trust in the therapist is fortified, and a constructive positive transference is reestablished.

Occasionally a strong eroticized positive transference serves as a denial mechanism for strengthening the repression of the negative transference. In other words, when anxiety mounts due to slow progress in therapy the patient regresses, becoming increasingly dependent and thereby decreasingly able to afford conscious awareness of a growing resentment toward the therapist for failing to cure him. His dependency "security" is defended by a heightened positive transference, which reinforces repression of negative transferential feelings.

Patients suffering with this transference ambivalence struggle are likely to express buried resentment indirectly, usually by means of resistance maneuvers in therapy. Such a patient, for instance, may begin to arrive late or forget appointments. There is the patient who arrives promply for, let us say, a noon appointment and then starts to complain that the hour complicates his business schedule, and so requests a 6 o'clock appointment. Then, when the doctor complies, the patient either fails to show up at all or is invariably late. Or, a patient whose anxiety had been alleviated by Valium® , 5 mg, t.i.d., now complains that the medication is useless and demands another drug. Should the doctor fall into the trap of changing the medication, the patient expresses gratitude but either fails to fill the prescription or combines the new medication with yet another type obtained from a friend—but you do not hear about this; you only hear that the patient "feels rotten," and in a matter of time he tells you it is all your fault. All this time, meanwhile, the patient is too involved in the power struggle to bring up important current anxiety problems in the sessions.

It is a good idea to interpret indirect expressions of negative transference before compliance becomes increasingly replaced by episodes of defiance. Whenever the patient's therapeutic progress is painfully slow and punctuated by occasional setbacks, usually the therapist can anticipate the patient's mounting frustration of dependency expectations. Unless foreseen and dealt with, eventually the patient will express resentment—sometimes with a vehement swing from dependent compliance to a defiant struggle for independence—often precipitated by a trivial matter.

In connection with resistance and mounting resentment, many a compliant schizophrenic patient will perseverate with minor complaints, session after session, and completely omit mention of existing important problems. Then suddenly such a patient will tell you he is very angry because you did not stop him from quitting his job, or leaving his wife, or from acting out in some other self-detrimental way —none of which he had hinted at in interviews. This exemplifies how a schizophrenic patient can harbor smoldering resentment for having to depend upon you, and then will precipitously take matters into his own hands and act out with extreme "independence," totally confused with regard to the importance of his actions. The therapist is then blamed for having failed to protect him from his plight. At this point, you are annoyed at the patient for having withheld the information, and annoyed at yourself for having overlooked these major symptoms while allowing the patient to endlessly perseverate on minor matters. You quickly put your countertransference to rights, and deal with the matter at hand. You cannot reply to the patient, "Why didn't you tell me all this before?"; perhaps your attitude had inhibited the patient from doing so. You might say instead, "That is a very important thing you are telling me; I am glad you explained it to me, and now we shall deal with it. . . ." Then you listen to the patient, interrupting only to ask for appropriate details of his plight and how it developed. You take advantage of this opportunity to open up new avenues of investigation while, hopefully, the patient is guided by your judgment to remedy matters. Perhaps this procedure will divert the patient from his aggression toward you to constructive assertion on his own behalf.

Here again, we realize how important it is to keep a finger on the pulse of a patient's ambivalent transference, as well as on each area of his functioning—social, sexual, and occupational—and to never allow a patient to perseverate exclusively on one topic for weeks at a time. Address youself to prevention!

When the patient's ambivalence suddenly swings to resentment and defiance in the transference relationship, the patient may angrily state, "You are the worst psychiatrist in the city!"; "I could sue you for negligence!" and so forth. Perhaps you are not the most competent and experienced therapist in the area, but the fact remains that the patient's statements indicate considerable projection on his part. Quite similarly, an angry child shouting at his parent, "I hate you!" is actually manifesting a great fear that the parent hates him. There are two sides to a coin. An angry child is basically a frightened child. Underlying every rage reaction there lurks a fear: that is an axiom. Also, a regressed patient who is angry at the therapist is a frightened patient. He desperately fears rejection; he fears that the therapist considers him too inferior to cure. Blame is then projected; he rejects the "inferior" psychiatrist. Immediate reassurance of acceptance is indicated in order to allay the patient's underlying fears.

As we know, experiencing rage expands self-esteem; fear shrinks it. When a patient expresses negative transference feelings, it is therefore therapeutic to respond in an accepting and supportive manner. In other words, when a patient pronounces you "incompetent" and "inadequate," it does not reassure him to list your credentials and point to framed diplomas. First of all, show your respect for his expressing honest feelings toward you. Accept the patient by perhaps replying, "I am competent to say that *you* are much more adequate than you realize," and "When will you respect *yourself*?" The patient's anger has already implied that he projects feelings of inadequacy and holds you solely responsible for his lack of progress. Therefore, by aiding and abetting his "fighting spirit," you begin to steer him away from passive dependency and toward constructive self-assertion in the transference relationship. Explain to the patient that the therapeutic process is a mutual endeavor; that when he provides you with insight into his thoughts, feelings, and life activities you, in turn, are able to provide him with interpretive insights—the tools which will guide him toward resolution of conflicts. At the same time, point out to the patient particular assets—intelligence, strength of affect, drive, and so forth—on which he can rely in the therapeutic task. Patients should be advised of these things early in therapy, and well-timed reiterations serve to prevent the development of pathological dependency.

It is important to deal with a dependent patient's expressions of negative feelings by accepting them and encouraging the patient to be self-assertive in the safety of the transference relationship. When negative feelings are not shown to be clearly acceptable to the therapist, the patient's ambivalence quickly swings and the anger is replaced by guilty fear that you, the resented authority on whom he must depend, will hate and reject him. The ego-expanding rage is gone; inhibiting fear returns! Self-recrimination leads to masochistic expiation, and the patient regresses to an even greater level of compliant dependency than that which originally had preceded the rebellious defiant rage.

What does it indicate when your patient announces intent to quit therapy? Is it that the patient must move to Kansas? Or does he feel "cured"? Or, does the patient feel worse than ever since receiving therapy? The unfortunate possibility could be that a patient's urge to quit therapy is an indication that the therapist had been amiss in dealing with certain anxiety problems. Perhaps the therapist has probed too deeply in very sensitive areas, or undermined the patient's self-esteem, or has been too supportive and promoted unnecessary dependency. Very frequently, particularly in the neuroses, the patient is attempting to escape anxiety connected with an emergence of emotional material from the unconscious. Regardless of the motivations, realistic and unrealistic, a neurotic patient who announces intent to quit therapy usually means what he says, at least at the time. In the case of schizophrenia it is rarely so simple.

A schizophrenic patient can threaten to discontinue treatment several times during the course of therapy, without actually indicating direct intent. Strong ambivalence is involved: The schizophrenic individual is likely to feel two opposite ways at the same time. It is quite possible the patient resents you and wants to withdraw, and at the same time does not want to withdraw due to a fear of inability to function without your help. Perhaps due to the tension created by the ambivalent struggle, the patient's rejection of the therapist indicates a tension-releasing swing in the transference from dependency to independence strivings. On the other hand, a patient fearing rejection from the therapist may jump the gun by rejecting the therapist first. In any event, were you to reply to your rejecting patient, "Well, all right, goodbye and good luck," the schizophrenic patient could be devastated.

Know your patient's ambivalent motivations as well as vicissitudes leading up to his threat to reject you and his therapy. (Later on we shall discuss methods for swinging a patient's ambivalence, but it can be touched on in this instance.) Try to enable the patient to reverse his decision without losing face. For this end, it might be appropriate to seemingly accept the patient's decision, and at the same time suggest that he return to the next session to discuss his future plans. Meanwhile, encourage him to express his grievances, but avoid being overly supportive. The patient must not receive the impression that he is the victor over you; should that occur, he will leave therapy to avoid retaliation or for fear he might destroy you further. Without arguing, point out the unrealistic aspects of his grievances, all the while supporting his self-esteem as well as validating your strength in terms of mirroring reality. Keep it brief; do not run over the hour—which the patient would interpret as weakness and clutching on your part.

Sometimes when a patient rejects therapy in great anger toward you, quite a different approach is indicated. Counter with a feigned rejection by stating, "If you want to leave therapy, you cannot return here; my schedule will become full; you must go to another therapist." The patient may then "condescend" to give you another chance. By knowing the dynamics of your patient's transference ambivalence, you are able to parry. For instance, when the patient's rejection of you is an expression of fear that you want to reject him, your apparent sudden rejection sometimes breaks the tension. The old technique of meeting aggression with aggression, withdrawal with withdrawal, tends to swing ambivalence in anybody, schizophrenic or not.

In conclusion, a patient's dependence-independence ambivalence conflict usually involves one or more other ambivalence conflicts, depending on the context of the presented problem at any given time, and interpretations should aim at the major conflicts presented. In schizophrenia the dependence-independence struggle will frequently appear in the transference setting. Resolving the conflict in the transference relationship should open the way for resolving it in many other life situations where it also appears.

The patient's expressions of transference feelings, positive and negative, should be anticipated and recognized when they occur. It is important to periodically appraise their constructive and detrimental components. (In the same way, it is important for the therapist to vigilantly appraise, rectify, and utilize his own ambivalent countertransference reactions—to which schizophrenic patients are particularly sensitive.) Actually, the ambivalent dependency-independence strivings in the patient can be utilized to benefit the patient's progress, provided they do not develop to extreme. Employ the transference as a pilot study: Teach the patient when, to what extent, and in which areas it is appropriate to be dependent for guidance or to be independently assertive. By reality-testing his ambivalence in the transference setting, the patient gradually learns how to reality-test in the environment, hopefully in accordance with his inherent assets and deficits and with realistic perception of environmental opportunities and limitations.

The therapist's role includes efforts to prevent the development of an extreme ambivalence in the transference, which interferes with progress in therapy. Should this occur, the therapist is obliged to ask himself how it might have been prevented: Perhaps the therapist committed major errors in technique. Perhaps the diagnosis had been wrongly made and an incorrect dynamic theory applied, thereby threatening the patient by undermining his neurotic defenses. Not rarely, a therapist neglects to adequately support the patient's self-esteem during the course of therapy. It is important to evaluate these factors and, when one or more is considered responsible for an upheaval in the transference situation, make appropriate correction in the therapeutic approach. Every therapist is subject to error; we can all learn from our patients, and it is the competent therapist who continues in the ability to do so.

CHAPTER 13

Double Bookkeeping in Self-Evaluation

Compensated schizophrenic patients who suffer greatly with feelings of inferiority often manifest a peculiar pattern of self-evaluation which might be termed *double bookkeeping*. In other words, they are preoccupied with feelings of extreme unimportance due to inferiority, yet equally preoccupied with the assumption that all their behavior is of utmost importance to their social environment. Of course, this is not true ambivalence in a qualitative sense insofar as there is no actual contradiction: Such an individual is consistent in terms of feeling that the enormity of his inadequacies render him enormously conspicuous. Ambivalence is present, however, in that these individuals manifest an all-or-none attitude concerning the self and their social environment with an extreme hypersensitivity and painful awareness of themselves in comparison to others. It is as though they carry around with them at all times a mental yardstick with which they continually measure their own ability and acceptability unfavorably to an extreme and measure that of other people favorably in exaggerated contrast. Social, sexual, intellectual and, in fact, all life areas of endeavor are involved in this measuring procedure. The problem must be dealt with in treatment, because these patients feel their total inferiority renders them so conspicuous as to be all-important to others in a negative sense; they are paralyzed by a hopeless bind of anxiety and social frustration.

The dynamic mechanisms for the development of the double-bookkeeping pattern in schizophrenia include those depicted in our "onion" chart (Figure 2-1), and, more specifically, are as follows: The inherent disintegrative and dysregulative processes hindered the individual's ability to cope with his social environment. Confusion led to maladaptation, and a growing sense of failure led to feelings of inadequacy, all compounded by repeated hurts and rejections inflicted by the environment. Anxiety curtailed self-mastery experiences required for maturation of self-esteem. Deep feelings of inferiority grew and became generalized: The individual became conditioned to an assumption of total inferiority.

Mounting anxiety repeatedly fed back to aggravate dysregulation and cause further inadequacy of performance and, feeling helpless to cope on his own, the anxious individual regressed to levels of greater dependency on the environment—an environment that already loomed hostile and rejecting of him for his assumed and real inadequacies. The individual sensed himself unacceptable and on the basis of gross inferiority to others assumed himself conspicuously unimportant.

The pattern of feeling important versus unimportant develops in those individuals whose autistic negative self-appraisal is compounded by a dereistic attitude that the environment is continually observant of their inadequate functioning and demeanor. Such an individual becomes acutely hypersensitive to his own negative attributes and defensively on guard, with fearful anticipation of hurt and rejection from the environment. Dereistic thinking becomes complex-bound, manifested by misinterpretation of the social environment in a self-referential way. In other words, while judging himself in terms of the negative, he goes on to assume that other people are also busy judging him inferior and unacceptable. Commonplace positive or neutral actions on the part of others are taken personally as indications of aggression or rejection aimed at him. Such a patient will tell you, "I am inferior, inadequate, and unacceptable; the world passes me by," and on the other hand will state, "Everybody sees that I'm a nobody; that everything I do is wrong. I can only anticipate hostility and rejection."

Any attempt on the part of the therapist or the patient's family and friends to objectively point out positive attributes either roll off the patient's awareness like water off a duck's back or are resentfully viewed as deceitful platitudes. The patient has long since blinded himself to his positive assets, and anxiety continues to prohibit him the luxury of their recognition. Self-distrust and distrust of the environment have so compounded anxiety that the individual becomes "locked" in the trap of negative self-esteem that grows to grandiose proportions. Thus, always on guard against the environment in his expectation of hurt and rejection, he increasingly misinterprets the behavior of others in a self-referential way, always with a feeling that any actions on the part of those around him are direct indications that his inadequacies are conspicuous.

This attitude pattern becomes conditioned over the years. It is not delusional (although it could become so), insofar as these masked schizophrenic individuals can be influenced by reasoning to recognize when their negative assumptions of hostility and rejection from the environment are unrealistic. However, the very large task in therapy is to influence the patient away from his extreme negative self-appraisal, to which he has become conditioned.

Treatment method for the schizophrenic double-bookkeeping pattern is suggested in the following clinical example.

Patient Jim is a 22-year-old single white Protestant hardware store salesman. He is a handsome man of strong athletic build, intelligent, well educated, and cultured. Jim's facial expression was stern, despite a basically warm and gentle personality. He was painfully self-conscious about his personal appearance as well as the "propriety" of his behavior. He claimed to have always felt quite shy and since adolescence had become increasingly withdrawn socially.

The main complaints Jim initially presented centered around marked feelings of social and sexual frustration. Although attracted to women, he explained, "I never attempt to date girls because I dread probable rejection." Upon questioning, he elaborated the feeling that he makes an unacceptable impression on anyone and everyone whom he encounters—without insight into the fact that his stern defensive facial expression more than suggests to people that he himself is rejecting. In short, his social and sexual frustrations were the result of his having become immobilized by great feelings of inferiority.

In the course of treatment, Jim related a typically disruptive experience to which he had reacted in his typical manner: "A very pretty girl came into the store today; I kept observing her out of the corner of my eye but was careful not to stare for fear that everybody would notice that I thought her sexually attractive. But, one of my co-workers who also saw her, looked at me and grinned. Naturally, I glared back at him in anger because he was probably thinking to himself, 'Jim has a dirty mind.'"

It was appropriate to deal with one of the several symptoms disclosed in Jim's brief account by offering him an insightful interpretation. The question is, which was the most disruptive symptom presented? Was it his symptom of sexual frustration, or a guilty fear connected with sexual fantasies, or a projected self-condemnation for sexual preoccupation? Or, was it that he misinterpreted a peer's shared reaction about the girl as indicating ridicule of him? Or, was it an anxiety expectation of a girl's rejection?

Naturally, selection of interpretation at a given time is made on the basis of thorough acquaintance with the patient's background, the diagnosis, knowledge of the patient's integrative potentials, and the dynamic mechanisms of the symptoms presented. Furthermore, it is important to recognize and evaluate any symptom patterns that the patient manifests repeatedly in a variety of daily life situations. Jim repeatedly manifested the double-bookkeeping symptom pattern, and it stemmed from a severe self-esteem conflict. Furthermore, his symptoms connected to sexual frustration were mainly secondary and a part of the symptom "package" of his primary problem, namely, social paralysis and frustration based on low self-esteem.

Many times during treatment Jim recounted various experiences exemplifying his inordinate sense of inferiority. For instance, he would complain that he had felt people laughed at his show of ineptitude, or were irritated by his slowness in writing sales receipts, or were gossiping about his bachelorhood, and so forth; his self-referential misinterpretations very often were triggered by ordinary actions and expressions of persons nearby. These feelings were based on anxiety and are manifestations of complex-bound thinking, rather than delusional ideations; Jim was readily able to recognize that they were illogical and unsubstantiated by fact. In any case, Jim felt his inadequacies were conspicuous.

Therefore, in response to Jim's recounted episode about his reactions to the pretty girl, interpretations were aimed at the dynamics of his double-bookkeeping symptom pattern. They are outlined essentially as follows.

What the symptom is: "Here, you show two opposite attitudes about yourself at the same time: You view yourself as so inferior and unimportant as to be unacceptable, yet you assume that everything you do is noticed by everybody, and for that you would have to be very important. How can a person be so unimportant and important at the same time? You are an honest man, Jim. If you did the store bookkeeping, wouldn't you count the company's assets as well as the deficits before arriving at the correct answer?"

Turning away from my own pseudologic (which a patient does not usually pick up) is contained in a follow-up interpretation of *why* I defined the symptom: "In assuming people take critical notice of you, you feel angry and defensive, which further prevents you from reaching out with positive feelings toward others and gaining friendly interchange."

"We must see *how* this problem evolved. Your social frustrations are due to anxiety about asserting yourself in relationships with others. In your anxiety, everybody becomes a potential critic and you are caught in a bind of fear that you will fail and evoke criticism. Anxiety has led you to become hypercritical of your every move and hypersensitive to those around you in expectation that they, too, judge you negatively." The patient is thus directed to focus on the problem of anxiety.

From *where* the anxiety is derived was reiterated: "It had been difficult for you to develop adequate social skills during your childhood because somehow you had been conditioned to strong feelings of inferiority. These inferiority feelings are at the root of your social and sexual frustration problem; they have made you feel too shy to assert yourself toward people. It is our task to explore the extent to which these inferiority feelings are based on actual inadequacies, and the extent to which they are derived from confused concepts about yourself."

Sometimes, depending on the patient's style of thinking, the schizophrenic is able to clearly grasp the relationship between anxiety and the self-esteem problem when it is summarized for him by means of a metaphor such as the following: "When alone in a forest at night, the unknown surroundings loom threatening. Confused by the lack of insight to guide you, anxiety governs your every move. On guard, you interpret all sounds as dangers that lurk in the darkness. You step on a twig and it snaps; you trip over something and fall. Terrible mistakes, these! Then, the gradual break of day throws light on the reality of your surroundings. An increasingly clear perception dissolves your unfounded fears. You at last feel secure; you venture forth and are able to find your way."

Remedial measures are always a crucial part of interpretation and deserve special emphasis when inferiority feelings are the predominant problem the patient presents. The patient must be reeducated to a realistic appraisal of his self as well as a realistic attitude concerning his environment. Only then can he "balance the books" of self-evaluation in reference to others. No patient can progress in therapy without self-esteem.

In Jim's case, again and again he was reminded of the reality principle: That no one is totally superior or inferior, fully adequate or inadequate, acceptable or unacceptable to all or to none, and so forth. There are no absolutes in human affairs and he, as does everyone, belongs somewhere along the broad spectrum of mediocrity, all told. In terms of specific assets and deficits, Jim was rated above average in intelligence but was presently far below average in self-confidence—the latter deficit required his use of intelligence to remedy.

He was reminded that all people resemble each other with regard to experiencing anxiety for one or a number of reasons; that when anxiety is based on inferiority feelings, all people react the way Jim himself reacts—with hypersensitivity to their negative attributes and hypersensitivity to the actions of those around them in anticipatory fear of hurt and rejection for assumedly conspicuous inadequacy.

Naturally, the conflict with regard to self-esteem and its effect on interpersonal relationships required reeducative interpretations many times in response to many presented situations before Jim could gradually loosen the knot of his conditioned negative attitudes and learn self-reality. In the context of a few typical experiences, interpretations offered him are exemplified as follows:

Example 1. "If a person is frowning angrily, and should he (God forbid) glance in your direction, you would tend to assume he is hostile due to some conspicuously unacceptable behavior on his part. Perhaps he actually *was* thinking about you, if you *really* did something outstanding. On the other hand, perhaps he frowned because he suffered a sudden back pain, or was reminded of a dent in his car, or recalled how angry he felt at his boss. In other words, the reality is that people are primarily much more concerned with their own personal experiences and problems than they are with those of individuals around them who are not involved in their lives."

Example 2. "If a group of strangers nearby are talking together and laughing, should any of them (God forbid) glance in your direction, you would tend to assume they are laughing about you for some reason. In reality, why should their behavior have any reference to you? Most likely one of them told the others a joke, or, if they were laughing *at* someone, most likely it concerned a person who is meaningful in their lives."

Example 3. "If sometimes you feel self-conscious about your dishevelled hair, or about tripping over a curb, you might assume people passing by all notice the fact and harbor critical thoughts about you. Some people may do so. But, in reality, why should people notice everything positive or negative about you? People are primarily concerned with their own good or bad appearance and behavior."

Example 4. "If a girl stares at you from time to time and (God forbid) should smile or look away and blush, is it impossible for you to assume that she thinks you attractive; that she, like you, is perhaps very shy? And if you knew she considered you sexy, would you consider she had a dirty mind? Would not her feelings be natural, normal? Here, you have the task of attempting to observe yourself honestly, and then to recognize that such things can happen to a handsome man."

These interpretations obviously contain a repetitious message in the context of each suggested problem, as exemplified. But it is only through repetition that the therapist can hope to loosen a patient's conditioned patterns and reeducate him to the formation of realistic attitude patterns. A word of caution is appropriate here, however. In all interpretations aimed to remedy a patient's self-esteem conflict, we must remember that although the patient needs to be made aware of his positive assets, he is unable to accept them until his conditioned negative opinions of himself begin to loosen their hold. This occurs gradually over a long period of time, and the therapist must guard against his own impatience. Attempts to prematurely "dose" a patient with positive insights will likely cause the patient to distrust the therapist and to rebel with "emotional indigestion," which will further strengthen his corrosive conditioned negative self-appraisal. One must feed him positive attitudes gingerly, gradually, and at specific times when succinct facts concerning the existence of his assets are obvious and irrefutable.

CHAPTER 14

The Success-Failure Conflict

Many pseudoneurotic schizophrenic individuals, especially, succeed in their chosen fields of work without much conflict. However, it is not uncommon to encounter these, as well as other masked schizophrenics, who, despite intelligence, abilities, and goal-directed drive, do not progress consistently in their life work. Close scrutiny often discloses a repetitive pattern of doing-and-undoing occurring in the lives of these people: They advance with appropriate effort, yet when success is in view they somehow happen to "miss the boat," either through blunders or default. In a matter of time they renew their efforts and progress nicely, only to again head for failure after progressing beyond a certain point.

Quite a number of schizophrenic individuals who manifest this syndrome are suffering with a specific ambivalence pattern, namely, a fear of success alternating with a fear of failure. It does not readily come to our attention when the anxiety connected with success and failure is sufficiently allayed by the doing-and-undoing acting-out processes. For instance, there is the individual termed "Jack of all trades" who attains success due to competence in one field, only to switch to an entirely different field of endeavor, thus roaming through life an intellectual hobo, changing careers as his level of competence is reached. We have all encountered such persons. I know a highly intelligent man with multiple talents who, within a period of 20 years, had been a competent horse trainer, a certified yacht captain, then a hunting guide, and then studied for the ministry only to quit before accreditation, presumably because he disputed the sect's interpretation of the New Testament. The last I heard he worked as a statistician for a railroad company. This man did not appear unhappy in his career-switching, or unhappy in his marital switching either: He left in his wake 3 wives. With each of them he had felt the warmth and security of the hearth unsettling.

Perhaps this man changed careers (and wives) due to Public Enemy Number 2, boredom. But I would wager that he was motivated to avoid the lurking spectre of anxiety, Public Enemy Number 1. He side-stepped career and marital successes when they loomed imminent and then his breadth of talent and charisma enabled him to sidestep failures, which he also would not have relished.

The individuals who come to our attention with this doing-and-undoing ambivalence pattern are those patients who struggle along and suffer great anxiety. They seek psychiatric therapy when the pattern seriously threatens their security in one or perhaps two major life areas. Picture the scholar, for example, who does exceedingly well in college but in postgraduate studies fails through default, probably striving for 6 or 8 years for a Ph.D. degree; first he is unable to settle on a topic for his dissertation and then he is unable to get himself to complete it. Or, picture the talented commercial artist who compulsively follows draft directions almost but not quite, and in his indecisions has difficulty meeting deadlines. Actually, the same dynamic pattern often underlies the fortunes-made-and-lost syndrome one hears about.

Schizodynamic Mechanisms in the Success-Failure Conflict

The dynamic mechanisms underlying the success-failure ambivalence pattern involve at least two major conflicts. First, there is the ambivalent all-or-none self-appraisal attitude carried by the schizophrenic. The patient harbors deep-rooted feelings of inferiority due to both actual and erroneously assumed inadequacies. A proper Gestalt is somehow missing. Large and small successes and failures are awarded equal, or reversed, value. A small task well done with a compliment from an authority will trigger anxiety, and the individual will react as though he seriously overstepped his bounds of capacity. Then, on the basis of one slight error, the individual will judge himself grossly incompetent and in brooding will disqualify his good achievements of preceding days. These reactions are extreme; they are insufficiently modulated by what should normally be a recognition of important existing aptitudes. Nor can the patient profit from positive past experience. Anxiety interferes. Grave doubts about his ability to either sustain a self-prescribed level of success or to avert an alternative of failure aggravate a feeling of helplessness, leading to an exaggerated fear of being annihilated by the environment.

Secondly, ambivalent all-or-none attitudes with regard to the environment lead the patient to view life as a kill-or-be-killed affair. He interprets assertions toward him as aggressive acts, just as he confuses his own assertion with aggression. Thus, assertion toward success carries with it the fear of retaliatory retribution, compounded by an assumption that he is weak and others strong. Yet, to become passive elicits fear of vulnerability to annihilation by the dog-eat-dog competitive environment. And there exists no middle ground on which to stand.

These all-or-none assumptions with regard to the self and the environment are not directly disruptive as long as the swinging pendulum moves not too far from center. But once the patient achieves a certain amount of success, or once he experiences some amount of failure, the all-or-none attitude concerning success or failure arouses anxiety. The conflict then mobilizes the patient to avert anxiety by shifting direction to avoid a showdown: Confrontation with success is tantamount to a life-or-death showdown, and confrontation with failure is tantamount to an equally ominous showdown. Thus, the patient asserts himself in one direction and then moves in the opposite direction in repetitive attempts to prevent the dangers he assumes inherent at either extreme.

This Sisyphean struggle often gives rise to a sense of *Weltschmerz* and to the feelings of futility many schizophrenics experience in terms of life achievement. Realizing they can never become "great," they will brood over the idea they are rapidly growing old and will have achieved "nothing" in life—there being no middle road.

The conflictual patterned behavior in connection with success and failure progresses in a cyclic manner according to the schematic diagram shown in Figure 14-1. These processes can be arbitrarily divided into four consecutive stages along what is actually a flowing cyclic course.

(1) DESIRE FOR (TOTAL) SUCCESS   "aggression"→   (2) FEAR OF SUCCESS

(4) FEAR OF (TOTAL) FAILURE   ←passivity   (3) DESIRE TO UNDO SUCCESS

Figure 14-1. SUCCESS-FAILURE CYCLE

In the first stage, the patient is obsessed with desires to succeed and compulsively performs with all-out assertion. He is competent, let us assume, in his business career and his anxiety is abated by his neurotic defenses. A crucial assumption nevertheless lurks in the back of his mind: "I have to be great or I am nothing." (Background conditioning largely determines an individual's criteria for "greatness"; it may be measured in terms of wealth, power, knowledge, fame, or perhaps all of these.) After a period of time, the patient's achievements earn him a promotion with monetary and other gains. A desired step toward success is now realized.

The second stage begins following the recognition of growing success. The patient experiences increasing anxiety about his ability to maintain his high level of performance. He becomes increasingly introspective and self-critical. He also becomes hypersensitive and misinterprets the behavior of those around him in a self-referential way. He gets the idea that he is being slighted by formerly friendly associates; that they are competitively jealous. At night he broods with insomnia, wondering, "Will my aggression lead to retaliation?" At the same time he thinks, "I cannot sustain the perfect performance people expect from me." He begins to regret having accepted the promotion. In other words, the obsessive-compulsive symptoms that had initially mobilized him no longer serve as a defense against anxiety. Quite the reverse, they lead to an increasing anxiety.

During the third stage he desires to recoil; to request a return to his former position, with the idea, "I never should have climbed so high." Anxious and tense, the patient begins to construct new neurotic defenses, perhaps hysterical or psychosomatic. He may suffer indigestion or backache, or develop headaches, or chronic fatigue. Perhaps he takes a brief sick leave from work on more than one occasion, and, because of difficulty in concentrating, he falls behind in a few assignments. Neurotic defenses fail, and anxiety gradually becomes connected to a gnawing fear of total inadequacy.

In the fourth stage, fear of total failure finally predominates the patient's thinking. Anxiety over anticipated rejection is compounded by depression. He ruminates in angry self-beratement, "I'm no good! I'll be fired from the job." He becomes increasingly tense and agitated, and begins to feel on the defensive. Mobilized by angry brooding, he gets the idea, "I'll show them I won't be beaten!" He feels motivated to avert seemingly imminent disaster. An urge to recoup increases; he directs himself to the tasks at hand and is again orientated toward success—with renewed obsessive-compulsive striving.

Differential Diagnostic Features
of the Success-Failure Conflict

Possible points of diagnostic confusion deserve mention. First of all, one often observes success-versus-failure ambivalence patterns operating in obsessive-compulsive neurotic patients. However, the dynamic mechanisms involved in the neuroses are entirely different from those in schizophrenia. The neurotic patient does not suffer massive dysregulation based on an inherent integrative impairment, and does not develop such extreme ambivalent swings. (If polar ambivalence occurs, one should reconsider the diagnosis of "neurotic".) The obsessive-compulsive doing-and-undoing behavior in the neurotic individual is probably based on specific early environmental anxiety mobilizing factors. In some neurotic patients it is traceable to repressed conflicts over sibling rivalry, or to repressed murder fantasies with guilty fear of retaliation from a domineering and jealous parent, or to a combination of these among other psychodynamic factors.

Of course, similar psychodynamic factors may be involved in some schizophrenic patients as well. However, in schizophrenia these psychodynamic mechanisms are not the causative factors at all. They may simply serve to influence the schizophrenic patient's selection of neurotic defense symptoms. Naturally, in treating the schizophrenic patient, this overlay of neurotic symptomatology must not be probed along the lines of the psychodynamic mechanisms applicable in treating the neurotic patient, no matter how tempting it may be to do so. Such a therapeutic approach would not lead the schizophrenic patient toward the roots of his conflict—namely, inherent faulty integration upon which dysregulatory responses to stimuli are structured. And what is most important to realize is that encouraging a schizophrenic to climb down the psychosexual ladder of the Libido theory or to analyze his conflicts in the context of any other theory of the neuroses is inviting the patient to decompensate: Should the frightening assortment of buried infantile sexual and aggressive fantasies be brought to light, it would foment an intensity of anxiety with which the schizophrenic patient would be unable to cope.

The phenomenon of alternating successes and failures is not to be confused with the pattern quite often occurring in bipolar manic-depressive psychosis. In that disorder, a drive toward success alternating with an abulia is mainly governed by endogenous affective cyclic shifts. Of course, external factors may occasionally trigger the speed of onset of the mood cycle, but the mood cycle itself is not "caused," nor is the rate of its periodicity altered, by external stimuli. Thus, in the manic-depressive psychosis, the successes or failures are actually secondary by-products of the manic or depressive mood; they do not have a primary relationship to anxiety, which they do have in schizophrenia. The dynamic mechanisms underlying the cyclic ambivalence symptomatology in schizophrenia are peculiar to that disorder alone. One must not be misled by any existing neurotic psychodynamic processes that may be superimposed. The treatment approach relies strictly on the diagnosis.

In schizophrenia, internal stimuli nevertheless do play a considerable role in both the timing as well as the intensity of the patients' ambivalent success-failure repetitive struggle. In dynamic terms, their marked dysregulation of responses is largely influenced by the underlying basic disintegrative process. Patients with poorly developed non-psychotic compensatory symptoms and patients with an especially low anxiety threshold may develop extreme and overlapping attitudes and motivations concerning success and failure. These individuals struggle against great anxiety odds. Seemingly they function like a car engine forever changing from third gear forward into reverse, and back, unable to maintain headway in one direction despite intense effort. In therapy, continual attention must be focused on the schizodynamic mechanisms responsible for the confused success-failure ambivalence struggle going on in these patients.

Dynamic Factors in Prognosticating

The patient who manifests repetitive strivings for success requires a strength of integration sufficient for the anxiety to serve as a mobilizing rather than a paralyzing force. And whenever a feeling of angry defiance is mobilized, it serves to expand the self-esteem and override the depression that usually is connected to feelings of failure—provided the depression has not reached paralyzing intensity. Thereupon, each successive step upward further abates anxiety and depression, until the patient again succeeds to the point where a surge of anxiety signals danger.

Obviously, the above-outlined success-failure pattern does not develop significantly in those schizophrenic patients who lack sufficient potential abilities. Nor does it occur in patients who are deficient in that ineffable attribute termed *drive*. Drive is an extremely important ingredient required for firing an individual's motivation to utilize his capabilities; motivation otherwise lies dormant, easily smothered by anxiety. In other words, passive-dependent personalities rarely strive to heights in accord with their inherent potentials, and should they experience failure, or threat of failure, they are more prone to react with a retarded depression than with an agitated depression. Such individuals are likely to attach themselves to a daily bottle of booze for solace rather than seek a solution to their problems.

It is obviously important for therapists to deal with the syndrome of a patient's alternating desire and fear connected with success and failure, because the pattern can seriously disrupt the patient's entire life. After a time the untreated individual can become "stuck" at either the success or the failure extreme for more than one reason.

With regard to the polar extreme of success (however one may define it), a power-driven individual can become stuck for the very same reason that had formerly motivated him to recoil from success, namely, the great fear of falling from the level of successful performance attained. As the saying goes, the higher you climb, the harder the wind blows. Thus, when considering himself in a precarious position, instead of compromising by retreating toward failure, the individual reacts by constructing greater and greater ramparts of defense against any possible loss of position gained. The ramparts consist of margins, or "cushions," of gain. They are constructed in defense against a fear that the success is actually a sham, perhaps the result of luck, a favorable misjudgment of him by his superior, or whatever. In any case, the higher he climbs, the higher he feels forced to climb to consolidate his gains; to secure his position. Guilty fear connected with his competitiveness is frequently involved.

Often actual aggression is required for the upward thrust to greater success. And, of course, this reinforces the patient's frenetic effort to construct further defenses against an increasing anticipatory fear of retaliatory annihilation from the environment. Such a patient is motivated for survival! It is more than just the "joy of the hunt" motivation commonly observed in neurotic individuals. It is more than the ubiquitous existential anxiety that propels individuals to accumulate "trophies" symbolic of immortality—although this motivation reinforces existing pathological motivations in all patients who compulsively strive for unlimited success. Oftentimes in this "Howard Hughes syndrome" defensive paranoid ideations strongly color the clinical picture.

Then there is the other extreme: Probably the large majority of schizophrenic patients who become stuck at some point in the ambivalence pattern end up at the failure end of the spectrum. There are a number of reasons to account for this. First of all, at some time or other such a patient is very likely to precipitate an actual downfall by impulsively reacting to his success in an adverse and unacceptable manner.

He unwittingly overplays his hand. The schizophrenic reacts more drastically to stress than does the neurotic patient. In reaction to an unconscious guilt, the schizophrenic patient will inadvertently "cruise" for punishment by scoring major blunders or defaults. Or, when the patient reacts to anxiety with defensive aggression, he will somehow manage to antagonize one or more persons crucial to his security and provoke hostile rejection. In any case, rather than retreating to safety by lowering himself down a few rungs of the ladder, he finds himself forcibly plummeted to the ground—irrevocably rejected, a failure. He has burned his bridges behind him.

An additional factor contributing to patients' becoming fixated at the failure end of the spectrum is important to mention here because it commonly comes to our attention in clinical practice. It is the factor of drive. Drive diminishes with the aging process, in some individuals gradually and in others not so gradually. However, by the time a patient has arrived well into middle-age, there is often a significant lessening of drive. (And as yet, the mitochondrial "batteries" cannot be recharged, despite continuing scientific search for some immortalizing "fountain of youth.")

As the years go by, therefore, the patient who at one time manifested the success-failure cyclic pattern gradually ceases to respond to an assumed threat of failure by swinging back with renewed striving toward success. The time in life arrives when anxiety and depression will override the patient's motivation to rebound. In some patients there is the additional factor of insufficient talents or skills to stimulate them in any particular field of endeavor. (It is an interesting observation that many highly creative people of genius caliber often maintain drive in their productive work well into old age.) Especially because of these drawbacks, it is important to recognize the success-failure ambivalence pattern early in the course of treatment and to direct therapeutic focus on the conflict as early as the presenting symptoms allow.

For those patients who continually repeat the success-failure cycle, the period of time involved for completion of the circuit varies among individuals and also varies for each individual, depending to a large extent on the quantity and type of external stimuli that bombard the patient at various times. The cycle may take a full course within a period of weeks, months, or years. For instance, the cycle could occur over a number of years in the teacher for whom promotions, or lack of promotions, are major factors which stir up anxiety connected with success or failure. On the other hand, for the speculator (a polite term for gambler) events may occur overnight that mobilize the patient's ambivalent swings. The astute therapist who knows his patient well

can usually learn to anticipate the types and quantities of environmental events that influence the rate and direction of the patient's success-failure responses.

In dynamic terms, the schizophrenic patient is unsure of himself, to
put it very mildly. Inferiority feelings and self-doubts are so strong
that, like a centipede counting each footstep, the patient constantly
questions himself, "Should I or shouldn't I?" and, "Was I right or
wrong?" in every little matter. He fears his own aggression; he fears his
own passivity. He makes tentative gestures in both directions as though
to say, "See how hard I am trying; I'm doing my best, but see—I'm
just a little boy and can never be a competent man." Obviously, no
schizophrenic really enjoys failure. But for such a patient the pain of
settling for a modicum of failure is far less than the anticipated pain of
consistently striving to achieve success at the risk of total disaster. The
patient settles in restless compromise by remaining on a childlike level
of achievement, namely, "If I'm careful not to climb too high, I won't
have far to fall." For such a patient, marked integrative impairment
obviates a fair prognosis regardless of any current therapy applied.

The Psychotherapeutic Approach
to the Success-Failure Syndrome

Now to discuss in general the therapeutic approach for patients who
do not suffer such marked integrative impairment and who possess
compensatory strengths. First of all, the most successful therapeutic
approach entails prevention. In other words, the therapist alerts himself to the directional trend of the ambivalence pattern in the patient
and must proffer interpretive interference during the incipient stage
along the transitional course toward either success or failure. Thus,
attention is focused on the conflict long before the patient has had time
to swing to one or the other polar extreme. For instance, the so-called
fortunes-made-and-lost syndrome obviously can be more successfully
resolved therapeutically before the patient reaches a fearsome pinnacle
of success, and before the patient falls into a fearsome abyss of failure.
This point cannot be overly stressed! When you catch the patient during the transitional periods, the pendulum is moving in the zone between the extremes; the patient's neurotic defenses are absorbing some
of the anxiety; the anxiety is not too intense. While suffering less anxiety, the patient is better able to relate to the therapist and is more readily influenced by interpretations aimed to resolve the ambivalence conflict. In other words, cut the vicious success-failure cycle at one or the

other of the two intermediate points. The target symptom is anxiety, nonetheless—and one needs no reminding that the neurotic defense symptoms are never tampered with.

If, for any reason, your interpretations are unduly delayed and given while the patient is in the throes of a polar extreme connected either with success or failure, you may find that interpretations aimed to show the patient the dynamic sources of the symptom pattern will stir up such intolerable anxiety that the patient may actually decompensate! In other words, this is not the time to inform the patient that his anxiety is derived from unrealistic expectations of retribution, or feelings of inferiority; he will not hear you; he already suffers a conviction that retribution *is* in order, or that he *is* inferior. Instead, immediately offer the patient strong supportive interpretations consisting of pointing out positive realities concerning the environment or himself. Show the patient in what ways his exaggerated concepts of external dangers connected with success and failure are realistically unfounded. By pointing out to him the ways in which he resembles the great majority of human beings, you can reassure the patient that he is not doomed, that life is a middle-of-the-road proposition, and so forth.

When treating any patient whose life is disrupted by a success-failure ambivalence conflict, keep in mind that the patient lacks clinical insight into the existence of the pattern. A patient will offer all varieties of rationalizations to account for a change of attitude and direction of performance from passive to assertive or vice versa. Projections onto the environment often appear plausible. For instance, a patient may explain that he quit his job because of personality clashes with his associates, which may be true—but what the patient does *not* tell you is how he unwittingly provoked the trouble. For this he lacks insight into the nature of his paranoid fears as well as his existing contact impairment. Interpretations for the patient take into account the current stage in the cycle and in which direction—toward success or failure—the patient is heading. In general, interpretation contents can be summarized as follows.

The *presented symptom* is defined for the patient as a process of backing and filling; that at times the direction of his actions indicate fear of success and at other times fear of failure. The presented problem is then defined in terms of the particular direction in which the patient is currently heading.

Why you give the interpretation at this time is explained to the patient, namely, that the repetitive extreme swinging from one direction over to the opposite causes continual frustration and disrupts any valid efforts he makes to gain gratifications in the life areas involved.

How this symptom pattern evolved is then explained by focusing the patient's attention on anxiety and noting that anxiety is connected with his all-or-none attitudes concerning both success and failure. When the currently presented symptom manifests the patient's incipient fear of success, the interpretation can be given: "If you succeed, you fear you cannot maintain it . . ."; or it might be appropriate to state, "You misconstrue your assertions toward success to indicate destructive aggression and therefore you fear retribution; competitive success arouses in you a fear of retaliation." Here again, it is usually appropriate to clarify for the patient the qualitative difference between assertion and aggression.

Similarly, when the presented picture demonstrates that the patient is going through the stage of recoiling from success, your interpretation again focuses on the target symptom, anxiety. You explain to the patient how his unwarranted fears of success lead him to retreat to a safe position. You remind the patient of his inevitable tendency to overshoot the mark; that he invariably heads toward failure even though he has no desire to fail. Point out the ways in which he is placing himself in a double-bind with these doing-and-undoing patterns of response.

Provided the patient has not been allowed to reach one or the other extreme stage in the success-versus-failure cycle, anxiety is usually not so intense as to prohibit your efforts to explain the *derivation* of the anxiety symptoms. Regardless of whether the patient is beginning to head in the direction of success or failure, the symptom derivations are dynamically the same—deep-rooted inferiority feelings and an exaggerated sense of inadequacy, based on confusion and dysregulation. When the stage of therapy is such that the basic self-esteem conflict can be pointed out to the patient, remedial interpretations must immediately and repeatedly place heavy emphasis on supportive measures appropriate to combat the patient's currently presented all-or-none attitudes.

Remedial measures aim to make inroads in reeducating the patient to realities with regard to the self and the environment. If the currently manifested anxiety is predominantly connected with imminent success, the patient needs to learn the extent to which the internal and external environmental factors that fomented the anxiety have realistic as well as unrealistic foundations.

The all-or-none attitude and responses to stimuli always require the focus of attention in treating the success-failure syndrome, as in treating all ambivalence phenomena in schizophrenia. In other words, the patient continually needs reminding that it is unrealistic to assume that any successful performance can be sustained at all times every day.

Repetition is required to condition him to realize that everybody experiences vacillation in performances with "up" days and "down" days, weeks, or months, due to a variety of internal circadian as well as external environmental factors over which no one is necessarily expected to have control. Furthermore, the therapist must repeatedly correct the schizophrenic patient's illogical penchant for negatively judging his self-worth on the basis of each performance of the moment. For instance, you will find it necessary to remind the patient that his failure to perform as well today as he had done yesterday does not prove him "stupid" or inept, but it rather should be accounted for on the basis of perhaps insufficient sleep and fatigue, or distraction by problems other than the tasks at hand, or a head cold, or whatever other realistic factors exist. Such simple realities are quite obvious to us. The anxious schizophrenic repeatedly overlooks them.

Again and again the patient needs reminding that the world is not actually a kill-or-be-killed propostion; that self-assertion is not synonymous with murderous aggression; that competition is a natural part of life's game; and that to win or lose from time to time does not warrant punishment by hanging.

When the fear of failure currently predominates, it is important to remind the patient that nobody is totally successful and, conversely, that everybody fails both in large and small ways from time to time, yet no person can be categorized as an absolute and total failure. This is another fact obvious to those of us who are not schizophrenic. Moreover, the patient needs reminding that it is very unrealistic to assume that one must either become great or else one becomes a nonentity, and that the vast majority of human beings throughout history who have enjoyed successes in their lives have not been designated historic monuments, yet in reality they cannot be classified as failures.

The aim in therapy is to influence the patient to "tone down" or to "moderate" existing extremes of attitudes in assessing success and failure. For this end, repetitive interpretations concerning simple everyday realities need be given the patient in the context of each disruptive symptom pattern as it is presented. Repetition is required in order to break up unrealistic conditioning of the past while gradually reconditioning the patient to the acceptance of reality. By means of periodic gentle prodding, the patient is put to the task of learning from past experiences that the relative successes he has achieved have caused no downfall, neither have the relative failures in his life culminated in disaster.

CHAPTER 15

Sexual Reproduction
Conflicts in Women

Sexual reproduction is so taken for granted by the medical profession that even obstetricians rarely question patients about their attitudes and motivations concerning pregnancy and the maternal role. Yet every woman harbors ambivalence with regard to her sexual reproduction. Due to the fact that the vast majority of women reproduce, and due to the fact that their attitudes and motivations for it are often laden with pathological conflict, this ambivalence deserves the psychotherapist's priority of concern.

Interestingly enough, society imposes no required credentials for the commonplace practice of motherhood, despite the fact that the quality of the future generation depends heavily on the quality of maternal nurturing. As David Levy stated, "It is generally accepted that the most potent of all influences on social behavior is derived from the primary social experience with the mother" (Levy, 1943, p. 3). From the viewpoint of preventive medicine, it apparently rests on the shoulders of the psychotherapist to concern himself with a woman's conflicts involving her past, present, or future pregnancies. Therefore, upon commencing to treat each and every woman in her fertile years of life, it is essential that the therapist investigate her desires and fears connected with pregnancy and motherhood—adaptive and maladaptive, conscious and unconscious. it is important to recognize these ambivalent patterns very early in treatment, preferably during the period of basic fact-finding.

For one thing, therapy aimed to resolve certain patterns of conflict can release a patient from pathological fears and enable her to adaptively fulfill her maternal role. On the other hand, early therapeutic aim to resolve certain other pathological conflicts can avert sexual reproduction detrimental to the woman's health and welfare and, thereupon, avert detriment to what would be unwanted or pathologically nurtured offspring (Klein, 1967). Many such unwanted children, in turn, contribute adversely to the human society already burdened with pathological sequelae of overpopulation.

As we know, female sexual physiology is cyclic and is far more extensive and complex than is that of the male. For the female, sexual intercourse leading to insemination initiates the sequential physiological processes of pregnancy, childbirth, lactation, and breastfeeding, and a long period of vigilant nurturing of the helpless infant. Normally, the maternal role is a relatively full-time career sustained until the child attains sufficient biological and psychological maturation to function independently. Thus, to become pregnant is the most important step in life a woman can take. Therefore, no responsible psychiatrist approaches a woman's pregnancy lightly, even though most patients are likely to do so, if they think about it at all!

Because the first experience of pregnancy leading to childbirth revolutionizes a woman's adaptation for more than a decade to follow, it is essential to consider the amount of stress these events are likely to provoke for her. The maternal role contains elements of stress even for the so-called normal woman. But, for the schizophrenic woman who suffers integrative impairment, the ability to cope with stress is curtailed and anxiety is easily mobilized, especially when she undertakes the maternal role. Despite the fact that a number of schizophrenic women benefit from pregnancy and function adequately as mothers, a great many first seek therapy because they are devastated by anxiety connected with child-rearing.

The therapist treating a masked schizophrenic patient cannot predict with complete accuracy how adequately the patient will cope with pregnancy, childbirth, and the maternal role. Fair predictions can only be tendered by the therapist who has thoroughly explored the patient's areas of integrative strengths and weaknesses and investigated all aspects of her confusion, anxiety, and ambivalence conflicts about sexual reproduction. The therapist cannot play God and assure the patient, "If you want a baby I'm sure it will be fulfilling," nor can he flatly state, "You should never become a mother; you could not endure the stress."

The therapist's role is to afford the patient insight into her pathological ambivalence conflicts in order to resolve them before she becomes pregnant, and to educate her to realize her inherent assets and limitations as they relate to stress factors with which she would be re-

quired to cope when assuming a maternal role. The final, and hopefully realistic, decision rests with the patient—with perhaps the exception of the poorly compensated anxious patient who requires supportive
objective guidance from the therapist.

Some patients spontaneously bring up the question of their sexual
reproduction early in treatment and will do so freely. However, a great
many young women completely ignore the subject in interviews. When
a schizophrenic patient expresses her desires or fears concerning pregnancy or maternity, an ambivalence conflict sometimes is readily discerned on the conscious level. Nevertheless, the therapist cannot assume
that these surface attitudes and motivations represent the total ambivalence picture. Further observations and questioning of the patient
might well disclose various verbal and nonverbal clues pointing to the
existence of unconscious conflicts. In a matter of time, the therapist
becomes able to delineate the patient's totality of ambivalence patterns
—adaptive and maladaptive, conscious and unconscious.

When a young woman patient begins treatment and makes no
mention of attitudes about her sexual reproduction, it does not indicate
that she never gives it a thought or that no conflicts exist. As we know,
many schizophrenic patients omit mention of major anxiety conflicts
and will even deny their existence when questioned. Thus, it becomes
necessary to explore the patient's sexual attitudes and behavior in general, because they contain some amount of confusion and ambivalence
conflicts in schizophrenia. We must endeavor to foresee potential problems and avoid the chance of the patient suddenly announcing, "I'm
four months pregnant, Doctor; help me out of it," or, "Congratulate
me, I'm pregnant with my tenth child—hope this one won't turn out a
rotter." Conversely, when pathological fears of pregnancy exist they
also require attention in order to free the patient for adaptive fulfillment of her maternal needs.

There are many faulty assumptions with regard to disorders of
human fecundity, and much continued research is needed (McFalls,
1979). It can be assumed, however, that mental illness is a factor.
Whether a woman suffers from neurosis, sociopathic personality, schizophrenia, or whatever, in our stress-provoking so-called civilization,
unrealistic ambivalent attitudes and motivations prevail in the area of
sexual reproduction, as they do in any other life area. The ambivalent
configurations we will discuss are schematized in Figure 15-1.

One or more of these conflictual desire-fear attitude and motivation
patterns (A, B, C, D, and E) exist in patients—whether vacillating on
the conscious level or fixed in the unconscious, whether "normal" or
pathological. Actually, a woman does not possess conscious and uncon-

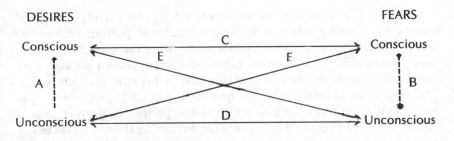

Figure 15-1. AMBIVALENCE PATTERNS CONCERNING SEXUAL REPRODUC-
TION IN WOMEN

scious desires for pregnancy and maternity without some amount of
conscious and unconscious fear or negative attitudes as well. Ambivalence configurations vary among patients, although one pattern usually
maintains predominance over the others in a given patient at a given
time.

The intensity of the ambivalence conflicts also varies among patients and exerts influence on their sexual behavior. Therefore, from a
preventive viewpoint it is important to recognize both realistic and
unrealistic elements present in the predominant pattern and the intensity of each element. Then, upon assessing the dynamic structure of the
predominant pattern, it is possible to predict the intensity of its influence to a considerable extent and thereby determine the direction in
which to initiate treatment. It is particularly important to recognize
the patient's unconscious attitudes and motivations because, of course,
these are likely to bear the strongest influence on her sexual reproductive behavior.

We shall now briefly discuss the various ambivalent configurations
(schematized above) connected with sexual reproduction—the conscious and unconscious desires in conflict with the conscious and unconscious fears—in terms of general clinical prediction and therapeutic
approach. Emphasis will be placed on schizophrenic patients' unrealistic attitudes and motivations.

Neither conscious and unconscious desires (pattern A), nor conscious and unconscious fears (pattern B), exists without opposition:
Although the procreative drive is biologically indelible, the super-
imposition of confusion and anxiety gives rise to ambivalence. The
tenuous nature of repressive mechanisms along with the regulatory impairment in schizophrenia compounds ambivalence, leading to polar
swings. The ability to make any prediction of acting-out behavior
varies depending on the strength of the positive or negative polar forces.

Conscious desires and fears (pattern C) can be readily perceived during fact-finding when it is the predominant pattern. However, oddly enough, most women patients manifesting this conscious desire-fear pattern rarely volunteer the matter in therapy, either because they accept their sexuality as an inevitable fate or because they are struggling with denial efforts. Careful questioning of all young women patients to discern this conscious ambivalence pattern is of great importance. It can be predicted that a woman harboring the conscious desire to become pregnant is very probably going to succeed, provided the desire is not outweighed by the conscious fear component in the ambivalent conflict. Conversely, if the conscious fear predominates she will probably succeed in avoiding pregnancy. However, if the positive and negative forces carry equal intensity, this becomes a determinant in itself. In other words, the patient is likely to relieve herself of the intolerable tension fomented by the conscious ambivalence struggle by "going over the hill" and becoming pregnant. Keep in mind, all the while, that there are always unconscious forces operating that complicate prediction.

The existence of unconscious desires and fears (pattern D) requires very thorough fact-finding and mental examination to discern. The existence of this unconscious conflict is easily overlooked. The pseudoneurotic schizophrenic patient not only employs mechanisms of defense against the return of repressed ideation and affect connected with sexual reproduction—denial, displacement, reaction formation, and so forth—but often manifests massive "blocking," which serves to protect her against otherwise overwhelming anxiety connected with the chaotic concepts of sexuality involved.

Naturally, the desire-fear ambivalence struggle festering below the patient's level of awareness foments enormous tension because of her inability to deal with any of the impulse components. Keep in mind that the schizophrenic cannot cope with tension and is particularly prone to releasing it through impulsive behavior. This acting out can occur in any life area—including the sexual—for which the patient may convincingly rationalize, thus complicating the issue even further. Actually, should pregnancy result from acting out, the tension promoted by the unconscious ambivalence forces is only relieved temporarily. Resurgence of tension occurs, because the unconscious conflict connected with pregnancy remains unresolved. Had the therapist not recognized the unconscious conflict nor anticipated the sexual acting out, he is now obligated to deal with the patient's anxiety connected with her pregnant status.

From the viewpoint of prevention, the therapist cannot expect to elicit the patient's unconscious attitudes and motivations directly, and therefore he must seek this data by indirect means, namely, by investigating her attitudes, feelings, and behavior toward men; her confusion about sexuality; and also her confusion about self identity, which may disclose feelings of "emptiness" or "contamination." And, of course, indirect clues are often afforded by examining the patient's dreams. There are many clues that can be picked up, as we shall soon discuss.

The coexistence of conscious desires and unconscious fears (pattern E) is extremely prevalent among neurotic as well as schizophrenic women, and is usually compounded by social pressures. For instance, a woman may consciously desire a baby to please members of her family, yet unconsciously equate pregnancy with death, or maternity with life entrapment. A patient in whom this ambivalence configuration is predominant is likely to find herself infertile. For one thing, unconsciously held fears of pregnancy (or maternity) seemingly influence the thalamic, hypothalamic, and pituitary axis and inhibit follicle-stimulating hormone production, causing an anovulatory cycle (McFalls, 1979, pp. 103-120). Physiological defenses can also include uterine tubal spasm, or early spontaneous abortion. Women suffering from this ambivalence struggle swamp infertility clinics, pleading for help. Their gynecologists relish the challenge; they employ specialized skills to crash through the patient's psychophysiological blockades with hormonal "weapons" such as Clomid® or Pergonal® , X-ray stimulation to the ovaries and pituitary, tubal insufflation, and, of course, tranquilizers and sedatives. This is often successful and, provided the patient's husband maintains adequately mature sperm production or is not rendered impotent by being treated as a "stud," the woman is "forced" to become pregnant, and perhaps then protected from spontaneously aborting by periodic progesterone injections. Of course, many women who manifest this ambivalence pattern need no such heroic measures in order to become pregnant. Interestingly enough, women indoctrinated by certain religious or ethical systems emphasizing fertility as an acceptance requirement rarely suffer "psychological" infertility.

It has been medically documented, however, that women who unconsciously fear pregnancy are more likely than the average to suffer complications during pregnancy and are more susceptible than the average woman to develop pre-eclampsia and eclampsia, as well as to have prolonged and difficult deliveries. For instance, it is common knowledge that tension due to fear and apprehension delays cervical dilation during labor and that these women respond to uterine contractions by countercontractions of pelvic floor musculature, which cause resistance and prolong the first stage of labor. This is also prevalent among women harboring unconscious fears of childbirth per se, or those who fear the ensuing maternal role.

Obviously, preventive psychotherapy is clearly preferable to therapy initiated after the patient becomes pregnant. However, therapy initiated after the fact that aims to resolve the unconscious unrealistic fears may enable an uncomplicated delivery and a smooth postpartum course. It is also true that when the patient's conscious desire for pregnancy is sufficiently strong to override an existing unconscious fear of childbirth itself, delivery may be uneventful and her success may serve to dissolve unrealistic fears in future deliveries. When a woman's "psychological" infertility is connected to an unconscious fear of assuming the maternal role, she is quite likely to become fertile soon after adopting a baby. This event is so commonplace it needs no documentation. Seemingly, upon realizing her competence in coping with the maternal role, her heretofore unconscious fears diminish. Such a favorable response cannot be relied upon, however: Many women who suffer this ambivalence pattern struggle with great anxiety when attempting to cope in their maternal role.

The coexistence of unconscious desires and conscious fears (pattern F) is very important to recognize because when predominant in a patient, she is usually as "fertile as a manure pile," as one patient lamented. Consciously fearing pregnancy, an intelligent and informed patient will employ one, or more than one, available contraceptive measure—or play a strict game of "Vatican roulette" if religiously so restricted—but is likely to become pregnant despite all. Her unconscious motivations overrule her conscious fears: She somehow is "careless" or forgetful in guarding herself against pregnancy.

When such a woman becomes pregnant, her conscious fears may lead her to obtain an abortion, yet she is likely to again become pregnant. She may have repeated pregnancies and repeated abortions, unable to understand why no contraception "works." All the while, the reliability of its application is sabotaged by her unconscious motivation for pregnancy. Moreover, women with this ambivalence conflict who carry pregnancy to term are likely to continue to reproduce—despite any economic, social, health, or other deterring contraindications—for so long as the unconscious desire to reproduce remains.

One tends to assume that unwanted pregnancies are accidental, but we must realize that such "accidents" are largely determined by unconscious motivations. Many pregnancies result following the unreliable use of prescribed contraceptives: Perhaps the woman's judgment is silenced during sexual arousal, or while intoxicated by a drug such as alcohol, or when told by her sexual partner that he is "sterile" (a common trick), and so forth. In such cases, one obviously must explore the role played by unconscious motivation.

It is nevertheless true that there are pregnancies that occur purely accidentally; no contraceptive measures, even when reliably applied, are 100% reliable, with the exception of successfully performed tubal closures. A pregnancy can be considered purely accidental also when a woman has been sexually victimized on the basis of extreme ignorance, mental retardation, gross overt psychosis, or when secretly drugged. Pregnancy as a result of rape is purely accidental, for instance, when a woman is assaulted by a singularly dangerous and armed assailant or by a group of overpowering men. On the other hand, there are women who are raped, and in some cases repeatedly raped, as a result of "poor judgment" in their behavior. Some of these women are unconscious of a seductive quality in their walk or attire, or are sexually provocative verbally, all of which connote forms of unconscious solicitation based on one or another psychodynamic factors.

From the viewpoint of therapeutic prevention, however, it is safer for us to assume that purely accidental pregnancy is quite rare: The forces of unconscious motivation are powerful determinants. Here again, preventive psychotherapy aims to resolve conscious unrealistic fears of pregnancy while simultaneously exploring the realistic and unrealistic components of the patient's unconscious desires before she becomes pregnant. The therapist should meanwhile encourage her to reliably employ contraceptive measures by alerting her to the tendency for unconscious self-sabotage.

Obviously, the above-mentioned ambivalence configurations are condensed and oversimplified; they omit mention of many possible prediction factors and preventive therapeutic approaches. Actually, ambivalence in schizophrenia can be so massive as to include the gamut of configurations involving sexual reproduction. Patterns may change in intensity in response to endocrine factors and to external stimuli, all of which can influence shifts in sexual attitudes and motivations. A patient's integrative impairment may cause repressive mechanisms to fluctuate, and occasionally unconscious desires and fears float to the conscious level to either augment or cancel conscious forces. Such possibilities naturally interfere with accuracy of prediction and lead to a quandary in treatment approach.

When an astute therapist discovers a potpourri of all-inclusive ambivalence patterns in a patient, it does not imply that he must tackle every sexual ambivalence problem immediately, or that such attempts are feasible. After all, patients will suffer problems quite unrelated to conflicts over sexual reproduction that may also require immediate and

ongoing attention. Nonetheless, it is important to make some prediction regarding those sexual ambivalence patterns that are predominant
and to deal with them therapeutically before the patient acts on them
in ways disruptive to her future adaptation. In other words, treatment
must be tailor-made in accordance with each patient's most serious and
urgent conflicts.

CLINICAL MANIFESTATIONS OF SEXUAL
REPRODUCTION CONFLICTS AND
DYNAMIC PROCESSES

What are the clinical manifestations of a schizophrenic woman's pathological ambivalence conflicts concerning her sexual reproduction?
What dynamic processes are involved and what treatment approaches
are indicated? In order to answer these questions, we must first explore
the schizodynamic mechanisms underlying the evolution of the clinical
signs and symptoms. Figure 15-2 schematizes the schizodynamic mechanisms (upper half of chart) that are the empirical bases for the signs
and symptoms of pathological ambivalence involving sexual reproduction (lower half).

At the core of her sexual conflict, the schizophrenic woman suffers
a so-called nebulous ego boundary. Occasionally a patient will express
this by stating, "I feel empty inside," or will tell you, "Something is
missing but I don't know what it is." Be alert to the possibility that the
patient's desperate need to find her sense of self may unconsciously
motivate her to become "fulfilled" by means of constructing a symbolic
self.

Confusion with regard to bodily integrity and functioning in schizophrenia is compounded by confusion as to what is concrete and what
is abstract. Not only are self and non-self ill-defined, but there is also
confusion between sexual and nonsexual components and functioning.
For instance, the schizophrenic tends to sexualize a concretized concept of self: A fetus may unconsciously serve as a symbolic representation of "ego." At the same time, however, the existence of the fetus may
also stir up the patient's anxiety connected with the disintegrative process, as it can represent a destructive "foreign body" such as a cancer-
ous growth that feeds on its host.

This exemplifies how pathological distortions of reality concerning
sexual reproduction have dynamic influence on the desire-fear ambivalence pattern in schizophrenia. In other words, the autistic-dereistic
processes superimposed on the confusion and anxiety influence the
ambivalence concerning sexual reproductive functions. Confusion and

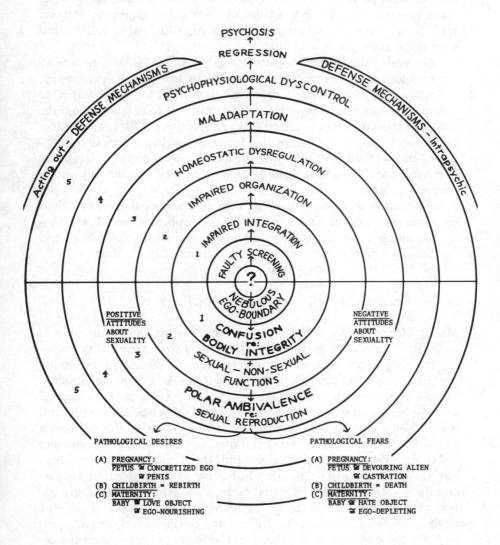

Figure 15-2. SCHIZODYNAMIC MECHANISMS UNDERLYING AMBIVALENCE
CONCERNING SEXUAL REPRODUCTION IN WOMEN

mounting anxiety also play a large role in fomenting great tension, which, in turn, compounds the existing dysregulation of responses, so that attitudes and motivations connected with sexuality swing to ambivalent polar extremes. On the one hand, sex is viewed as "good"; it is imbued with pleasure; it is synonymous with love. On the other hand, sex is viewed as "evil"; it is a form of destructive aggression imbued with pain. Thus, the schizophrenic woman will harbor antithetical unrealistic concepts of sexuality.

The ambivalence conflict between desires and fears may involve all sex components and functions connected to intercourse, pregnancy, childbirth, and maternity. This is very important for the therapist to recognize from the viewpoint of preventive medicine. During the course of therapy, clues pointing to aspects of this conflict can at times be gleaned, directly or indirectly, from the patient's verbal productions. And (at the risk of sounding paranoid) it is far more preferable to overread than to overlook possible clues whenever treating any young woman patient.

We shall now briefly exemplify some of the clinical clues and their dynamic evolution in the context of the schizophrenic patient's pathological ambivalence conflicts concerning pregnancy, childbirth, and maternity. A treatment approach can thereupon be outlined.

Pathological Desire vs. Fear Concerning Pregnancy

Many schizophrenic patients are vaguely aware that something is basically wrong; that something is missing in their personality make-up. Inability to define it compounds their anxiety. Yet, upon becoming pregnant these feelings often are dissipated. As I have mentioned, when a young woman patient remarks to you, "I feel empty, hollow," or complains that something is missing in her psychological structure, it could be a clue handed to you on a platter that for this woman a fetus somehow represents "ego fulfillment"; that the symbol becomes the thing. (With this possibility in mind, the therapist should continually check the patient's reliability in her use of contraception and ascertain the status of her menstrual cycles.) In such case, seemingly the fact of pregnancy serves as a compensatory mechanism of defense against psychotic pan-anxiety. The woman begins to feel content, perhaps for the first time in her life, and the feeling of contentment may continue throughout the course of her pregnancy.

The physiological changes brought about by pregnancy normally have a beneficial influence on a woman's vegetative homeostasis. The "ego fulfillment" phenomenon can occur on a psychodynamic basis as well. The patient's pan-anxiety and symptoms connected with it may almost become subclinical. When this occurs, the psychiatrist may forget having observed any indisputable signs of the nebulous ego structure, although they had been obvious prior to the patient's pregnancy. Observing that the patient now relates quite rationally and calmly, he may conclude that she merely suffers from a mild neurosis, after all! To the therapist's dismay, however, pan-anxiety and related symptoms of schizophrenia resurge sooner or later during the patient's postpartum period, perhaps ushered in by severe depression (Normand, 1967).

Unrealistic motivations can also appear in the framework of neurotic dynamic mechanisms in pseudoneurotic schizophrenia. The patient's desire for pregnancy can be an expression of conscious or unconscious competitiveness with a sibling or with the mother, or it can be an expression of penis-envy, for example. On a conscious level, it is well known that a woman may purposefully become pregnant to "hook" a man or to consolidate a marriage. Some women desire pregnancy to alleviate guilt for a past abortion or miscarriage. Women also seek pregnancy in attempting to prove female adequacy—just as some men measure their masculinity in terms of their ability to impregnate women.

Now, the same schizophrenic patients who present clues indicating a desire for pregnancy also may furnish clues indicating a fear of pregnancy. Perhaps a patient will state, "I fear I'm falling apart; that I'll go to pieces!" Although this may simply be a valid expression of her fear of losing control of her mind, it may also indicate a deep-rooted inexplicable fear of some disorganizing force operating within her body. It is common for a schizophrenic individual to displace a lurking fear of mental disintegration over to a lesser fear: That of a tangible physical disintegration. It is natural to fear an enemy that is concealed in darkness more than one that can be concretely measured. Thus, by means of displacement, a pregnancy could carry the connotation of physical pathology. As an additional mechanism of defense, the patient who unconsciously equates a fetus with a destructive alien force may further displace this ideation and express all manner of hypochondriacal fears. Perhaps she will fear a devouring tumor in her stomach, in her brain, or wherever, which will drain away her strength and eat her up. One of the many dynamic hypotheses concerning anorexia nervosa relates to a distorted body image as well as a displaced fear of pregnancy with the attitude, "If I eat, I am aggressive, and something evil will grow in my stomach." The same displacement sometimes applies to psychotic obsessions and compulsions involving fears of disease from dirt and germs. Patients' dream content often offers similar symbolic expressions of pregnancy fear.

Although the idea that pregnancy is somatically destructive relates to the schizodynamic concept that sexuality connotes violence and aggression, the fear is often compounded by "common knowledge" dealt to the patient over the years by the social environment, namely, that pregnancy destroys a woman's figure, rots her teeth, and generally robs her of her youth, vitality, and perhaps of her life. Here, treatment should include reeducation to sexual "facts of life."

Pathological Desire vs. Fear Concerning Childbirth

Although making no mention of sexual matters in interviews, a patient may suddenly profess, "Doctor, I'm joining a religious group; it provides rebirth through Jesus." You do not have to be very paranoid to recognize the possible significance of the metaphor: Childbirth is dereistically equated with rebirth. In other words, the patient harbors an unconscious desire to "give birth" to the concretized self in the form of a baby. However, should you in fact open up the subject of her sexual aims, this same patient may respond, "I'm afraid to ever have a baby." Or, "My mother almost died when I was born." Actually, the fact that morbidity and mortality as a result of childbirth do occur on rare occasions enables the hypochondriacal, hypersuggestible schizophrenic patient to rationalize her defensive, irrational fear of childbirth. This complex-bound thinking can be so conditioned in a patient that reeducating her to accept correct positive realities concerning the normal sexual reproductive process requires therapeutic perseverance in resolving the underlying ego-integration conflict.

Pathological Desire vs. Fear
Concerning the Maternal Role

Unless her pathological attitude toward motherhood is dealt with in therapy, a schizophrenic patient is likely to act on an unconscious desire for rebirth by becoming pregnant, carrying the conceptus to term, and nurturing the "new self." Such a woman perhaps will have told you, "Ever since I was a little girl I have wanted a baby," or, "When I have a baby I'll give it everything I had been denied in life." Actually, many neurotic women are similarly motivated on a different dynamic basis. Both the neurotic and the schizophrenic woman may suffer low self-esteem traceable to early maternal deprivation. However, in schizophrenia, deep feelings of inadequacy are based on integrative impairment. Therefore, if therapy aims at the schizophrenic's neurotic dynamics—even though they may seem valid—it cannot enable her to resolve her unrealistic desire for a baby because her inherent defect prevents her from ever fully gratifying her emotional need to be a complete self. She not only will continue to equate a baby with a "new self," but will be obsessively motivated to make it a successful self. Undertaking the maternal role might assuage her feelings of futility and personal failure—but only temporarily. In the maturational process, no child could meet her magical expectations for self-perfection; after a time her sense of failure will be compounded. In her ambivalence, her feelings toward her child will swing to the negative pole.

Incidentally, one of the dynamic processes underlying the so-called battered child syndrome includes a woman's search for a sense of self by means of her baby's unqualified love for her. Many such women partially identify with their once-battering mother in the need to hold complete control over the completely dependent baby. The mother attempts to maintain this control in an autistic-dereistic manner. For instance, she will interpret her baby's smile as: "He loves me!" and thereupon her maternal response is stimulated. However, when the baby cries it will mean to her, "He doesn't love me; he rejects me!" and this so-called narcissistic threat inhibits her maternal response. In anger, she "punishes" the baby for its unpardonable sin, whereupon the baby responds with additional crying. Feeling a loss of control over the love-object compounds her anger. She becomes increasingly punitive, moreover, because the helpless baby's responses provoke her guilt feelings. Over a period of time a vicious circle becomes established. In some cases, the mother's ensuing angry rejection of the baby leads her to finally batter the poor little creature to a pulp—an increasingly popular indoor sport among mentally ill mothers in our overpopulated and sociopathic current society.

Another basis for the pathological desire for a baby stems from a great sense of loneliness suffered by so many schizophrenic individuals. Time and time again a schizophrenic patient will lament, "I am unable to sustain close relationships; I feel unloved and unlovable; I am terribly lonely!" This could indeed clue you to her unconsciously equating a baby with an unqualifying love-object, and the urge to put all her love into one bassinet in order to gratify a symbiotic love-dependency need. Obviously, a baby cannot magically solve her lifelong loneliness problem, which is dynamically prefaced on an impairment of her ability to attain or sustain social contact. Incidentally, many teenaged unwed mothers, whose numbers have reached epidemic proportion, fall into this category. All may go fairly well in the mother-baby relationship for as long as the symbiotic bond is strong, but as the maturing child develops increasing autonomy, the mother's expectations crumble; her sense of loneliness is revisited along with growing resentment and rejection of the child.

During the course of therapy, many schizophrenic women present subtle clues indicating predominant fears of assuming a maternal role. Of course, denial of the fear is a common defense maneuver supported by social pressures, mainly the idea that the universal experience of motherhood is a demand she is expected to meet. Occasionally, however, one encounters women patients who overtly dislike children, and in whom all maternal drive is repressed. Such attitudes are often conditioned by sibling conflicts during childhood, or are perhaps due to partial identification with a sado-masochistic mother who cultivated the patient's guilt for having caused her a life of frustration and suffering. Oftentimes for the emotionally deprived patient, children represent hateful rivals as well as enslaving tyrants.

In schizophrenia, a woman's conscious dislike for children can be traced to a much deeper dynamic issue: Considerable autism is involved. Absorbed in anxious defense of her fragile self, she can ill-afford the luxury of experiencing maternal love. For her, there can be no pleasure connected with the maternal role. A baby is viewed as an ego-threat: It is controlling and renders its mother a helpless slave (Benedek, 1959); it is an oral-aggressive creature who victimizes its mother and "sucks her dry." It is understandable that for such a woman the protracted responsibilities connected with the maternal role are intolerable. Even the simplest tasks involved in child care provoke intense anxiety and rage.

Such a schizophrenic woman, especially if untreated, may "accidentally" become pregnant and have a child, or have more than one, depending on her patterns of ambivalence conflict. In attempts to repress hostile feelings for her child, she may exemplify the overprotective mother (Levy, 1943). She may develop a pattern of maternal overindulgence. Or, she may become a compulsive mother obsessed with fears that the child will get hurt, sick, or will die from a terrible disease. These fears may be punctuated by sudden irrational ideations and impulses—to cut the baby's fingers when clipping its nails, or to toss the baby in the incinerator, and so forth. The masked schizophrenic does not yield to such impulses, but may suffer haunting guilty fears of doing so. Trapped in ambivalence conflict of feelings in her relationship to the child—love and hate; fear and rage—the mother will very likely project these feelings onto the child, and in a matter of time the child's anxiety reactions to her double messages will thus compound the mother's stress, with which she is already unable to adaptively cope.

The maternal role is feared by many women insofar as it interferes with, prevents, or nullifies a gratifying career. However, for many a patient this is a rationalization of the fact that her so-called career exists in fantasy only. Perhaps the fantasy arose out of a desire to escape maternal responsibility. Perhaps the woman lacks true potential for achieving progress in any area of interest, or lacks ability to consistently sustain an effort toward any goal. The typically schizophrenic all-or-none concept that a person must become an outstanding success or else is a nobody may also block her strivings. Yet, she may continue to fantasy success in a career because she looks with disdain upon becoming "only a mother," especially if she is confused about her female identity.

There are a great many other dynamic features in the syndromes mentioned, which give rise to conscious and unconscious desire-fear ambivalence patterns. It is the therapist's task to explore and recognize those that are realistic and unrealistic, predominant and subsidiary, in all matters related to the patient's sexual reproduction.

Treatment of Sexual Reproduction Ambivalence Conflicts

The appropriate treatment approach for women who manifest unrealistic attitudes and motivations in any aspect of sexual reproduction requires recognition of the ambivalence patterns involved. These must be determined early in treatment and the predominant conflicts must be given priority of attention. Their significance for her future adaptation must be delineated for the patient. How the unrealistic patterns evolved must be interpreted to her; their derivations must be traced to the ways in which the schizodynamic mechanisms interacted with early environmental conditioning. Mainly, the ambivalence struggle needs to be interpreted as it relates to the patient's anxiety structure and underlying self-esteem conflict.

The importance of supporting the patient's shaky self-esteem with positive interpretive reinforcement cannot be overemphasized. In the remedial process of reeducating a patient to reality about sexuality and body image, keep in mind that simple facts which are common knowledge to most people are often received as "big news" to the schizophrenic. The therapeutic task is to reeducate the patient to the reality of her self, its sexual and nonsexual aspects. Confusion and conditioned misconceptions about her sexual integrity and functions must be resolved. She must be made aware of her areas of integrative assets as well as liabilities in the context of her ability to cope with all aspects of sexuality, including the maternal role. The realistic pleasures to be expected as well as the problems involved in the maternal career often must be elucidated for her. When her sexual reproductive ambivalence conflicts are resolved, the woman is able to decide whether or not to become pregnant, at what time, and under what realistic circumstances, so that she can aim toward goals appropriate to her abilities, desires, and needs.

Another point is worthy of mention. Occasionally, one encounters a schizophrenic woman who fears pregnancy for the valid reason that she is aware of her actual limitations, causing her to feel inadequate to cope with the stresses involved in the maternal role. Provided the therapist also recognizes that her integrative impairment realistically justifies her fears, he is able to offer her constructive support. Here, it is essential to bolster her self-esteem. Whether schizophrenic or not, a woman's recognition of an existing psychological inadequacy to function adaptively in the basic biological role of maternity deals a monumental blow to her female pride. To say the least, it severely compounds her existing feelings of inferiority. Thereupon, the therapist must play a very active role in counteracting these feelings with every possible realistic means of support at his professional disposal.

An important preliminary supportive measure is to turn the patient's sense of failure into a sense of pride in successfully facing her handicap and dealing with it realistically and adaptively. She can be helped to recognize that, in her particular case, decision to forego motherhood proves her strength of judgment. Furthermore, the therapist can lead the patient forth to cite examples of successful well-adapted women who have chosen to limit childbearing or forego it (depending on the patient's case), for valid reasons comparable to those posed by the patient. In the continuing course of therapy, the patient can then be influenced to explore her areas of interests, talents, and available opportunities with the aim of appropriately developing compensatory sources of gratification and fulfillment. It is often not difficult to encourage a schizophrenic patient to appreciate that her mind is "superior" to that of other mammals because of the human capacity for symbolic creativity; that the human female has the unique ability to be much *more* than simply biologically creative.

When employing such remedial measures, it is important that the therapist keep keenly in mind the values and interests of the patient as well as her integrative potentials. In other words, watch the patient's transference! The patient must not be allowed to ingratiatingly espouse what she may consider the therapist's values, interests, or talents: She must be shown respect and appreciation for those characteristics that are hers alone. Naturally, this moves the patient toward developing a realistic sense of self. Because the quantity and quality of compensatory potentials vary markedly among patients—whether in areas of scientific research, talent in the fine arts, needlepoint, culinary skills, or whatever—it is essential that the patient choose to strive in a direction in keeping with her own experiences, preferences, and abilities. In any event, she must not be pushed to aim too high, nor encouraged to aim too low. Furthermore, one must tacitly encourage the patient's feelings of pride along with every step she takes toward success in this remedial process.

It is imperative to realize that, no matter how handicapped with psychosis or no matter how strongly a woman may deny having maternal feelings, the biological drive to sexually reproduce is indelible and exists in all women on the conscious or unconscious level. When this drive is thwarted, some psychophysiological reverberations are bound to result, even though sometimes they are subtle and indirectly manifested. This becomes apparent when the woman approaches middle age, particularly for the one who must come face to face with the fact she has not borne, and is no longer able to bear, children. Therefore, in treating a young woman patient who determines not to bear children for one or another adaptive reason, the therapist must endeavor to pave the way for her emotional acceptance of the fact of her biological "failure" by conditioning her to appreciate her past and current areas of "success," so that eventual menopause will not provoke a depressive reaction, anxiety, bitter rage, or other manifestations of grief and frustration.

In summary: Every woman harbors ambivalent attitudes and motivations concerning her sexual reproduction. These are rarely presented as complaints. Acting out is more likely to occur—often to the detriment of the patient and society. Preventive medicine requires that the therapist conduct four simultaneous procedures whenever commencing to treat women in their fertile years:

1. Apprise the patient of a basic psychotherapeutic rule, namely, that she make no life-altering decisions, including that of pregnancy, until her main conflicts are explored and sufficiently resolved.

2. Influence the patient to employ reliable contraceptive precautions early in treatment and to keep the therapist informed of her monthly menstrual cycles.

3. Make early and continuous search for attitudes and motivations

concerning all aspects of sexual reproduction; make predictive evaluation of predominant pathological ambivalence patterns and deal with them therapeutically.

4. Aim therapy to constructively exploit the patient's self-interest motivations by affording her an increment of insight into benefits to be accrued by adaptive, rather than maladaptive, sexual behavior.

In conclusion, I would like to point out that all people (including therapists) are self-interest motivated in everything they do. I refer to Masserman's (1968, pp. 251-261) First Principle of Biodynamics, "Motivation: The behavior of all organisms is actuated by physiological needs." On the psychophysiological level, this is translated to mean that the behavior of all individuals is actuated by psychophysiological needs—in other words, egocentricity.

By appealing to this indelible biological fact of egocentricity, we motivate patients away from self-injurious behavior and toward self-beneficial behavior, including sexual behavior. Therefore, a therapist is best able to influence human motivations by affording patients insight into ways and means for adaptively serving their self-interests, present and future. In the matter of a woman's ambivalence concerning her sexual reproduction, as in other life matters, the pendulum swings in response to self-interests as they are felt or perceived. The therapist aims to influence the patient's emotional attitudes by affording her insight into the fact that her greatest self-interest benefits are to be gained from adaptive rather than maladaptive sexual reproductive behavior.

CHAPTER 16

The Social Contact-Withdrawal Conflict

The pattern of withdrawal from interpersonal relationships alternating with a breakthrough in effort to make emotional contact is well known in schizophrenia. For some patients, this intermittent symptom pattern is very problematic and requires intensive therapeutic attention; for other patients it occurs but is not disruptive; and for others it may occur to such a mild extent that it is difficult to clinically discern. When the contact-withdrawal symptom pattern is predominant and disruptive, one observes the schizophrenic all-or-none ambivalence policy operating. The patient will vacillate—over a period of weeks or months—from an extreme state of passive withdrawal to aggressive and hectic contact with the environment. Such repetitive ambivalent actions can, of course, markedly interfere with the patient's adaptation in all life areas, when allowed to continue untreated.

In dynamic terms, the extent of the ambivalent contact-withdrawal swings are largely determined by the patient's regulative impairment. The schizodynamic mechanism is based on the inherent integrative impairment, which gives rise to confusion in the individual's perception of reality concerning the self in relationship to the social environment. Thus, responding to internal and external stimuli in a dysregulative manner, the individual gets into situations whereby he makes a great many "mistakes" when attempting to relate to the social environment. He realizes he is somehow inadequate; he feels it very strongly. He recognizes that somehow he is unacceptable, and becomes convinced of an inferiority, which he cannot clearly define in the morass of ego-confusion.

Suffering with the ever-present anxious anticipation of rejection, the schizophrenic patient grows hypersensitive, manifesting a keen ability to pick up minimal clues of negative reactions from the environment. Autism and dereism compound anxiety, and the hypersensitive individual misinterprets the behavior of those around him in always self-referential and negative terms. Extraordinary tensions develops over a period of time due to the great anxiety the individual experiences in all efforts to relate to people. All the while, such a schizophrenic carries the tacit assumption that he alone suffers; that everybody else is confident, happy, and adjusts competently in interpersonal relationships. (It is no small wonder that when Christmas bells are ringing, the psychiatrist's schedule is full: These schizophrenic patients react to greetings of "Merry Christmas!" and songs of joy and goodwill toward men with feelings of terrible isolation, loneliness, and resultant depression.)

Tension and frustration mount to an excruciating peak at those times when the individual reaches an extreme point in either the contact or withdrawal phase of the ambivalence swing. It is, in fact, the schizophrenic patient's inability to tolerate tension and feelings of frustration that triggers into motion the ambivalent turnabout reaction whereby the pendulum begins its swing away from one pole toward the opposite pole. The recurrent dynamic pattern is schematized in Figure 16-1.

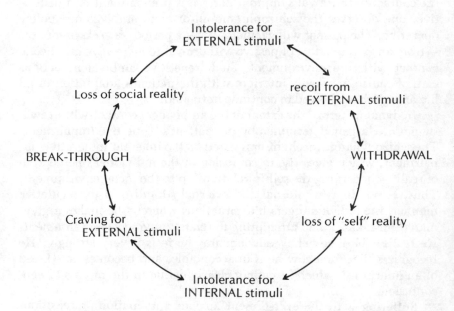

Figure 16-1. THE CONTACT-WITHDRAWAL CYCLE IN SCHIZOPHRENIA.

The course of events can be clinically described as follows. At some point in time the schizophrenic individual suffers intolerable tension and frustration connected with attempts to cope with external stimuli. The anxious individual has perhaps suffered increasing conflict with many people on the job or socially. He feels an urgent need to recoil from all efforts to continue environmental relationships. The urge to withdraw has become acute and in interview he complains, "I cannot tolerate any contacts with people; I feel irritable; I have to get away from it all!" So, he withdraws.

He chooses to remain at home, perhaps in his room all day, or perhaps he moves around his home area but avoids all social contacts. In the craving to be alone he states, "I hate it when the phone rings; why do people have to bother me!" He may offer his therapist reasons for canceling appointments. Of course, it is very important at this time for the therapist to insist that regular contact be maintained in therapy. He should explain to the patient, "I understand your need to be left alone, but you are troubled and I cannot help you unless I see you." Otherwise, the patient's withdrawal will compound his suffering, due to an ensuing bombardment of internal stimuli.

While in the state of extreme withdrawal, the schizophrenic patient initially may attempt to glean some amount of self-gratification by means of hobbies or particular work interests. In a matter of time, however, he begins to feel bored and complains of difficulty concentrating and a lack of sustained interest in anything. A growing sense of isolation gives rise to an inexorable feeling of loneliness—much more profound than that ever experienced in neuroses. Deprived of external stimuli, after a time the confused schizophrenic becomes hypersensitive to, and disorganized by, internal stimuli.

A feeling of detachment develops. Episodes of depersonalization occur with increasing frequency and the patient will tell you, "Everything seems unreal; it is as though nothing is alive, not even me." In other words, the sense of self, or so-called ego-identity—nebulous to begin with in schizophrenia—becomes lost when the patient is deprived of human contact. The individual lacks a "point of reference" with which to gauge the self; there is nobody to serve as an "ego-mirror." The patient now feels a burst of relief when the phone rings, and will tell you, "I'm glad when the delivery boy comes to the door; it is nice to talk with someone." Sometimes the patient actually feels as though he is disintegrating; in a sense, this is happening. Trapped in the chaos of internal stimuli, the patient often broods over the futility of life with feelings of despair, exclaiming, "What is the use; what is the use!" Thus, depression grows out of the anxiety in the isolated schizophrenic individual, punctuated by irritability, impatience, and self-intolerance.

Flooded with internal stimuli, the patient appears very tense and feels unbearably frustrated. In order to break away from intolerable inner sources of tension, the individual begins to crave external sources of tension. He may express a need for exciting stimulation, stating, "I must see some movies that are full of violence and murder—to make me feel alive again." In the drive to make contact with external reality, an increasing urge to seek human contact develops. Paradoxical as it may appear, the patient now experiences an excessive craving for environmental stimuli from which he had formerly withdrawn—in order to escape the intolerable internal stimuli currently suffered. The pendulum thus begins its swing toward the opposite pole.

The patient may break through and relate to the environment quite precipitously with frenetic effort to make human contacts. However, in an effort to quell pan-anxiety the patient is likely to prime his courage with one or more drugs of choice—marijuana, "uppers," "downers," and especially alcohol. These people one always can find frequenting pubs, drinking it up and whooping it up; or they crash somebody's wild party and will appear to have a marvelous time of it while making very superficial contact with those around them. If the patient is a woman, she is likely to accept free drinks and will sleep with her bene-factor or anyone else who gives her friendly attention. The schizo-phrenic patient desperately craves acceptance and, starved for love, will concede to sometimes bizarre requests in efforts to attain some modicum of sensational social satisfaction.

Meanwhile, having broken through the isolation barrier, you may find the patient misses appointments, or arrives late, telling you he is "terribly busy" or has a hangover, or will give some other excuse. Ac-tually, the patient may be quite busy searching for work or catching up in his work, if he is able to return to his job. In social contacts, the pa-tient may initially function quite affably on a superficial level. How-ever, the honeymoon does not last long.

In a matter of time, the schizophrenic patient runs into the prob-lem of contact impairment. The patient is rigid and inflexible. In re-sponse to people he overreacts and underreacts. His judgment is poor: He overestimates and underestimates situations and people. Of course, he has difficulty relating on an affective level and, confusing assertion with aggression, is prone to attacking others for assumed hostility or rejection on their part. For instance, he will react in a defensively ag-gressive way, without recognizing the particular social situation realis-tically required pleasant assertion. Such a patient senses that somehow his social behavior is unacceptable, but is unable to understand why and will complain, "People accuse me of acting hostile, yet when I cor-rect myself and sit passively, they tell me I'm a party-spoiler, so I never know what I'm supposed to do." Tension and feelings of frustration mount.

Many schizophrenic patients manifest the "chameleon syndrome" in desperation to "belong." The patient may recount to you, "I try to show interest in politics (or art, business, philosophy, gourmet cooking —whatever interest characterizes the group) but, when I try to share my opinions, people turn away or look at me askance." Of course, if the patient manifests dereistic thinking, social contact breaks down because he is unable to hold to the conversational points. Sometimes, however, the chameleon act serves well for a time when the patient comes in contact with his own kind. Actually, the schizophrenic has an affinity for other schizophrenics and a bunch of pseudophilosophers can have quite a nice time together. I know one patient who sat up almost a whole night discussing with friends the weighty matter of whether it is easier to love or to hate.

Unfortunately, however, those schizophrenic individuals who feign a role in attempting to "belong" end up rejected and frustrated, mainly due to contact impairment. Confused as to what other people think and feel and why they react the way they do, the patient may take a lot of drinks in an attempt to allay anxiety, only to compound the inevitable contact impairment.

In a matter of time, the patient finds himself unable to cope with the stimulation from the environment he had formerly so craved. Even brief and benign interpersonal contacts flood him with anxiety. Feeling tense and very frustrated, he becomes edgy and irritable—especially toward people who seemingly enjoy gratifying interpersonal contacts. Acutely aware that such gratifications are beyond his reach, the patient feels left out, hurt, and will lament, "I cannot continue this effort any longer; everything I do causes me trouble." The patient has moved in full cycle from withdrawal to contact, and now begins again to recoil from the environment.

When treating patients who manifest the ambivalence pattern of excessive contact alternating with extreme withdrawal, the therapist's timing is of utmost importance. The two preferable times for therapeutic intervention are while the patient moves at one or the other intermediate points in the cycle between the ambivalent extremes of either contact or withdrawal. This cannot be overly stressed. Unlike the well-integrated neurotic patient, the schizophrenic is unable to regulate ambivalent responses and become stabilized within the range of reality limitations short of polar extremes. Obviously, when struggling to function while at either ambivalent pole, the patient is least able to relate to the therapist, because of intense anxiety, and the therapist is least able to influence the patient with constructive interpretations. Therefore, therapeutic intervention is required in order to intercept the patient's reactions long before they have extended to an extreme.

Therapeutic approach involves three main aspects: *Preventive intervention, adjustment of medication,* and *interpretive procedures.* We shall briefly discuss these aspects of therapy as used during the intermediate phases of the ambivalence, namely, the period of imminent withdrawal, and the period of imminent breakthrough.

THERAPEUTIC APPROACH DURING THE PERIOD OF IMMINENT WITHDRAWAL

Preventive Intervention

The therapist anticipates the directional trend of the patient's ambivalence by alerting himself to the significance of the patient's verbal and nonverbal expressed attitude and behavior. The astute therapist will not be misled by a schizophrenic patient's bland façade, which sometimes conceals an undercurrent of enormous anxiety and anxiety-related feelings accompanying mounting tension and frustration. The level of these feelings stemming from excessive external stimuli can usually be gauged before the patient commences to act out excessively.

During the period of imminent withdrawal, the patient may show signs of irritability and hostility directed toward the environment. He may wallow in self-pity for assumed or actual hurts and rejection. His self-esteem appears very low. Naturally, should he express a desire to avoid human contacts and be allowed to completely withdraw, he will brood over failures and his self-esteem would be further lowered. However, a certain amount of withdrawal from environmental stress has curative value: It allows the patient to lick his wounds, as it were, during which time the therapist can proffer support and engage the patient in realistic appraisal of his self and the environment.

Feeling defeated, the patient is undoubtedly quite depressed. Severe depression is often averted by counselling the patient to "keep moving!" You want the patient to keep moving in order to prevent his brooding and becoming mired down by internal stimuli. So, you push the patient, but you do not want to push too hard and you are careful to mobilize the patient in an appropriate direction. Naturally, you do not attempt to steer your patient back to the stage of social breakthrough, because he has just been there and can no longer tolerate the external stimuli. Therapy aims to gently, but firmly, nudge the patient to focus on whatever areas of interest and abilities have in the past enhanced any sense of self-worth. He should be encouraged to engage in some type of work or hobby that can be enjoyed in solitude, or requires only objectively held relationships—such as card games, for one good example. Every small step of progress is important and for each step taken the patient should be commended.

The patient should be encouraged to schedule himself somewhat, mainly because unstructured withdrawal causes the schizophrenic individual to become detached due to bombardment by internal stimuli. A not-too-rigid routine of "doing something" offsets the patient's tendency to view himself as a "nothing." Even slight daily accomplishments not only reduce tension but also afford steady doses of self-gratification and counteract frustrations inflicted by the external environment—all serving to moderate the intensity of the patient's withdrawal.

Adjustment of Medication

During the early withdrawal period, the therapist may deem it appropriate to readjust the patient's medication with the aim of reducing the tension, irritability, and anxiety to a level whereby the patient can relate in therapy rather than act out in a negativistic or excessively withdrawing manner. But you do not want to prescribe medication that will make the patient feel dopey or groggy, because that could promote withdrawal and feelings of detachment. The patient is discouraged, so any neuroleptic medication should also aim to elevate his mood and mobilize drive. Yet if you prescribe a stimulant at this time, it might make the patient "climb the wall" by increasing the tension. Perhaps a tricyclic would serve well, alone or in combination with a mild tranquilizer. In other words, medication that lifts the patient's mood while cutting tension and anxiety places the therapist in a favorable position to influence the patient with insights into the dynamic nature of the ambivalence pattern and to begin the process of reeducating the patient to reality concerning the self and interpersonal relationships.

The Interpretive Procedure

The interpretive procedure is, of course, the major part of therapy during the intermediate phase of the ambivalence cycle prior to withdrawal. Allow the patient to fully relate the disruptive symptoms (some of which we have described) and encourage him to connect them with precipitating life events.

Define for the patient the symptoms that he presents. For instance, the patient can perhaps be told, "You are extremely tense, and feel very frustrated in your contacts with people, so now you have an urgent desire to withdraw and avoid these people."

Explain why you focus on these symptoms: "Now you want to remain alone, but in the past when you isolated yourself, your loneliness and brooding put you into a state of confusion"—or mention whatever symptoms seem more relevant. Also, remind the patient that the past withdrawal reactions culminated in breakthrough reactions that perpetuated the vicious circle of suffering. These interpretations clarify for the patient the ambivalence pattern and the reasons why it must be dealt with. In other words, the patient learns that the extremes of withdrawal and breakthrough reactions both foment tension and anxiety symptoms. Of course, the patient requires additional dynamic insight before appreciating that he can do anything about the problem.

Interpret for the patient how the urgent desire for withdrawal evolved from intolerable tension and frustration that developed because of interpersonal conflicts and rejection. Trace the evolution of the resultant anxiety back to the more basic anxiety related to the patient's feelings of inadequacy because of futile attempts to establish interpersonal contacts.

When interpreting the derivative basis for the withdrawal pattern, do so in terms of the patient's particular contact-impairment difficulties. Include the factor of confusion and its dysregulating influence. In other words, the patient needs to understand that as a result of confusion in attempting to relate to people in an "acceptable" manner, anxiety and mounting tension culminate in extreme all-or-none responses to external stimuli—thus compounding the entire conflict.

Naturally, you cannot go so far as to explain that the confusion with regard to the self in its relationship to the environment is based on an innate integrative impairment; the patient would thereupon feel helpless to do anything about it. However, it is important for the patient to grasp an understanding of the relationship between confusion and dysregulation with its all-or-none ambivalent responses. Upon enabling the patient to resolve particular points of confusion, you can more readily influence him to recognize the nature of his contact impairment and in what ways his past reactions toward the environment led to particular conflicts and rejections. The therapist then focuses on teaching the patient how to modify certain of his dysregulated responses and react in a more realistic manner to remedy existing conflicts. Herein lies the great importance of remedial interpretation. All dynamic interpretations must conclude with lessons in self-image reality and the reality of adaptive interpersonal relationships.

No patient is able to act on the basis of reality insights afforded him —nor can he even remember interpretations given him—unless remedial interpretations counteract his negative self-esteem ledger. For this, the patient's realistic assets, including social ones, must be reviewed in the context of each ambivalence and dysregulative problem presented.

Keep in mind that the patient begins to recoil from interpersonal contact because he can no longer tolerate exposure to these external stimuli. He feels terribly inferior and tends to assume that everybody else is competent; that everybody else has importance; that everybody else is successful. And he tends to feel that he alone is unacceptable. In the reeducation process, these all-or-none assumptions must be directly dealt with, over and over again and in many different ways, in the context of the presented problem. Sometimes a hypothetical situation serves to point up the unreality of these assumptions. For example, you can tell him: "When any person is acquainted with 9 people, the chances are that 3 of the 9 will consider him adequate and acceptable, 3 others may feel indifferent about him, and the other 3 may reject him —for realistic or unrealistic reasons of their own." Or, had the patient explained a desire to withdraw because of intolerable anxiety connected with efforts to relate, you might reassure him that, "If there are 9 people in a room, 3 probably suffer no social anxiety, 3 may suffer occasional anxiety, and another 3 may be flooded with anxiety all the time."

Regardless of a therapist's individual interpretive style, the important thing is to teach the patient the Gestalt of various realities concerning human relationships and at the same time aim to correct the patient's penchant for judging himself solely on the basis of rejection by others. It is interesting that the schizophrenic tends to assume that those who judge him negatively are correct and anyone who judges him for positive attributes is either wrong or lying. It is important to remind the patient of such tendencies and how experiences of assumed or actual rejection compound existing contact impairment by further lowering self-esteem and elevating the level of anxiety.

THERAPEUTIC APPROACH DURING THE PERIOD OF IMMINENT BREAKTHROUGH

Preventive Intervention

Sometimes it is difficult to gauge the patient's ambivalent turnabout. Forewarning symptoms are not always clear-cut and the patient's shift can occur with surprising suddenness. For instance, the patient may fail to appear for the next session or two—or even for two or three weeks if he is dipsomaniacal. (Incidentally, quite a number of alcoholic patients manifest this pattern of explosive social contact followed by sudden withdrawal. A therapist would have to be very imprudent not to recognize that treating an alcoholic patient in a one-to-one relationship cannot be efficacious; such patients require some form of group therapeutic involvement, to say the least.)

In any case, an astute therapist carefully perceives signs and symptoms that indicate a patient is on the brink of a breakthrough from environmental withdrawal. The patient is tense, restless, and probably suffers agitated depression. Feelings of detachment and other anxiety-related symptoms may include the patient's fear of "going crazy." A great amount of reassurance is required at this time, and probably more frequent therapeutic sessions.

It is realistic to show empathy for the patient's expressed need for environmental stimulation. However, until you have had an opportunity to give interpretive therapy, you want to avert the patient's impulsivity and importune acting out with social entanglements. You attempt to "steer" the patient toward whatever channels of activity will release tension and ease frustration without causing him to run headlong into the problem of contact impairment. Naturally, the therapist would not suggest, "What you need is close contact with people to get your mind off yourself," any more than he would advise the patient to remain cooped up alone until he has resolved the contact impairment conflict, a task that cannot be accomplished in a vacuum. Thus, the patient can initially be encouraged to approach the environment on a relatively impersonal plane. Going to "horror movies" with a companion or two might serve to gratify the craving for excitement, for instance, but alcoholic "binges" are bound to lead to interpersonal altercations. Early interpretations should aim to avert such acting out.

Adjustment of Medication

Adjustment of medication may also be indicated to lessen the patient's inner tension and prevent impulsive and aggressive acting out. It is first essential to determine whether or not the patient is dosing himself with drugs, because you do not wish to complicate the patient's disordered state by creating untoward synergistic or antagonistic drug reactions. Actually the choice of medication is a matter of common sense. Obviously, the patient should not be taking disinhibiting depressants such as barbiturates and alcohol, nor should he indulge in stimulants such as amphetamines. Keep in mind that any existing depression at this time is secondary to anxiety, and disinhibiting medication could mobilize the patient's aggressive acting-out impulses. Sometimes during this period of stress the already prescribed psychotropic drug need only be stepped up in frequency or dosage for a brief time.

Interpretive Procedures

Interpretive procedures run parallel to those given the patient who suffers imminent withdrawal, but are aimed in the opposite direction.

First of all, the symptom pattern is defined for the patient, namely, that an intolerable inner tension causes a craving for external sources of tension to serve as relief, and so he feels an urge to break out of isolation and seek contact with the external environment. Here, also, the cyclic course of the ambivalence pattern is reviewed with the patient, and the direction toward which the patient is now heading made clear. However, it is obvious that the therapist cannot leave the patient dangling by merely defining the symptoms and their likely consequences, because the patient cannot draw conclusions about how to apply this information in his daily life. Dynamic insight and reeducation to reality are required.

How the patient's craving for external sources of tension evolved can be appropriately interpreted in connection with the effects of isolation from external stimuli by noting that the patient became increasingly bombarded by internal stimuli when deprived of external reality reference points and lost contact with a realistic sense of self. From the viewpoint of symptom derivation, it is important that interpretations enable the patient to grasp an understanding of the relationship between confusion, dysregulation, and the resultant all-or-none ambivalence responses.

At this intermediate phase prior to breakthrough, the patient's unrealistic and confused self-image requires remedial attention. And, of course, the patient requires further education concerning reality about the self in relationship to others, with special emphasis on middle-of-the-road attitudes. The patient can be encouraged to explore opportunities for social contacts that are not too emotionally demanding (in the light of the patient's specific integrative handicap) and yet which can afford some degree of interpersonal gratification. In other words, the patient's particular contact impairment configuration must be understood by the therapist; within that framework the patient can be given enough rope to move forward, but not enough rope with which he could hang himself.

As the patient commences social assertion, problems of contact impairment must be dealt with in the context of the patient's particular all-or-none attitudes and misconcepts about himself and interpersonal relationships. For example, in the past perhaps the patient had repeatedly misinterpreted responses of refusal to his invitations as personal rejections, reacted with hostility, and thus actually created the very rejections he had feared. Or, in the past the patient may have manifested a pattern of continual joviality in all efforts to relate, without recognizing that the appropriate behavior in certain situations was seriousness. Here, it is helpful to teach the patient how to profit from particular past experiences of contact impairment. In other words, the patient can benefit from examples in his past by applying newly gained reality insights to cope with future encounters of a similar nature.

In teaching the patient realistic attitudes and behavior in interpersonal relationships, keep in mind that a schizophrenic patient often fails to perceive the significance of the simplest, most commonplace human interactions: He will fail to respond to situations when assertion is normally expected, and he will overreact to situations which normally should be ignored. Moreover, the schizophrenic's empathy is often delicately tuned to pick up the negative, yet the individual can be completely blind to positive affect manifested by other people. These factors of contact impairment require repeated attention in remedial therapy.

In conclusion, I would like to tender a speculation with regard to the apparent energy dysregulation involved in the contact-versus-withdrawal ambivalent behavior in masked schizophrenic patients. At one time, tension related to frustration and anxiety stemming from internal stimuli seemingly triggers a hyperkinetic response and the individual aggressively seeks external stimuli. At another time, tension related to frustration and anxiety stemming from external stimuli appears to trigger a hypokinetic response and the emotionally exhausted individual recoils with "passive" withdrawal from external stimuli. When these phenomena occur in masked schizophrenic patients, it reminds one of the catatonic syndrome in which a state of excitement with marked aggression toward the environment alternates with a stuporous withdrawal that shields the individual from the environment. This pattern of dysregulation, observed in both the masked and catatonic schizophrenic syndromes, may only be superficially comparable and perhaps is dynamically unrelated in the two conditions. However, it would be interesting to investigate whether or not such masked schizophrenic patients would manifest a catatonic picture of ambivalence, should they decompensate into an overt psychotic state.

CHAPTER 17

Emergency Intervention: Swinging the Patient's Ambivalence

It is not rare for a therapist to be confronted with a patient who suddenly becomes "stuck" or "fixated" at an ambivalent extreme and acts out, or threatens to, on an emotionally charged idea. In such case, a patient makes an impulsive decision that is often quite threatening to his security and/or to that of other people, or to that of the therapist. For instance, a patient may suddenly announce he has quit his job in reaction to a perhaps minor frustration. A patient may phone you at 3 A.M. to tell you he is about to kill himself. A patient may exclaim he intends to beat up his wife when he leaves your office. Last, but not least likely, a patient may make an aggressive and assaultive move on you during an interview.

When such emergency situations occur, they are usually triggered by some stress-provoking situation, but occasionally they seemingly occur like a bolt out of the blue and the therapist cannot readily recognize precipitating factors. Such events place the therapist in a rather nerve-racking position, to say the least, and require immediate therapeutic intervention.

Prevention is not always possible. It requires a therapist's thorough knowledge of the patient. By keeping aware of anxiety conflicts currently disruptive to the patient, and by familiarity with the types of situations likely to trigger a polar fixation, the therapist can sometimes predict the likelihood of this phenomenon's occurring. Thereupon, preventive measures can often be expedited and the patient's precipitous behavior forestalled. However, because prediction and prevention cannot be guaranteed, it is imperative to understand a few principles of therapeutic technique for dealing with possible emergencies.

205

The technique employed is reliant on recognition of the dynamic mechanisms involved in the derivation and evolution of the fixation phenomenon—as is treatment of any other presented disruptive symptom. The same symptom picture occurs to some extent in so-called passive-aggressive personality disorders and in neurotic individuals who tend to hold back their feelings until the tension becomes so intolerable that they precipitously act out. However, the underlying dynamic mechanisms are essentially different in schizophrenia. We are discussing the masked schizophrenic individual, and the schizodynamic mechanisms are the main factors responsible for the "fixation" syndrome.

In dynamic terms these individuals suffer confusion due to the integrative impairment, and marked dysregulation operates on more than one level of functioning. The patient is prone to swinging from passivity to aggression, from compliance to defiance, or vice versa. In fact, any number of ambivalent reaction patterns can develop, the type of patterns considerably influenced by the patient's past environmental conditioning. These dysregulatory patterns give rise to maladaptive behavior and the patient makes many "mistakes" in relating to the environment, which compounds his sense of inadequacy. Mounting pan-anxiety aggravates the existing ambivalence and then, when some stress-provoking event occurs in the patient's life, tension becomes intolerable and an all-or-none reaction is triggered. Thus, a single event in the patient's daily routine can be the straw that breaks the camel's back, so to speak, causing the patient to suddenly release tension by taking a rigid, unyielding stance of one sort or another. He impulsively makes a decision and is likely to act on it suddenly. Needless to say, these consequences often require the therapist to intervene by inflicting a counter-stress with speed equal to that taken by the patient's sudden stance.

In the process of emergency intervention, timing of interpretation is essential! The therapist must quickly deliver a succinct and forceful verbal (and nonverbal) response to the patient's "fixed" attitude, decision, or act. The aim is to jolt the patient loose, as it were; to shock the patient from one fixed position by provoking a pendular swing toward an opposite position. In other words, the therapist must introduce counterstimulation to quickly reduce the impact of the emotional stimulation that triggered the patient's adverse behavior. It is analogous to influencing an individual to suddenly about-face when poised on the brink of a precipice and preparing to jump. The therapist has not the luxury of time to engage the patient in calm discussion with show of emphatic understanding of his symptom behavior. Only at a later time —perhaps during the same interview, perhaps not—does the therapist investigate with the patient the triggering stressful factors that had arrested his ambivalence vacillations.

The emergency intervention utilizes the patient's positive or negative transference to directly influence the schizophrenic all-or-none ambivalence tendency. On one occasion it might necessitate changing the patient's transference attitude from aggressive defiance to passive compliance. In another instance it might be therapeutic to goad the patient into aggressive defiance, depending on the patient's current transference attitude and the nature of his unrealistic stance at the time. Here again, these influences must be accomplished quickly and succinctly.

In order to quickly swing a schizophrenic patient's ambivalence, or anybody's ambivalence, for that matter, it is important to apply the following principle: React in a direction concordant with that of the patient's move. Whether the patient moves on the level of thought, affect, or behavior this rule is generally valid. Step back when the patient steps back, and the patient will most probably step forward. Similarly, when the patient moves forward aggressively, an aggressive countermove by the therapist will most likely cause the patient to automatically move back.

This principle is exemplified by the following early experience of Sandor Rado when he was a young physician in Hungary. According to his account, Rado was enjoying a day at the beach when one of his friends urgently whispered to him, "Don't look now, but an angry-looking man is approaching behind you and I suspect the hand in his pocket is aiming a revolver at you." Whereupon, Rado turned and recognized the man as one of his patients. Briskly advancing toward the patient Rado issued an angry verbal assault, "How dare you rudely interrupt my holiday! Go home this instant, and whatever you have to discuss can wait until I see you at your appointed hour on Monday!" The patient mumbled an apology and slinked away (Rado, 1946). Now, had Rado run back in fear when the man approached him aggressively, would the patient have shot him? We don't know, but it could be that had he not quickly reacted in concordance with the patient's move, the psychiatric world would have lost the brilliant innovator of the adaptational frame of reference so vital for scientific method in psychiatry.

Actually, the common-sense rule of concordant reaction applies when dealing with ambivalence in any animal. The postman most bitten by vicious dogs is the one who shows fear and retreats. There are two alternative moves which the postman could make: Either to move aggressively toward the dog in concordance with its anger, or to move with a show of friendly intent in concordance with the dog's underlying fear of man. In short, in order to reverse an object's ambivalence stance, fight fire with fire.

Very often a series of back-and-forth steps is required in the therapist's choreographic repertoire before a patient's fixed ambivalent position is loosened and its direction reversed. During the emergency intervention process, the patient may at first vacillate between compliance and defiance, or passivity and aggression, and the therapist may need to move back and forth concordantly before the patient's ambivalence becomes correctively influenced. The parrying procedure is comparable to "playing the line" when fishing: As the fish approaches, the bait is dangled; when the fish retreats, the bait is drawn back, and so on until the stimulating effect of repetition finally leads the fish to be hooked. This applies in dealing with patients who become "stuck" at the pole of extreme passive withdrawal when assertion is realistically indicated. Conversely, this applies in dealing with patients who take an aggressive stance when a period of calm and passive deliberation would be the appropriate response to a situation.

I would like to first illustrate the instance in which the patient inappropriately withdraws in response to a crucial stimulus. A patient I once treated suddenly stated upon his arrival at the office, "Yesterday the job I'd been searching for was offered me, but I shall turn it down." Here you can observe that when an employer came forward the would-be employee stepped back. Naturally, the therapist has not time to explore the patient's rationale for rejecting the long-sought job offer— fear of success versus failure, or fear of entrapment, or whatever— because the moment of opportunity for the patient was of crucial importance. In response to his move of defiance, I countered with the move, "*Don't* take it if it's not the job you *want*," and added the hint of the consequence by suggesting that he would get another opportunity, "perhaps in a year or two." The patient began to vacillate; he became uncomfortably undecided, wondering what to do. He became annoyed that I failed to contribute an opinion and merely nodded as he wavered back and forth. Toward the end of the session he asked, "Should I take the job?" to which I replied, "Well, you *might* want to give it a try—if it doesn't work out you have *nothing* to lose."

At the next session the patient announced he had accepted the job offer. The emergency was over for the time, but dynamic interpretations were of a parrying nature with aim to consolidate the gain. For instance: "Jumping into the unknown is often quite frightening, you know? But once you familiarize yourself with your work you will feel less anxious," and "By the way, remember that you don't have to perform perfectly in order to be adequate." By tuning in to the content and level of a patient's anxiety in the situation confronting him, the therapist may also gently continue to parry where indicated.

Of course, parrying steps in conducting therapy do not always yield success. For instance, had the patient with the job offer maintained his stance and rejected the opportunity, it could indicate he was not as yet psychologically prepared for the leap. In such case, the therapist might let the entire matter drop and resume working with the patient on the related conflicts. Sometimes, when a therapist drops the subject of the presented ambivalence conflict, it is interesting to observe that a patient will resent being "turned off" and may doggedly reintroduce the subject. Or, he may even reverse his stance and accept the opportunity he had threatened to reject—in seeming defiance of the "rejecting" therapist. If he should later ask the therapist, "Did I do wrong to accept the job?" the therapist could parry with a casual comment, "I don't see anything wrong in your giving it a try," or offer some noncommital reassurance. This enables the patient to assume his decision is his own; that he allowed himself to be neither pushed nor pulled; that he had simply done what he wanted to do. Naturally, whenever a patient takes any step toward success he is entitled to full credit for his progress.

A sudden ambivalence fixation is sometimes determined by a patient's tyrannical conscience mechanism. For example, a talented young professor who was struggling to support his family was unjustifiably fired from his research post by a jealous department head. Taken off guard by this sudden incident, the professor manifested a shock reaction: He made no effort to defend himself against the aggressor, and directed his rage into self-beratement. Moreover, when a longtime friend, the dean of faculty, came to his aid, he angrily lashed out at him, "Leave me alone; don't involve yourself; I'm bad luck for you." He lamented to his therapist, "I'm tired of struggling all these years; I might as well give up; my wife and children would be better off if they left me now."

Fighting fire with fire, the therapist berated the patient for his self-beratement with a sudden command, "Stop ranting as though in helpless defeat! How dare you reject your friend so insultingly! You owe him a gross apology; go see him now and don't come back here before you have arranged to cooperate with him!" The patient complied without hesitation. Here, emergency intervention aimed at the target of the masochistic patient's sadistic "superego" and forcefully loosened its fixed hold. The patient was maneuvered to put his conscience to work *for* him rather than to whip himself with it. Guilt connected with failure was redirected to a feeling of guilt for accepting defeat. Self-punitive rage—which the patient had displaced onto his friend, the dean—was rechanneled over to self-defensive rage against his real enemy, the department head. Having thus externalized rage appropriately, the patient's sense of self-esteem expanded sufficiently to enable him to aggressively cope with his emergency problem.

DEALING WITH TRANSFERENCE AGGRESSION

Now to discuss applying emergency intervention when patients threaten to act out with aggression against the therapist. There are cases in which patients have suddenly assaulted a therapist with homicidal intent, but usually these are overtly psychotic patients who move under the influence of delusions or hallucinations. Nevertheless, occasionally a seemingly compensated pseudosociopathic schizophrenic patient will suddenly become overtly psychotic, with a show of violence provoked by some stressful situation, and emergency intervention is required. The same applies in cases whereby a patient threatens aggressive self-destruction. Not all such emergencies can be prevented even by therapists who know the patient well and are vigilantly aware of the patient's current conflicts. Therefore, it is important to know how to apply emergency intervention for dealing with such sudden aggression.

Let us assume that you, a male therapist, are confronted by a burly male patient who suddenly manifests emotional dyscontrol in his negative transference and unexpectedly converts verbal abuse into physical assault. Perhaps enraged by some frustrating assumed rejection, he impulsively makes a move to punch you in the face. What should you do? As in Rado's case, you do not try to run from your office, because the patient will surely present a karate chop to the back of your neck. Nor do you counterassault him with clenched fists, because in defensive rage the patient will hit you first. You might stand up and move forward, certainly, but attack the patient with verbal thrusts. At the same time, of course, angrily berate him for interrupting his own session; for denying himself his urgent right to express a verbal assault; for defeating himself in therapy—in the context of whatever current problems are presented. Here again, you show anger *for* the patient with aim to swing his transference ambivalence. This form of counter-aggression may not always succeed, but the fact remains that any other tactic is less likely to reverse the patient's aggressive stance. In other words, you will be attacked if you show fear, and if you threaten physical force you violate the Hippocratic oath and betray your patient's trust forever.

Now let us assume that a female therapist observes her male patient approaching her with obvious intent of sexual assault. Attempts to evade the patient and run are contraindicated; if she does so, the patient is likely to chase her down the hall in hot pursuit. Instead, it would be best to immediately move toward the patient and attack with a verbal assault, "You make me very angry by interrupting your session with such behavior. Sit down this instant and explain yourself!" In response to such sudden counterassault, the patient will most likely comply and begin to verbalize in his defense. If he projects and accuses you of sexual provocation, don't argue; listen and analyze.

In brief, any aggressive assault by the patient toward the therapist, regardless of intent, is best met with a strong and sudden verbal counterassault. The patient is likely to respond by reversing his stance— provided the therapist had not misdiagnosed the patient, and provided the patient has not suddenly decompensated into a state of catatonic excitement—in which case a perceptive therapist would have been forewarned of the possibility by keeping aware of the patient's anxiety level, the precipitating environmental situation, and the growing negative transference.

To briefly digress on this issue, when in a state of acute catatonic excitement, patients are unresponsive to psychotherapy: They cannot listen to reason, and counteraggression further incites their aggression. In the emergency clinic or on the ward, these patients are more dangerous than patients in the throes of psychomotor epilepsy or pathological intoxication. They can exert the strength of 3 or 4 men and can kill without forewarning. When interviewing such patients alone, which would be foolish to do, never turn your back on them for an instant, and make certain several hefty attendants are on the alert to intervene.

INFLUENCING THE SUICIDAL PATIENT

Returning to our topic of emergency intervention when treating aggressive patients, there is the prevalent problem of patients directing aggression against themselves, namely, the problem of threatened suicide. Many, not all, such confrontations can be foreseen and prevented. Even patients who manifest seemingly mild depression must be questioned as to any suicidal ideation. In fact, many patients who are severely depressed may omit mention of their suicidal ideation in interviews, unless questioned. Suicide can result from a therapist's failure to adequately recognize and respond to a patient's repeatedly presented symptoms, which are directly or indirectly related to depression. Furthermore, severely depressed patients are most likely to kill themselves when they are beginning to emerge from deep depression and their energy is mobilized; therefore, prescribing an antidepressant stimulant such as an amphetamine to patients who are paralyzed by depression is generally contraindicated.

Fortunately for the patients, those harboring suicidal ideation will usually vacillate for some period of time before acting out on a final decision. The therapist must keep aware of this ambivalence struggle and deal with it therapeutically. In their ambivalence, sometimes patients make suicidal gestures, such as "taking an overdose" or wrist-slashing: When only a gesture, the ambivalence pendulum has swung to an extreme and the patient is crying out for help. This event should have been anticipated by the therapist in many cases. It is a matter of utmost importance, because sometimes the patient miscalculates and the suicidal gesture results in death. Obviously, therefore, whenever a patient admits to suicidal intent, or acts out in desperation with a suicidal gesture, emergency intervention, usually hospitalization, is indicated.

Therapeutic technique in dealing with a potentially suicidal patient relies on many factors besides the degree and acuteness of the depressive picture. The patient's diagnosis, anxiety structure, ambivalence patterns, and, of course, the contributing environmental circumstances and precipitating events must all be recognized by the therapist. These combined factors point to the affect-laden motivation connected with a patient's suicidal ideation or threat.

Therapeutic intervention relies a great deal on the depressed patient's conscious or unconscious affective motivation as well as ideational motivation for suicide. One or two predominant motivating forces are usually discernible. First, the suicidal act may represent an aggressive attack on one or more people in the patient's life, including the therapist. Here, suicide would serve as a punitive measure aimed to arouse guilt in the survivors, and as an act of ultimate defiant rejection. Secondly, suicide would serve as an escape from the intolerable pain of depression when the patient feels helpless to surmount it and life appears hopeless. An individual can also be motivated to escape intractable physical pain—for instance, that due to terminal cancer—although here the act is not true suicide but simply taking the matter of an already imminent death into his own hands.

When a large component of the depressed patient's motivation for suicide consists of rage directed toward the environment, a suicidal threat can be an aggressive act aimed to arouse guilt in some person or persons. You, the therapist, must react to it in the framework of the transference relationship and treat it as a personal rejection. Assumedly, the patient's suicidal threat carries the implication, "I shall kill myself and *then* you'll be sorry!" You meet such a message head-on with the fact that, quite to the contrary, "Killing yourself will make me (and others) angry at you!" In other words, aim to jolt the rejecting patient out of his aggressive stance by aggressively threatening counterrejection. This maneuver is usually successful, provided, of course, the patient is not overly psychotic with a delusional assumption of somatic immortality, which is a prerequisite for overriding the basic drive for survival. Keep in mind, you only reject the rejecting component of the patient's personality, not the total patient.

Here, it is sometimes a grave mistake when a therapist impulsively shows totally rejecting negative countertransference feelings, but not always. I know a psychiatrist who impulsively reacted to an angry patient's threat of suicide by exclaiming, "Don't kill yourself; it will ruin my reputation!" To his surprise, the patient withdrew his threat. Why? The therapist's remark had clearly indicated he would resent the patient, rather than feel guilty. If a therapist should be so aggressively tactless as to exclaim, as did one psychiatrist when awakened at night by a patient's phoning his suicidal intent, "If you want to kill yourself, call an undertaker, not me," this total rejection could be disastrous. The patient may elect to live, yes; but out of anger for the callous rejection he may decide to revenge himself by committing character assassination of the doctor for his unprofessional conduct. More importantly, however, playing Russian roulette in the name of therapy can cost a patient his life, especially if the patient's suicidal motivation is largely to escape the intolerable pain of depression. The therapist must know his patient well, and also be fully in command of his own countertransference before initiating any emergency intervention.

When a patient's threat of suicide is based on a feeling of lack of hope that he ever will emerge from an agonizing depression, the motivation is largely a matter of pain-riddance. Interpretation must immediately first show the patient understanding: "You feel trapped in a deep dark pit; you feel that there is no way out." Once the patient feels that the therapist understands, he is likely to be receptive to further interpretations. The therapist then aims to mobilize the patient out of his suicidal stance by offering an alternative to suicide. Here, I consider it imperative to actually promise the patient that by accepting a succinctly proffered treatment plan—prefaced on immediate hospitalization—his depression will lift. Promising relief is not unwarrantable insofar as depression is often self-limited even without treatment, and insofar as current antidepressant medications afford relief in a very high percentage of cases (as also does ECT treatment).

When influencing a patient to accept hospitalization, do not plead; do not argue. Explain to him his need for a stress-free setting with a fully competent medicinal regime in order to quickly and effectively relieve him of depression. Of course, a patient's reaction to promises of help is often quite paradoxical due to ambivalence. Some patients willingly comply with the therapist's plan of treatment; others object strenuously; and other patients vacillate between compliance and defiance. The therapist must apply different tactics accordingly.

Should the patient flatly reject your stated alternatives to suicide and tell you, "You don't understand, Doc; I don't want to live," or, "I've made up my mind and would rather die than go to a nut house," and refuse to discuss the matter, it is clear that the patient will not listen to reason. He may react in anger and stomp out of your office and slam the door. Do not chase after him. Wait. Perhaps the patient will run in front of a truck, but if you chase after him he will be more likely to do so. Here again, when the patient backs off, you also back off. (Often one has little choice.) Such a patient will then probably return, perhaps within a few minutes, or will telephone you later and condescendingly agree to discuss the matter of hospitalization.

Should the patient remain in your office and defiantly refuse hospitalization, you might respond, in accordance, "All right, don't go to the hospital." If the patient then forwards the idea that you can cure his depression by other means, agree that it might well be possible to do so—but that this will prolong his suffering, which you cannot guarantee he will want to tolerate. An alternative parrying tactic consists of diversion. For instance, when the patient refuses to accept hospitalization you can comment, "Forget it, then," and quickly change the subject. You might proceed to question him about his health. Interestingly enough, ambivalent schizophrenic individuals who contemplate suicide often express anxiety about their health at the very same time. They will tell you that they fear a heart attack or cancer, and so forth. Try to elicit expressions of hypochondriacal fears and descriptions of somatic symptoms. This could afford an opportunity to suggest that a thorough medical checkup, including an electrocardiogram, a G.I. series, or appropriate laboratory tests are important. Still backing off from the idea of hospitalization, the patient's ambivalence may thus swing from the desire to die over to a concomitant fear of dying. Hopefully, the patient's concerns may subtly be rechanneled into actually fearing his own suicidal impulses, and he may himself initiate a request for hospitalization.

There are many possible intervention tactics that can be employed, depending on the therapist's "style" when confronted with apparently suicidal patients. One of the possible tactics worth mentioning entails actually siding with a patient who adamantly considers suicide. You can show that you understand how intolerable life obviously seems to the patient, that you recognize how he suffers. Then, question the patient concerning his plans for suicide. Male patients often prefer violent methods; women usually select wrist-slashing or drugs. You might express your aversion to any painful methods your patient contemplates, and mention nonpainful alternatives. Such discussion may arouse the patient's feelings of repugnance and disgust for your seemingly cold objectivity. Thinking that you are condoning suicide may swing his ambivalence, resulting in rejection of your suggestions and in retreat from his own contemplated intent. This then affords you the opportunity to change the subject to the alternative methods of hospital treatment for depression. The patient may now perseverate on this theme and question you about various drug treatments. Your responses explaining these alternatives may elicit a show of interest in what methods would apply for his case, and as the patient begins to veer toward accepting one or the other treatment possibility, you parry the issue. Dangling the bait, you perhaps then comment, "I might have difficulty finding a hospital that can accept you today; I would be willing to pull rank and try—but I can't unless you tell me what *you* want. It is entirely up to you."

At the point when the patient tells you hospitalization would be acceptable, hesitant willingness to cooperate with his decision can dispel his hesitation. Then, exploiting schizophrenic intolerance for frustration, you can comply with the patient's request by stating, "Let me phone X hospital now, and if they won't accept you I'll talk to the director at Y hospital. . . . Meanwhile you decide who you want to contact at home to bring your overnight bag to the hospital for you," and so forth, concerning practical matters.

To summarize: In dealing with potentially suicidal patients, no therapeutic intervention tactic can be guaranteed successful, but the principle of parrying by reacting in accordance with the patient's ambivalent moves is best applied. The technique varies with each patient, with each confronting situation, and also varies with each therapist's personal style of approach.

Methods for hospitalizing a suicidal patient usually proceed by a series of steps. The first step aims to redirect the patient from the intent of suicide to that of self-preservation by offering promise of pain-riddance through therapeutic alternative. The second step aims to swing the patient's transference ambivalence from the defiance stance over to compliance with the therapist's plan for hospitalization. The next step

entails activating the schizophrenic tendency to perseverate in an initiated direction by diverting the patient's attention to means for fulfilling the therapeutic intent, namely, attaining admission to the hospital.
It is important that with each step along the way the patient feels
neither pushed nor pulled by the therapist, but that he is simply using
the therapist to effect his own decisions.

The procedure described is usually ineffective—and is in fact inap-
plicable—when dealing with suicidal patients who suffer a markedly
agitated depression. Such patients are extremely anxious and tense.
They are impulsive and not likely to postpone acting on a suicidal
intent. Unable to think rationally, they are deaf and blind to any attempts at psychotherapeutic influence. Sometimes, however, the
anxiety in these agitated patients becomes quickly reduced when they
are interviewed under sodium amytal, and they are able to relate. It is
often possible to elicit a patient's cooperation for this interview by explaining, for instance, "I would like to give you some medication now,
to relieve you of the anxiety you are suffering so that you can describe
your grievances clearly for me to understand."

Sodium amytal disinhibits patients: They thereupon pour out their
grievances—with the exception of emotionally rigid and angry patients
who are strongly paranoid, catatonic, or suffering from an organic
brain disorder. Assuming that you know that your masked schizophrenic patient's pattern of faulty integration and emotionality does
not fit these criteria, a sodium amytal interview serves well. The disinhibiting drug relaxes the patients and they ventilate a great deal of rage
and fear. Actually, it is a favorable prognostic sign when patients
quickly begin to feel less anxious, less depressed, and are able to relate to
the therapist. The suicidal crisis can often be resolved during the interview—at least temporarily. Sometimes these effects are lasting, for
some inexplicable reason, especially when followed up with intensive
psychotherapy.

However, for the suicidally depressed patient who submits to the
sodium amytal interview but remains unresponsive, it is sometimes
necessary to terminate the interview by injecting the amount of drug
required to narcotize the patient for hospitalization by ambulance. It is
never an acceptable procedure to trick a patient into hospitalization
except when this is considered necessary for saving the patient's life.
Even so, when such a patient awakens he will rant and rave against the
therapist for the deceit: He may never trust you or your profession
again. On the other hand, should hospital treatment relieve the patient
of his depression, the recovered patient will most likely realize the
merit of your actions—although he may later seek another therapist.

CHAPTER 18

APPENDIX

The Sodium Amytal Interview: An Adjunctive Diagnostic and Adjunctive Therapeutic Measure

The technique for using sodium amytal in interview is worth discussion because it can serve as a valuable tool for purposes other than the emergency intervention described in the previous chapter. The sodium amytal interview can be applied as a diagnostic tool, a prognostic indicator, and can be applied for a number of therapeutic purposes. When employed for any of these purposes, keep in mind that sodium amytal interviews serve only as auxiliary measures, not primary measures. As we shall discuss, the drug depresses the higher cortical centers, thereby disinhibiting the patient and rendering him more accessible for effective contact with the therapist.

In my opinion, sodium amytal is preferable to currently popular drugs, such as diazepam, because amytal tends to have a euphoric effect, which elevates the patient's self-confidence, thus leading to more freedom of verbal production. Other barbiturates can be used, such as sodium Pentothal® or Brevital®. The former requires extreme caution during injection due to its marked respiratory depressant effect, and even a skilled therapist would be wise to have ready an ampoule of injectable ephedrine as well as Benzedrine® to counteract any possible sudden apnea. Brevital® is an ultra-short-acting barbiturate that has the advantage of quick recovery from its narcotizing effect; but the disadvantage lies in the difficulty of maintaining the patient at a stable level of sedation for any length of time during the interview.

Regardless of the purpose for which sodium amytal is applied, it must be realized that the drug itself does not do the work; the work is done by the physician and its efficacy requires considerable clinical experience. When using sodium amytal for diagnostic and prognosticating purposes, the interviewer must know the diagnostic criteria and dynamics of the various disorders—manic-depressive, schizophrenic, neurotic, organic, and so forth. If the patient is recognized to be schizophrenic and sodium amytal is used for therapeutic purposes, the interviewer must know the patient's particular schizodynamic configuration and the patterns of conditioning underlying the symptom picture.

Now to briefly outline the technique of applying intravenous sodium amytal for interview purposes. Generally, 7.5 grains of sodium amytal are dissolved in a syringe with 20 cc of sterile water. The therapist injects about one grain (approximately 2½ cc) slowly during the first minute or so, keeping close watch on the patient's respiratory rate. The needle is retained in the patient's cubital vein. By questioning the patient, the interviewer ascertains when a state of relaxation is attained, at which point injection continues more slowly in order to sustain the patient on that desired level of response throughout the 30- or 45-minute interview. The drug is never introduced in such a manner that the amount injected causes the patient to become befuddled or drowsy. A total of 3 to 7.5 grains is usually sufficient to influence the emotional state of the patient most favorably and to maintain him in a communicable state (Hoch, 1947).

As an adjunctive diagnostic method, a sodium amytal interview is applicable for patients who are unable to relate their attitudes and feelings in routine mental examination. The drug serves as a decorticating agent and thereby "loosens up" the patient, rendering him temporarily accessible for ascertaining the true nature of his psychiatric or organic mental disorder. Sodium amytal influences preeminently the affective state: By removing the patient's inhibitions, the full array of symptoms can often be disclosed. The depressed or agitated patient relaxes, communicates. The schizophrenic patient who had heretofore seemingly appeared to be in good contact with reality will sometimes respond to questioning by describing hallucinatory and delusional experiences that had not been verbally disclosed during nondrug sessions. And, of course, the drug will frequently reveal the overtly psychotic elements in a schizophrenic patient's bizarre chain of thought, disclosing processes and content of hallucinations and delusions that were previously blanketed.

Sodium amytal is especially useful for differentiating between organic and so-called psychogenic symptomatology, for example, in posttraumatic amnesias. The psychogenic conditions usually clear up during the interview, while amnesias of organic origin do not. Here again, in organic disorders the affective symptoms such as depression, manic or excitement states, as well as anxiety are markedly reduced or eliminated during sodium amytal interview. In this way, any existing organic intellectual impairments become manifest. Sodium amytal can aggravate intellectual impairments in organic disorders—such as in Alzheimer's or Pick's diseases, cerebral arteriosclerosis, and especially frontal lobe impairments. On the other hand, manifestations of intellectual integrative impairments in schizophrenia are reduced by the anxiety-reducing effects of sodium amytal. For a long time people have attempted to find a method for differentiating organic conditions from psychiatric conditions: As yet there are no infallible diagnostic methods. However, sodium amytal, when properly applied, could be quite a valuable indicator, despite the method's shortcomings.

As a prognostic indicator in psychiatry, sodium amytal is also useful, due to its disinhibiting influence on the patient. It shows the therapist the amount of affective component responsible for the patient's disturbance, as opposed to the amount of intellectual impairment present. The more the affective component and the less the intellectual component present in the symptom picture, the better the prognosis, generally speaking. For instance, if the schizophrenic patient is mute and remains uncommunicative during the sodium amytal interview, it could indicate that the patient suffers from catatonic withdrawal which, of course, involves quite an amount of organicity and forebodes a poor long-term prognosis. Conversely, when a mute patient pours out affect-laden material during sodium amytal interview, it is a favorable prognostic sign, because it indicates the prior lack of communication was due to some psychological inhibition.

The therapeutic value of the sodium amytal interview extends beyond its use for emergency intervention, as we have mentioned. This interview technique is applicable when treating patients who are uncommunicative on the basis of either consciously held or unconscious inhibitions, and it is especially useful when treating patients who are in the throes of a severe affective upheaval, when the precipitating factors need to be explored. The sodium amytal serves not only to disinhibit the patient but also affords quick temporary relief from painful symptoms so that the patient can relate to the therapist. By thus rendering the uncooperative patient cooperative, the sodium amytal makes the patient accessible to psychotherapeutic influence.

Depending on the patient's therapeutic needs, the interviewing therapist either questions the patient regarding certain symptoms or allows the patient to free-associate on topics that at the time require full description and attention. The therapist must know what to search for in questioning the patient. In then responding to the patient's verbal productions, he must know how to steer the patient to disclose anxiety-provoking material pertinent to the existing conflicts.

Within each sodium amytal interview, it is also important to give the patient insightful as well as supportive interpretations concerning the conflictual material disclosed. An interview can continue for 50 minutes or so, toward the end of which time it is always appropriate to give remedial suggestions aimed to lessen the patient's conflict and alleviate anxiety and other symptoms disclosed by the interview. The salient dynamic factors revealed during the interview can later be brought to the patient's attention for synthesis during routine nondrug interviews.

For example, let us assume that during the sodium amytal interview your patient is relieved from intense anxiety and discloses for the first time his bizarre sado-masochistic sexual fantasies and accounts of sexual acting-out behavior. Having dropped his defenses at this time, you cannot simply respond to his flood of material without comment: The patient needs supportive interpretation in order to trust your acceptance and understanding. Therefore, you interpret to the patient that the conflictual material disclosed now shows you that he is confused about his bodily integrity and sexuality; that this can be remedied. This enables the patient to pour out additional attitudes and feelings connected to the insights you have just afforded him. Then, when it is time to terminate the interview, your remedial interpretations hint at reality with regard to sexuality—and the patient will feel motivated to seek your help for resolving his conflicts in interviews to follow. Then, during the subsequent drug-free interview, the salient dynamic factors of his conflicts are reintroduced; they are reinforced with explanations and elaboration, to be employed for synthesis.

When the sodium amytal interview is employed as an adjunctive procedure in therapy, it should be repeated about 2 or 3 times a week or, if necessary, even daily. However, the number of sessions beneficial for the patient is limited. If the patient does not respond with this therapeutic measure after 10 or 12 sessions, it is very unlikely that it will be beneficial at all. In any case, interviews without the drug are the main part of therapy even for those patients who have made progress during the course of sodium amytal interviews. The reason for this is that the disinhibiting effect of the drug usually melts away anxiety, tension, and depression only temporarily; in order to remove these symptoms on a long-term basis, continued psychotherapeutic follow-up is required with the patient not sedated and able to focus attention on the dynamic mechanisms that had influenced the symptom development. Sodium amytal serves as an auxiliary interview procedure aimed to make the patient more accessible and responsive to psychotherapeutic influence.

Not only is sodium amytal limited as a therapeutic tool, but there are inherent dangers to this technique: The relaxing and symptom-relieving effects may lead to a craving for barbiturates in some patients. Actually, however, a similar drug craving can occur for nonbarbiturates, such as diazepam, insofar as patients may crave the treatment more for the drug effect than for the psychological help afforded by it. However, it is usually possible to cut the drug transference in the same way as one can resolve the patient's emotional transference to the therapist.

It should be stressed, nevertheless, that especially for treating anxiety states in pseudoneurotic schizophrenia, in the neuroses, or for patients who have suffered a superimposed trauma, and clearly in cases of so-called traumatic or war neuroses, a series of sodium amytal therapeutic interviews can be curative of the disorder—provided the treatment technique is applied early and skillfully.

In conclusion I would like to state again that, for some unknown reason, a series of sodium amytal interviews has a remarkably sustained beneficial effect on some patients. This may be due to a number of factors. Perhaps for some patients it opens up an avenue of hope when they experience a drug-effected reprieve—perhaps the first they have ever experienced—from long-standing symptoms that they had long assumed were part of their fate.

It is also quite probable that the drug itself exerts some chemical influence on the hierarchy of regulatory homeostatic mechanisms and fortifies their stabilizing effect in response to stress. It is also probable that during the course of this adjunctive treatment the drug serves to initiate a disruption of conditioned patterns of pathological reactions to stimuli. Although psychotherapy continues to be the primary therapeutic technique, sodium amytal interviews seemingly serve to accelerate the therapeutic process for many patients.

It is important that the therapist be flexible in his therapeutic approach. He should not take the stance, "I treat patients only organically because I belong to this sect" or "I am treating the patients only psychotherapeutically because I belong to that sect." We should treat the patient with all means available and with what is best for the patient. How can we be dogmatic when we still don't know what the schizophrenic disorder is?

If you treat schizophrenic patients whose compensatory defenses have been shaken, and if some drug reduces to a very large extent patients' anxiety, perturbation, and many vegetative manifestations, your way is then clear to deal psychotherapeutically with these patients more swiftly. Many of the psychotherapeutic machinations used to quantitatively reduce the symptoms of the patient can be given over to the drug and the psychotherapy can concentrate on his more important adaptational difficulties. I believe psychotherapy combined with adjuncts such as drugs needs more research, indeed, but meanwhile this method permits us a far more effective therapy of schizophrenia than we had in the past, even though the etiology of the disorder is unknown.

References

Introduction

Committee on Nomenclature and Statistics of the American Psychiatric Association. *Diagnostic and statistical manual of mental disorders* (3rd ed.). Washington, D.C.: American Psychiatric Association, 1980.

Goldstein, K. *The organism*. New York: American Book Co., 1939.

Hoch, P.H. The etiology and epidemiology of schizophrenia. *American Journal of Public Health*, 1957, 47, 1071-1076.

Hoch, P. H., Cattell, J. P., Strahl, M. O., & Pennes, H. H. The course and outcome of pseudoneurotic schizophrenia. *American Journal of Psychiatry*, 1962, *119*(2), 106-115.

Hoch, P. H., & Polatin, P. Pseudoneurotic forms of schizophrenia. *Psychiatric Quarterly*, 1949, 23, 248-276.

Kety, S. S., Rosenthal, D., & Wender, P. H., et al. *The types and prevalence of mental illness in the biological and adoptive families of adopted schizophrenics*. Oxford, England: Pergamon Press, 1968.

Chapter 1

Bleuler, E. [*Dementia praecox or the group of schizophrenias*] (J. Zinkin, trans.). New York: International Universities Press, 1950. (Originally published, 1911.)

Bleuler, E. [*Textbook of psychiatry*] (A. A. Brill, trans.). New York: Macmillan, 1930.

Buss, A. H., & Buss, E. H. (Eds.). *Theories of schizophrenia*. New York: Atherton Press, 1969.

Deutsch, H. Some forms of emotional disturbance and their relationship to schizophrenia. *Psychoanalytic Quarterly*, 1942, *11*, 301-321.

Hendin, H. *Suicide in Scandinavia*. New York: Doubleday, 1965.

Hoch, P. H. *Treatment of the pseudoneurotic form of schizophrenia.* Paper presented at the annual meeting of the American Psychiatric Association, Chicago, April 1961.

Hoch, P. H., & Cattell, J. The diagnosis of pseudoneurotic schizophrenia. *Psychiatric Quarterly*, 1959, *33*, 17-43.

Hoch, P. H., & Polatin, P. Pseudoneurotic forms of schizophrenia. *Psychiatric Quarterly*, 1949, *23*, 248-276.

Kallmann, F. J. The genetic theory of schizophrenia. An analysis of 691 schizophrenic twin index families. *American Journal of Psychiatry*, 1946, *103*, 309-322.

Kallmann, F. J., & Barrera, S. E. The hereditoconstitutional mechanisms of predisposition and resistance to schizophrenia. *American Journal of Psychiatry*, 1942, 98, 544-550.

Kernberg, O. Borderline personality organization. *Journal of the American Psychoanalytic Association*, 1967, *15*, 641-685.

Knight, R. Borderline states. *Bulletin of the Menninger Clinic*, 1953, *17*, 1-12.

Perry, J. C., & Klerman, G. The borderline patient—a comparative analysis of four sets of diagnostic criteria. *Archives of General Psychiatry*, 1978, *35*, 141-150.

Schneider, K. [*Clinical psychopathology*] (M. W. Hamilton, trans.). New York: Grune & Stratton, 1959.

Strahl, M. O., & Lewis, N. D. C. (Eds.). *Differential diagnosis in clinical psychiatry—the lectures of Paul H. Hoch, M.D.* New York: Science House, 1972.

Zilboorg, G. Ambulatory schizophrenia. *Psychiatry*, 1941, *4*, 149-155.

Chapter 2

Bleuler, E. [*Dementia praecox or the group of schizophrenias*] (J. Zinkin, trans.). New York: International Universities Press, 1950. (Originally published, 1911.)

Flekkoy, K. Psychophysiological and neurophysiological aspects of schizophrenia. *Acta Psychiatrica Scandinavia*, 1975, *51*, 234-246.

Mahler, M. S. *On human symbiosis and the vicissitudes of individuation: Infantile psychosis.* New York: International Universities Press, 1968.

Masterson, J. F. *Psychotherapy of the borderline adult: A developmental approach.* New York: Brunner/Mazel, 1976.

Strahl, M. O., & Lewis, N. D. C. (Eds.). *Differential diagnosis in clinical psychiatry—The lectures of Paul H. Hoch, M.D.* New York: Science House, 1972.

Stransky, E. Nature of schizophrenia. *Jahrb. f. Psychiatry u. Neurology*, 1929, *46*, 217-254.

Chapter 3

Aichhorn, A. *Wayward youth.* New York: Viking Press, 1935.

Fries, M. Personal communication, 1946.

Kallmann, F. J., & Barrera, S. E. The hereditoconstitutional mechanisms of predisposition and resistance to schizophrenia. *American Journal of Psychiatry*, 1942, *98*, 544-550.

Strahl, M. O., & Lewis, N. D. C. (Eds.). *Differential diagnosis in clinical psychiatry—The lectures of Paul H. Hoch, M.D.* New York: Science House, 1972.

Chapter 4

Levenson, A. *Basic psychopharmacology for health professionals.* New York: Springer Publishing Company, 1980.

Strahl, M. O., & Lewis, N. D. C. (Eds.). *Differential diagnosis in clinical psychiatry—The lectures of Paul H. Hoch, M.D.* New York: Science House, 1972.

Chapter 6

Hoskins, R. G. *The biology of schizophrenia.* New York: Norton, 1946.

Chapter 7

Rubin, E. *Visuell wahrgenommene figuren.* Copenhagen; Gyldenalske, 1921.

Chapter 9

Adler, A. Study of organ inferiority and its psychic compensations. *Nervous and Mental Disease Monograph Series*, 1917, *24*.

Rado, S. The theory of schizotypal organization and its application to the treatment of schizotypal behavior. In *The out-patient treatment of schizophrenia*. New York: Grune & Stratton, 1960.

Chapter 10

Kallmann, F. J. Twin and sibship study of overt male homosexuality. *American Journal of Human Genetics*, 1952, *4*(2).

Chapter 11

Jung, C. G. [*Collected papers on analytical psychology*] (2nd ed.) (C. E. Long, trans.). London, England: Bailliér Tindall & Cox, 1917.

Jung, C. G. [*The integration of the personality*] (S. M. Dell, trans.). New York: Farrar, Rinehart, 1939.

Nietzsche, F. [*Thus spake Zarathustra*] (T. Common, trans.). New York: Random House, 1905. (Originally published, 1884-1885.)

Chapter 12

Despert, J. L. The early recognition of childhood schizophrenia. *Pediatrics*, 1947, 680-687.

Chapter 15

Benedek, T. F. Sexual functions in women and their disturbance. In S. Arieti (Ed.), *American handbook of psychiatry* (Vol. 1). New York: Basic Books, 1959.

Klein, H. Obstetrical and gynecological disorders. In A. M. Freedman & H. I. Kaplan (Eds.), *Textbook of psychiatry*. Baltimore: Williams & Wilkins, 1967.

Levy, D. M. *Maternal overprotection*. New York: Columbia University Press, 1943.

Masserman, J. H. Comparative and clinical approaches to biodynamic therapy. In J. H. Masserman (Ed.), *Animal & Human* (Sciences and Psychoanalysis Series, Vol. 12). New York: Grune & Stratton, 1968.

McFalls, J. A., Jr. *Psychopathology and subfecundity*. New York: Academic Press, 1979.

Normand, W. C. Postpartum disorders. In A. M. Freedman & H. I. Kaplan (Eds.), *Textbook of psychiatry*. Baltimore: Williams & Wilkins, 1967.

Chapter 17

Rado, S. Personal communication, related to a group of psychoanalytic students during a lecture on ambivalent mechanisms in obsessive behavior, 1946.

Chapter 18

Hoch, P. H. Narcodiagnosis and narcotherapy in the neuroses and psychoses. *New York State Journal of Medicine*, 1947, 47(24), 2694-2698.

Index